The Legal Status of International Non-Governmental Organizations

Nijhoff Law Specials

VOLUME 85

The titles published in this series are listed at brill.com/nlsp

The Legal Status of International Non-Governmental Organizations

Analysis of Past and Present Initiatives (1912–2012)

By

Rephael H. Ben-Ari

MARTINUS NIJHOFF PUBLISHERS

LEIDEN · BOSTON
2013

Library of Congress Cataloging-in-Publication Data

Ben-Ari, Rephael Harel, 1972-
The legal status of international non-governmental organizations analysis of past and present initiatives (1912-2012) / by Rephael Ben-Ari.
pages cm. -- (Nijhoff law specials; volume 85)
Includes bibliographical references and index.
ISBN 978-90-04-25436-7 (pbk. : alk. paper) -- ISBN 978-90-04-25437-4 (e-book) 1. Non-governmental organizations--Law and legislation--History--20th century. I. Title.
KZ4850.B435 2013
341.2--dc23

2013022820

This publication has been typeset in the multilingual "Brill" typeface. With over 5,100 characters covering Latin, IPA, Greek, and Cyrillic, this typeface is especially suitable for use in the humanities. For more information, please see www.brill.com/brill-typeface.

ISSN 0924-4549
ISBN 978-90-04-25436-7 (paperback)
ISBN 978-90-04-25437-4 (e-book)

This book is printed on acid-free paper.

CONTENTS

Acknowledgements vii

Introduction 1

I Contextual Historical Analysis of Past Initiatives 5
1.1 An Optimistic Start: The Quest for International Legal Personality 5
1.2 Uniform Universal Status: A Transnational World Vision 9
1.3 Selection, Registration, and Order: Political Reliability vs. Expertise 11
1.4 Gaining New Momentum: UN Consultative Status Arrangements 13
1.5 *De Facto* Legal Status: False Promise of Consultative Arrangements 17
1.6 Resemblance to IGOs: The Quest for Functional Legitimacy 23
1.7 Disapproval of International Status: INGOs as *National* NGOs 26
1.8 *International* NGOs: A Socio-Political *Non*-Legal Phenomenon 29
1.9 Non-Governmental *Non*-Community: Whose Status? 32
1.10 The Turn to Regionalism: Pan-European Intellectual Environment 35
1.11 In Search of Political Support: Supranational Action 41
1.12 Intermediary Observations: Discrete Doctrinal Approaches 45

II New Initiatives and Developments 47
2.1 INGOs Accountability Charter 2006 47
2.2 Guidelines on International Human Rights Fact-Finding Visits and Reports (The *'Lund-London Guidelines'*) 2009 52
2.3 Reports of the Committee on Non-State Actors of the International Law Association (ILA) (2008, 2010 & 2012) 55

III Evaluation of New Developments and Current Trends 65
3.1 Doctrinal Evolvement 65
3.2 Resemblance to IGOs 74
3.3 Tensions within the Non-Governmental Community 78
3.4 Authors of Initiatives 81
3.5 INGOs' Disinterest 82
3.6 European Focus 84

IV Conclusions and Future Prospects 87

Bibliography 95

Appendices 103
1. Reports on International Status of INGOs 107
2. UN Consultative Arrangements 135
3. Regional Arrangements (Council of Europe) 163
4. New Initiatives 183

Index 201

ACKNOWLEDGEMENTS

I wish to acknowledge the generous sponsorship of the Hauser Global Law School Program of the New York University School of Law, which allowed me to complete the research upon which this book is based. I wish to thank Professor R. Stewart, and Professor J. Weiler, for their academic sponsorship, as well as the participants in the 2011–2012 Hauser Global Fellows Forum for their insightful observations.

I also wish to thank Professor Y. Zilbershatz, Deputy President of Bar-Ilan University, for her moral and academic support. Finally, special gratitude goes to Mr. Alan Stephens, for his friendship and for his inspiration.

INTRODUCTION

> It would be difficult to imagine an intellectually more stimulating subject than the one proposed here for our study. It has its roots in a long and varied history and leads on to the most topical and concrete problems of world structure and organization. ... But however fascinating the subject ... may be, any solution to the problem is, as it always was, extremely difficult to find ...
> (M. Merle, *'Report on INGOs and their Legal Status',* Colloquy on *'The Role of INGOs in Contemporary Society',* Parliamentary Assembly, Council of Europe, 1983)

The last several decades have witnessed a tremendous growth in the number of international non-governmental organizations (INGOs) with world-embracing memberships. Their number has grown from 6,000 in 1990 to 26,000 in 1999,[1] and currently probably exceeds that figure by far, reaching 40,000 according to some estimates.[2] Using the mass media and other channels of information – the Internet in particular – issue-oriented INGOs have proved capable of forming worldwide coalitions. Consequently, many INGOs claim to act as a 'global conscience',[3] representing broad public interests. In this way, INGOs have become a source of power and legitimacy in world politics, developing new social, political and legal norms, either by directly lobbying governments, intergovernmental organizations (IGOs), and transnational corporations to change policies, or by mobilizing public opinion indirectly.[4] Nonetheless, being unelected,

---

[1] See J. Nye, *Soft Power – The Means to Success in World Politics*, (2004), p. 90.

[2] See *Yearbook of International Organizations – Guide to Global and Civil Society Networks 2009/2010, Union of International Associations*, Ed. 46, Vol. 1B, App. 2–3, pp. 2999–3000. The answer to the question 'How many INGOs are there?' is a complex one, and depends on the mode of classification and criteria applied.

[3] See H. Anheier, M. Glasius, M. Kaldor, *Introducing Global Civil Society*, in H. Anheier, M. Glasius, M. Kaldor (eds.), *Global Civil Society Yearbook 2001*, pp. 16–17.

[4] Account of the vast literature dealing with INGO activity is clearly beyond the scope of this work. For an outline of the main trends in the analysis and current understandings of the function of INGOs – see R.H. Ben-Ari, *The Normative Position of International Non-Governmental Organizations under International Law – An Analytical Framework* (2012), pp. 47, 53–70.

unaccountable and unrepresentative, their activities raise difficult questions of legality and legitimacy.

Policy and international relations studies have focused considerable attention on non-state actors, and INGOs in particular, as a locus of power outside the state system.[5] The conceptual transformations in these domains frequently demand the attention of international lawyers working within interdisciplinary frameworks to adopt a normative agenda that corresponds to perceived changes in the structure of world affairs. However, the discourse regarding the normative position of INGOs under international law is not new. In fact, it has made progress over the last 100 years. The need for an international convention to regulate the status of INGOs was realized within international forums as early as 1910, and the first draft proposal was ready to be presented in 1912. The many stages that followed in the long sequence of developments dealing with the matter were apparently built on lessons drawn from previous attempts. It is, therefore, surprising that most of the registered proposals and related reports are relatively unknown to international lawyers or historians of international law,[6] and that a systematic analysis of the many attempts to regulate the status of INGOs has not, heretofore, been undertaken.[7]

In this work, we endeavor to review and evaluate the 100-year sequence of attempts to propose a formal status for INGOs. We demonstrate how this analysis provides an invaluable perspective that is essential for an informed review of contemporary attempts and theoretical trends, relevant to the ongoing consideration of the

[5] See generally B. Arts, M. Noortmann, B. Reinalda (eds.), *Non-State Actors in International Relations*, (2001); R.A. Higgot, R.D. Underhill, A. Bieler (eds.), *Non-State Actors and Authority in the Global System*, (2000); G. Kreijen (ed.), *State, Sovereignty and International Governance*, (2002).

[6] For some mention of early proposals, see S. Charnovitz, *Two Centuries of Participation: NGOs and International Governance*, *Michigan Journal of International Law*, Vol. 18 (1997), p. 183, 189. See also S. Charnovitz, *Nongovernmental Organizations and International Law*, *American Journal of International Law*, Vol. 100 (2006), p. 348, 356–357.

[7] See, generally, R.S. Rodgers, *Facilitation Problems of International Associations – The Legal, Fiscal and Administrative Facilities of International Non-Governmental Organizations – An International and Comparative Law, Organization, and Policy Study*, (1960), pp. 117–118. Rodgers was one of the very few who reviewed certain attempts to ameliorate a formal status for INGOs.

position of INGOs under international law. Unfortunately, most contemporary writers – whether jurists, socio-political scholars, or INGO activists – who deal with the normative aspects of INGO activity, neglect this crucial perspective. In part one of the book, we will provide a detailed chronology of past attempts to regulate the position of INGOs (1910–1990s). This synopsis will set the stage for a contextual-historical analysis, which will outline an evolutionary doctrinal sequence, evolving on the basis of normative and political considerations. In the second part of the book, we will review some new developments (2006–2012) that reflect significant trends in the contemporary discourse regarding the legal position of INGOs. In the last part of the book, we will evaluate these developments against the benchmark derived from the analysis of past attempts, and will then offer some ideas as to how this discourse might progress in the future.

Chapter One

CONTEXTUAL HISTORICAL ANALYSIS OF PAST INITIATIVES

1.1 AN OPTIMISTIC START: THE QUEST FOR INTERNATIONAL LEGAL PERSONALITY

The year 1910 was significant in the history of the evolving discourse concerning the legal status of INGOs under international law.[1] In that year, the Union of International Associations (UIA) was established following a resolution of the First World Congress of International Associations.[2] This forum was the first to propose that a '*super-national status* be established *through diplomatic convention,* for the use of international associations without lucrative object, which, by reason of their nature or aim cannot or do not wish to be subject to a fixed society legislation'. In that same year, the International Law Association (ILA) adopted a similar resolution calling 'to establish by *diplomatic convention,* an *extra-national* or *super-national statute* or *governing law* which may be adopted by international associations formed for no profit'.[3] Most significantly, however, the matter was discussed for the first time by the Institute of International Law (Institute). These discussions led to the formulation of the first *Draft Convention on the Legal Status of International Associations* presented by the Institute's member, von Bar, in 1912.[4]

---

[1] Due to the informality and ill-documentation characterizing INGOs' conferences at the time, it is possible that earlier relevant proposals, resolutions and records are no longer available – see R.S. Rodgers, *Facilitation Problems of International Associations – The Legal, Fiscal and Administrative Facilities of International Non-Governmental Organizations – An International and Comparative Law, Organization, and Policy Study*, (1960), p. 119.

[2] See *UIA – Selected Reports, Papers and Studies on International Legal Status of NGOs*, App. 4.1, p. 1, available on: http://www.uia.org/legal/index.htm (hereinafter: UIA).

[3] See ibid. The resemblance of the resolutions is due to the fact that both were inspired by the same persons and attitudes – see Rodgers, op. cit. note 1, p. 119.

[4] For the draft's text, see UIA app. 4.1, op. cit note 2.

The 1912 Institute Proposal (C.L. von Bar)

The aim of the draft convention was to enable states signatories to grant 'legal personality' to 'international associations of public utility'. Associations seeking recognition as an 'international legal person' had to forward copies of their constitution to an international bureau[5] – the heart of the registration and supervisory machinery, which was to be established by the states signatories.[6] Recognition would be granted by all governments that had not previously refused to do so. Refusal by a state to grant recognition on its territory, whether initially, or following a change in the constitution of the association, required no explanation.[7]

The draft convention was a significant departure point that set the basis for most future developments. It seems to have been the first of its kind, dealing directly with the issue of the status of INGOs under international law, and raising the question of their international legal personality (ILP) as a major concern. It was, therefore, indicative of the fact that the problem of legal personality was indeed the reason for the early legal interest in INGOs.[8] This finds further support in the written comments to the proposal that elaborated on the intention to find a solution to a reality in which it was impossible to establish an INGO without being dependent on a national jurisdiction.[9] However, the over-simplified proposal

[5] No further requirement regarding the constitution's content or the association's character was mentioned.

[6] Neither the draft, nor von Bar's written comment on it elaborated on the composition of the bureau or its international legal status.

[7] In the same spirit, revocation of recognition at any time was to be made by a simple notification to the bureau; such revocation however was without any retroactive effect.

[8] See Rodgers, op. cit. note 1, p. 120, 122–123. Von Bar, in his short eight-article proposal, did not define exactly what he meant by 'ILP'. Although some doubts were raised regarding whether he meant 'ILP' as we regard it today, von Bar was clearly aware of the 1910 UIA/ILA mandates that considered a 'super-national status', and was influenced by them in his work. Given the modern context of the term, it may be assumed that he really meant 'internationally recognized legal person'. This conclusion is in line with other indications regarding his intellectual viewpoint on the structure of the international community as an overarching universal system – see L. Reydams, *Universal Jurisdiction: International and Municipal Legal Perspectives*, (2003), pp. 30–31 & fn. 13–14.

[9] See Comment, UIA app. 4.1, op. cit. note 2, pp. 3–4; relevant associations however had to be genuinely international in character, and not national associations with international goals.

completely ignored delicate issues, such as the contents of the status of ILP, the composition of the registering 'international bureau', and the problematic position of INGO officials as foreign nationals *vis-à-vis* the host state.[10] It clearly, therefore, did not aspire to the establishment of any balanced system of control between states and INGOs. The following Institute proposal reflected a significant development in dealing with the formulation of an international status for INGOs.

The 1923 Institute Proposal (N.S. Politis)

In 1923, Politis[11] presented a proposal for a *Draft Convention Relating to the Legal Position of International Associations*. The proposal was intended to grant international associations 'an international status which is compatible with the requirement of public order'.[12] The fundamental assumption underlying the proposal, set out in its preamble, was that the encouragement of the development of INGOs was essential to the general interest of the international community. To this end, it was considered necessary that associations 'be at liberty not to have exclusive ties with any given country'. Politis explained that it was not possible to find, in those countries where the associations pursued their activities, such legal protection as was required by their interests, and that the legal status recognized by one state was not automatically recognized by other states. Consequently, international associations were unable to enjoy an adequate degree of capacity and freedom to pursue their activities everywhere. In view of these problems, the draft convention suggested a scheme by which states parties would grant legal protection by conferring upon international associations the 'status of legal entities' or by 'recognizing the legal status acquired by them in another contracting state'.[13]

---

[10] See as well Rodgers, op. cit. note 1, pp. 120–121, 124.

[11] Nicolas Socrate Politis, an Institute member, became central to discussions and research on the topic.

[12] See UIA, op. cit. note 2, App. 4.5, p. 1. Politis spoke about 'international status', avoiding the term 'ILP'.

[13] See ibid, art. 1. 'International Associations' were broadly defined as 'associations of a private character which pursue, without any profit motive, an objective of international interest'.

The proposed system of recognition was to be administered by a permanent central bureau made up of 'special delegates or diplomatic representatives' of states parties. This bureau would function as a depository, responsible for registration; it did not reserve power to refuse registration. With effect from notification by the bureau to signatory governments, the association would enjoy 'the benefits attaching to the legal status acquired' within all states parties. States nevertheless reserved the right to refuse recognition of the legal status if the nature of the association's aims or the attributes of its members appeared to them to constitute 'a danger to the public order of their countries'. Significantly, refusal motivated in this way could be contested by the refused association by way of an appeal to the then World Court – the Permanent Court of International Justice (PCIJ), on the grounds of an *ultra vires* action.[14] The proposal further indicated that international legal status provided associations with certain internationally secured rights.[15]

Unlike von Bar, Politis understood that a universal status required the specification of certain secured rights, without which the formulation of such status would be meaningless. Furthermore, he clearly realized the need to set up a more balanced universal system of control, providing protection to states and INGOs alike by suggesting an improved international bureau, supervised by a diplomatic (that is, state-controlled) commission. However, the provision of the right of appeal by an INGO to the World Court shows that Politis envisioned INGOs, at least potentially, as equal to states and IGOs within the overall scheme of the international community, in terms of the quality of their aimed-for universal status.[16] Unsurprisingly, the inclusion of this revolutionary mechanism in the comprehensive scheme led observers to regard the proposal as a premature and largely Utopian exercise.[17] In any case, it seems that Politis tried to stretch

---

[14] In any case, a definite refusal resulted in deprivation of the relevant association's right to maintain establishments only within the refusing country.

[15] Such as bringing actions at law, entering into contracts, possessing real and movable property, receiving gifts and donations, protection of name and seal, acquisition of fiscal privileges, and access to courts.

[16] The term 'international community' was explicitly used by Politis in his proposal's Preamble.

[17] See Rodgers, op. cit. note 1, pp. 121–124; See as well UIA app. 4.5, op. cit. note 12, p. 10. Rodgers noted that 'Politis must have known that an INGO could not be a

the notion of a universal status to the greatest possible extent, and in so doing, clarified the depth of revision that would be required. It is also clear that Politis viewed the acquisition of a universal legal status as a process that should develop into a rule of customary law.[18] In these respects, his proposal demonstrated how radical the idea of a unified universal status was, as well as how far-reaching its implications were for the fields of international law and international relations.[19]

1.2 UNIFORM UNIVERSAL STATUS: A TRANSNATIONAL WORLD VISION

Clearly, the early Institute proposals reflected the understandings underlying the broadly delineated 1910 mandates of the UIA and the ILA. Both made clear that the acquisition of the international status was based on the *desire of international associations not to be subject to any national jurisdiction*, by reason of *their nature or object*. The ILA, the Institute, and the UIA – themselves newly established highly-motivated INGOs, formed to strengthen international law[20] – were obviously acting against the blossoming private transnational

party to a dispute before the World Court, that is, could not be a full subject of international law in the eyes of the court' – see fn. 2, p. 121.

[18] See generally, Rodgers, ibid, p. 122. According to Art. 7 of the Politis proposal, even a refusal to grant recognition by a certain state on the basis of public order that had been approved by the PCIJ would have a limited effect, only within the confined territory of the refusing state.

[19] In any case, it is noteworthy that Politis had already made a cautious concession with regard to the notion of a uniform universal status, when he suggested a second-best scheme by which states would recognize 'the legal status *acquired by associations in another contracting state*'. This option was not easily reconcilable with Politis' otherwise broad normative vision, as it suggested an alternative system of 'mutual recognition' that theoretically conflicted with that of a single universal status. An explanation can be found in Politis' desire to set up a more balanced system of control than that established by von Bar, one that would give protection to states and INGOs alike – see Rodgers, ibid, p. 124. As we shall see, by mentioning this relatively more realistic (albeit, in his view, second-rate) possibility in his proposal, Politis, in fact, opened the way for future writers to pursue this path.

[20] See S. Charnovitz, *Two Centuries of Participation: NGOs and International Governance, Michigan Journal of International Law*, Vol. 18 (1997), pp. 194–195, 212. The Institute and the ILA were both established in 1873, the American Society of

associations and the evolving modes of private action evident at the turn of the century and the early days of the League of Nations. The expanding scope of international cooperation at the time was marked by increased NGO influence on international governance, apparent in the development of mixed international conferences that brought together government officials and individual NGO representatives.[21] Von Bar and Politis corresponded with leading jurists who invited international lawyers to be attentive to the phenomenon of groups working successfully to influence intergovernmental policymaking, pointing out the need for regulation of international associations in order to 'effectuate their formation and functioning', and, most importantly, to ensure that states' acts would not 'retard and hinder their existence and activity'.[22] They were thus inspired to develop, through international law, more direct forms of INGO advocacy.[23] Intellectually and normatively, this quest was not unreasonable during a period of numerous conferences, conventions and congresses emphasizing the expansion of the rules of international law and the close network of international relations.[24] Furthermore, since the distinction between the 'IGO' and the 'INGO' was yet to be crystallized, and many intergovernmental conferences

---

International Law in 1906, and the UIA in 1910. Between 1872 and 1914, 26 law-related INGOs were created, and became highly active in the conclusion of landmark treaties and facilitated the success of intergovernmental conferences. Encouraged by their own achievements, and becoming self-aware of their growing capacity to influence governments, they were clearly motivated to promote the legal position of INGOs.

[21] See ibid, p. 191, 208. The First and Second Hague Peace Conferences, of 1899 and 1907, are two significant examples of the many cases of pre-League NGO involvement in international meetings that undoubtedly influenced von Bar and Politis. Since the 1850's and until the late 1920's, INGOs have stimulated the development of international regimes and provided technical expertise in various fields. Their extensive participation in the work of the League of Nations and the ILO has further strengthened their position as influential international actors – see pp. 200–208, 212–245.

[22] See S. Charnovitz, *Nongovernmental Organizations and International Law, American Journal of International Law*, Vol. 100 (2006), p. 348, 349, quoting S.E. Baldwin (1907), W. Kaufmann (1908), and Elihu Root (1911).

[23] See ibid, p. 356. See as well Charnovitz (1997), op. cit. note 20, p. 183, 189, quoting W. Kaufman, who supported Politis' proposal by arguing that international law was no longer solely about relationships among States but also about relations among individuals and associations.

[24] See M.N. Shaw, *International Law (6th ed.)*, (2008), p. 28.

had yet to be transformed into 'international organizations',[25] the time was ripe for such an endeavor. Apparently, in view of the growing cooperation between governments and INGOs and the demonstrated need of INGOs' expertise and input,[26] the Institute's proposals were not expected to raise many practical problems or foster much political opposition.

All in all, it is important to note that the initial interest in the legal position of INGOs was clearly derived from the problem of ILP and its related topics, such as public registration and order.[27] The working assumptions of the pre-Second World War drafters, who were INGO activists and worked under the mandates of INGO-forums, were that (1) the development of international associations was essentially beneficial to the interests of the international community, and that therefore, (2) they should be at liberty not to be tied exclusively to a certain state. Evidently, this logic was expected to spur states to grant *all* INGOs a uniform universal status.

1.3 SELECTION, REGISTRATION, AND ORDER: POLITICAL RELIABILITY VS. EXPERTISE

The optimism that characterized the initial quest for ILP, based on a highly positive and autonomous view of the INGO community, could not last long. This was a direct effect of world politics: the Second World War was not preceded by any comparable optimism such as that which existed before the First World War; what had been a European crisis became a world crisis.[28] The international ideological strife, which proved to be 'so dangerous to the peaceful work of at least the technical INGOs' passed from regional to global levels. Due to the rapid pace of events in the interval between the World Wars, the Institute's proposals were put aside and earned little mention by academics, diplomats, or even INGO officials.[29]

---

[25] See Charnovitz (1997), op. cit. note 20, pp. 198–199.

[26] Charnovitz suggests a general cyclical pattern, in which the involvement of INGOs rises when governments need them and falls when governments and international bureaucracies gain self-confidence – see ibid, p. 190.

[27] See Rodgers, op. cit. note 1, p. 120, 124.

[28] ibid, p. 125. See also Charnovitz (1997), op. cit. note 20 p. 246.

[29] See Rodgers, ibid, p. 125.

Evaluating the background against which the early proposals were drafted, it is important to note the growing concern with the problem of INGOs' political reliability. Politis was obviously writing against the political background of the First World War,[30] and although von Bar was writing before the entry of the Soviet Union into world politics, he must also have been concerned with the problem of control over politically unreliable organizations.[31] Before the Second World War, however, the two main factors that affected INGO involvement[32] – the needs of governments and their agencies on the one hand, and the capability of INGOs on the other hand – were balanced. In other words, INGOs could dependably supply the demands of governments. The early involvement of INGOs was clearly marked by good leadership, expertise, and reliable funding.[33] One main reason for INGOs' strength at the turn of the century was that it was propelled by elites that gained INGOs' credibility.[34] Consequently, although the period of von Bar and Politis was not characterized by much political freedom or high INGO memberships, organizations were generally trusted as being professional and reliable – and expectations for helping them achieve an upgraded status were accordingly high. In the following years, as world tensions heightened and the number of INGOs grew rapidly, the disenchantment of states and IGOs with INGOs increasingly reflected the former's political concerns.[35] On the one hand, governments were relying more on the expertise of IGOs' secretariats, while on the other hand, INGOs' credibility was derived more from broad

30 Politis must have been aware of 'the possible threat which the Comintern posed to Western parties, just as the Bolsheviks would be aware of the threat posed to their position by the Labour and Socialist International and the predecessors of the International Peasant Union – see ibid, p. 124.

31 Rodgers explains that since the struggle between the Western Allies and the German Alliance was hardly one involving persons committed to an international ideology, the precedence to von Bar's concerns should be found either further back in history, in the internationalism associated with certain revolutionary periods such as the early Napoleonic, or in religion – see ibid.

32 See Charnovitz (1997), op. cit. note 20, p. 269. These factors underline Charnovitz's suggested 'theory of NGO involvement'.

33 See ibid, p. 270.

34 Ibid.

35 See ibid, p. 247, 249.

membership and less from credible leadership.[36] Furthermore, some leading INGOs willingly joined the game of power politics, becoming political allies of certain states and IGOs and applying more and more direct pressure on governments, thus setting back the cause of INGO participation.[37]

1.4 GAINING NEW MOMENTUM: UN CONSULTATIVE STATUS ARRANGEMENTS

Under these circumstances, the lack of optimism and the stagnancy that characterized the Cold War era meant that new momentum was needed to revive discussions about the legal status of INGOs. Such momentum was provided by the adoption of the UN Charter and the incorporation of Article 71 as a result of significant INGO lobbying and drafting efforts.[38]

Article 71 UN Charter & ECOSOC Consultative Status

Article 71, under Chapter X dealing with ECOSOC, instituted the formal status of INGOs within the UN system.[39] This provision, the single reference in the Charter to 'INGOs' and their first documented recognition as such in international law,[40] enabled ECOSOC to

---

[36] See ibid, p. 269.

[37] See ibid, p. 264, 269.

[38] See ibid, p. 249, 257–258.

[39] According to Art. 71, 'ECOSOC may make suitable arrangements for consultation with NGOs which are concerned with matters within its competence. Such arrangements may be made with international organizations and, where appropriate, with national organizations after consultation with the Member of the UN concerned'. Suggestions to expand the consultative arrangements to include the General Assembly, and to establish a single system of NGO accreditation for all UN bodies have failed – see *Report of the Panel of Eminent Persons on United Nations-Civil Society Relations* (the *'Cardoso Report'*), UN Doc. A/58/817 (June 11, 2004), pp. 52–60; *Report of the Secretary-General in Response to the Report of the Panel of Eminent Persons on United Nations-Civil Society Relations*, UN. Doc. A/59/354 (Sep. 13, 2004), pp. 6–9. As of Nov. 2011, there were 3536 NGOs in consultative status with ECOSOC. Annually some 400 organizations apply for consultative status, while on average, between 200 and 300 applications are recommended for approval by ECOSOC each year – see UN DESA NGO Branch on: http://www.csonet.org (Jan. 2013).

[40] See M.A. Olz, *Non-Governmental Organizations in Regional Human Rights Systems*, *Columbia Human Rights Law Review*, Vol. 28, No. 1, 1997, p. 307, 314.

establish restricted official relationships with INGOs.[41] This article, in fact, formalized the extensive consultative relationships which existed during the years of the League of Nations,[42] and reaffirmed the value of INGOs' contribution.[43] Consequently, it was heralded as 'one of the most original and promising innovations made by the Charter', reflecting how 'in almost prophetic manner, the founding fathers of the UN recognized the importance of the notion of participation'.[44] Furthermore, the provision set up a model for other UN specialized agencies as well as access to all of the bodies under ECOSOC.[45]

Over the years, ECOSOC has expanded considerably the scope of application of Article 71, by adopting authoritative interpretations thereof, and by reviewing and modifying its Rules of Procedure.[46] Within this framework, the consultative status was understood to fulfill two fundamental purposes: (1) enabling the Council and its bodies to obtain expert information and advice, and (2) providing a forum for INGOs which represent important elements of public opinion in a large number of countries.[47] Noteworthy is ECOSOC Res. 1296(XLIV) of 1968 which formed the legal basis for decisions concerning INGOs' consultative status.[48] According to this resolution, the organizations concerned, which were not established by

---

[41] R. Lagoni, *Article 71*, in B. Simma (ed.), *The Charter of the United Nations – A Commentary*, (1994), p. 904.

[42] D. Otto, *Nongovernmental Organizations in the United Nations System: The Emerging Role of International Civil Society, Human Rights Quarterly*, Vol. 18 (1996), p. 107, 109; see as well Charnovitz (1997), op. cit. note 20, p. 250.

[43] After their role had withered during the war years – see Charnovitz, ibid, pp. 250, 257–258.

[44] *Report of the Council Committee on NGOs*, UN Doc. E/5257/Add.1, (April 9, 1973), p. 1, as quoted in *International Law Association (ILA) Australian Branch, The International Status of Human Rights Non-governmental Organizations* (1978), p. 8, fn. 2. The provision was included mainly due to NGOs lobbying in the Charter's drafting conference – see p. 13; see as well Charnovitz (1997), op. cit. note 20, pp. 249–250.

[45] See Charnovitz, ibid, p. 249, 253–256. For further institutional arrangements applying NGOs' consultative or observer status see H.H.-K. Rechenberg, *Non-Governmental Organizations*, in *Encyclopedia of Public International Law*, Vol. 3 (1997), p. 616.

[46] See generally Rechenberg, ibid, p. 614.

[47] See *ECOSOC Res. 1296 (XLIV), Arrangements for Consultation with NGOs*, (May 23, 1968), paras. 13, 14.

[48] See Simma, op. cit. note 41, p. 904; see Appendices, 2.1.

intergovernmental agreement, had to be international in structure, thus construing as exceptional the participation of national NGOs in accordance with the language of Article 71.[49] Following a review of the rules governing the consultative status, as reflected in ECOSOC Res. 1996/31,[50] the criteria for eligible NGOs were expanded in a manner that no longer regarded the access of national NGOs as exceptional. Furthermore, this resolution set the goal of facilitating a balanced regional representation.[51]

Article 71, initially viewed as an indirect form of recognition of the importance of INGOs in the opinion of governments, was increasingly criticized after two or three decades for being based on an anachronistic UN-NGO relationship, which positioned INGOs as supportive adjuncts to states.[52] Consequently, the consultative system was frequently viewed as reflecting a continuing and pervasive tension in the UN arrangements for cooperation between states and INGOs, enshrining a defensive state-centric approach.[53] Otto maintains that Article 71, in fact, limited earlier practices, by confining mandated consultation to areas covered by ECOSOC and by limiting involvement to 'consultation', in contrast, for example, to 'participation without vote'.[54] Furthermore, many assert that the actual operation of Article 71 is controversial,[55] creating Western-biased arrangements.[56] Considering that governments decide on

---

[49] See Olz, op. cit. note 40, pp. 314–316. INGOs were required to prove (1) a representative character, (2) a recognized international standing, (3) the representation of a substantial proportion of major sections of the population or of the organized persons within the particular field of competence, covering (4) a substantial number of countries (at least three) in different regions. Furthermore, organizations must qualify as democratic in process. Organizations were further divided into 3 categories of 'General' and 'Special' status, and a 'Roster' category, all in accordance with their relevance to ECOSOC fields of activity- see Rechenberg, op. cit. note 45, pp. 615–616; Charnovitz (1997), op. cit. note 20, pp. 252–253.

[50] *ECOSOC Res. 1996/31, Consultative Relationship between the United Nations and Non-Governmental Organizations*, (July 25, 1996); see Appendices, 2.2.

[51] See Olz, op. cit. note 40, p. 316. See as well Charnovitz (1997), op. cit. note 20, pp. 253, 266–267.

[52] See Otto, op. cit. note 42, p. 140.

[53] See ibid, p. 127.

[54] Ibid, p. 109.

[55] See, for example, Simma, op. cit. note 41, p. 903.

[56] See Otto, op. cit. note 42, p. 111, 121; Otto explains that Western-dominated NGOs are more likely to have the resources to develop international standing, arguing that the exclusion of national organizations from ECOSOC accreditation

ECOSOC applications, commentators further maintain that the UN consultative arrangements are maneuvered in a way which is inconsistent with movement towards recognizing NGOs' diversity and deepening their role in the international community.[57] Whatever the case may be, it is well acknowledged that decisions on admission, classification, suspension or withdrawal of an INGO, taken by ECOSOC's Committee on NGOs,[58] are highly motivated by political considerations.[59] Furthermore, due to the workload of ECOSOC and the growing number of NGOs and INGOs seeking consultative status, the quality of the accreditation and verification process taken by the committee has been widely criticized.[60]

Evaluating Article 71 arrangements, one must recall that the granting of consultative status to an INGO does not mean, conjointly, the transfer of rights, immunities and privileges of a member of ECOSOC or the UN to that organization.[61] Nevertheless, some commentators, like Rechenberg, claim that if an NGO is granted consultative status by an IGO, it simultaneously acquires 'a certain *international* legal status, albeit not that of a subject of international

---

operates to 'specifically disadvantage Third World NGOs'. Simma notes that, by far, the most organizations in consultative status are from Western industrialized countries – see ibid, p. 912.

57 See Otto, ibid, ibid.

58 Pursuant to ECOSOC Res. 3(II) (June 21, 1946), the Committee, currently consisted of 19 Member States, is the intergovernmental organ designated to consider applications for consultative status.

59 See Rechenberg, op. cit. note 45, p. 615; Simma, op. cit. note 41, p. 907; *'Cardoso Report'*, op. cit. note 39, p. 52. See also F.A. Vabulas, *What is a Seat on the ECOSOC NGO Committee Worth? Exploring the State Motivations and Benefits of Granting UN Access to NGOs, American Political Science Association 2011 Annual Meeting Paper*, available at SSRN: http://ssrn.com/abstract=1900279; J.D. Aston, *The UN Committee on NGOs: Guarding the Entrance to a Politically Divided House, European Journal of International Law*, Vol. 12(5), (2001), p. 943.

60 See I. Rossi, *NGOs in International Law: Has Regulation Come to a Halt?, Institute for International Law* (Leuven University), Working Paper No. 123 (Feb. 2008), p. 14. See as well *Report of the Secretary-General*, op. cit. note 39, paras. 30, 34, pp. 8–9; D. Brakman Reiser, C.R. Kelly, *Linking NGO Accountability and the Legitimacy of Global Governance, Brooklyn Journal of International Law*, Vol. 36 (2011), p. 1011, 1054–1059, 1069–1070, who note that monitoring by the Committee on NGOs fails to materialize the potential of the accreditation standards.

61 Rechenberg, op. cit. note 45, p. 616; Simma, op. cit. note 41, p. 903. The consultative status is more restricted than the observer status (Arts. 69, 70 UN Charter) – see ibid.

law'.[62] The essence of this 'status' short of personality remains, however, peculiar and blurred,[63] and one may conclude that the mere enjoyment of a consultative (or observer) status does not correspond to any of the corollaries of the acquisition of ILP. Whatever the case may be, it is hardly disputed that the scope and nature of INGOs' involvement has expanded beyond the ability of relevant UN arrangements, based on a compromise arrived at more than 65 years ago between advocates of INGOs' participation and opposing states, to embrace and to effectively regulate.[64]

1.5 DE FACTO *LEGAL STATUS: FALSE PROMISE OF CONSULTATIVE ARRANGEMENTS*

Initially, the creation of the consultative status inspired optimism and expectation. It provided a new framework for the discourse on the position of INGOs, applying different balances to those conceived by the early Institute proposals. Subsequently, the mandate of the first session of the Conference of Consultative Non-Governmental Organizations (CCNGOs), that gathered in 1948 INGOs that had been granted consultative status with ECOSOC, was modified to consider *the very desirability* of a convention granting

62 Rechenberg, ibid, p. 617. See as well P. Malanczuk, *Akehurst's Modern Introduction to International Law* (7th rev. ed., 1997), p. 97, and compare with Simma, ibid, p. 913, fn. 105.

63 An explanation for Rechenberg's formulation may be that, according to his view, the existing consultative arrangements provide a framework for an on-going evolution, and it may well be that the essence of the consultative status will expand over time; being adaptable and temporary, these arrangements may gain new meaning in view of changing conceptions regarding INGOs normative status in general. Rechenberg's observation should therefore be read in the light of his general assessment that, 'in the long run a uniform applicable code of provisions regulating the requirements, rights, privileges and immunities, obligations and responsibilities of NGOs when acting in the international scene will be indispensable' – see ibid, pp. 617–618.

64 See Otto, op. cit. note 42, p. 109; Charnovitz (1997), op. cit. note 20, p. 268; Simma, op. cit. note 41, p. 904, 914, where he maintains that the consultative status 'is narrow in its scope and limited in its content'. See as well Rossi, op. cit. note 60, who maintains that it becomes less and less clear whether further formalization of NGO arrangements within the UN would improve the current situation, and that 'no model has been found to guarantee full participation of NGOs in a manageable and meaningful way' that would convince both NGOs and Member-States – p. 8.

the status of a legal entity under international law to INGOs *with a UN consultative status*.[65] Neither the desirability of the international status, nor the group of INGOs that were supposed to enjoy it, continued to be taken for granted. The working assumptions of von Bar and Politis were thus nullified, and consequently the uniform universal status mechanism corresponding to these preliminary assumptions became open to question. The way was opened for the reconsideration of optional legal mechanisms, as well as the ranking and grouping of relevant INGOs. Moreover, the new arrangements under ECOSOC seemed to provide some practical solutions to the old problems of registration, control and order.[66] Accordingly, discussions were channeled to the confined review of the legal position of INGOs with consultative status. This was clearly a major turning point in the discourse on the normative position of INGOs; from then on, this discourse was closely linked to their UN status, and the ECOSOC arrangements were applied as a proxy for evaluation.

Proposal of the CCNGOs, 1948

Despite a preliminary decision to cover the granting of an international status to *all* INGOs, the Conference's study committee[67] decided to concentrate its work on the status of *consultative* organizations. This decision was based on the evaluation that the granting of international status to all INGOs was expected to raise difficult problems of control. Accordingly, the committee was presented with an initial proposal which suggested that ECOSOC, functioning as an international registration bureau, would grant requesting INGOs legal personality and related facilities. ECOSOC would exercise full discretion in its decision on an applicant INGO; its decisions would be final and binding. Registered INGOs would then be supervised by ECOSOC, in accordance with rules provided for by a UN General Assembly resolution.[68] Finally, an international UN

---

65 See Rodgers, op. cit. note 1, p. 127; See also UIA, op. cit. note 2, App. 4.6, p. l.

66 See Rodgers, ibid, p. 128.

67 The unique committee was chaired by the former Legal Advisor to the League of Nations, Professor Habicht, and was consisted of representatives of 11 leading INGOs, the Institute and the UIA.

68 See UIA, app. 4.6, op. cit. note 65, p. 2. The proposed 'UN General Assembly Resolution on the Granting of International Juridical Personality to Certain

convention would accord binding force to the recognition of personality and specify its contents and legal implications.

The study committee rejected this scheme, primarily because it could not support a system that granted political control to states and IGOs. Members of the committee, being INGO officials, generally thought that a political organ like ECOSOC could not produce proper decisions regarding INGOs' entitlement to personality.[69] Consequently, the committee decided to adopt a completely different approach while *renouncing the idea of establishing recognition of ILP*. Alternatively, it requested that recognition be based on *personality recognized in the consultative INGO's state of incorporation*, that is to say, recognition in each country of the legal status acquired in the country where the organization was legally constituted. In other words, the committee decided to concentrate on finding a *practical solution to the problem of conflicts-of-laws* arising from INGOs' cross-border activities, instead of recognizing INGOs' ILP.[70]

Following further discussions, the committee's rapporteur, Kopelmanas, prepared a *Report on the Legal Status of INGOs* which is intellectually significant even today.[71] This report acknowledged that the problem in law was indeed to provide the associations with 'the capacity to have rights and obligations' on the international plane; the practical needs of the vast majority of INGOs could

Consultative NGOs', suggested that the GA would express its opinion that the possession of 'an *international juridical personality independent of states* but recognized by them' was essential since 'the lack of a firm legal status prevents the INGOs from fulfilling completely their role and aims', or being 'of any real assistance to the UN'. The declarative part acknowledged that recognition of personality required assurances that it would be granted 'only to *truly international organizations of acknowledged importance* which can furnish every guarantee as to their integrity'.

69 See Rodgers, op. cit. note 1, p. 128. Some members were of the view that 'international supervision might be the one point on which divergent political systems could combine, to the detriment of the INGOs', while others felt that 'international political tensions would push INGOs one way and then another'. Others believed that the ECOSOC diplomats were not sufficiently expert in the problems with which they dealt.

70 See also ibid, p. 129.

71 See UIA, op. cit. note 2, App. 3.3; see Appendices, 1.1; Professor Kopelmanas, Director of Research at the National Scientific Research Centre (Paris), and Legal Advisor to the UN Economic Commission for Europe (UNECE).

only be fully satisfied by basing their legal capacity in foreign countries on an imperative rule of international law.[72] However, it had to be recognized that it would be impossible to obtain concessions from states for the benefit of *all* associations; a choice based on the principles of importance, usefulness, and legitimate purposes therefore had to be made from associations wishing to enjoy international status. Furthermore, if it was indeed intended to free INGOs from the bonds which attached them to national legal systems, it would not be sufficient to attach them formally to the international legal system, leaving them 'entirely free from any real subjection to a higher social order of a government nature'. Rather, it was essential 'to replace the control exercised by the domestic l egislation, with an equivalent control by international law'. Thus, an effective subjection of INGOs to the international system not only demanded registration but also ongoing supervision of their activities.[73]

This conclusion was followed by another decisive observation concerning the overall calculation of interests by INGOs when it came to considering the attachment of international status. The report acknowledged that whatever might be the methods of international control, they would always appear *more onerous* than the corresponding obligations devolving upon NGOs under certain domestic legislation. Since internal systems had general means of controlling all legal acts performed on their territory, they could afford to be more liberal in their supervision of associations than the international legal system, which in view of its general organization would have been obliged to stress the specific measures for controlling the NGOs granted the benefits of international status.[74] It was therefore 'perfectly natural' that INGOs should resign themselves to the 'practical disadvantages' of attachment to a domestic legal system, rather than accept a regime which would result in restriction of their freedom of action. Consequently, it had to be realized that the

---

[72] See ibid, p. 3.

[73] See ibid, pp. 5–6. This task could not be assigned to a 'subordinate *administrative* body', but had to be given to 'an important *political* body', bearing sufficient weight with states.

[74] See ibid, p. 6.

basis of the system of recognition still[75] had to depend on a formal attachment to national jurisdictions, while concurrently obtaining recognition of the status acquired in the state of constitution by other states, through an international convention.

Proposal of the CCNGOs, 1949

In view of these developments, in 1949, the CCNGOs suggested a draft convention entitled *Preliminary Draft Agreement Designed to Facilitate the Work of NGOs having Consultative Status.*[76] The draft was based on the distinction between international and domestic NGOs established by ECOSOC, as part of its function under Article 71, thus avoiding the need to create a new international registration body or to introduce a special procedure. The distinction was necessary in order to distinguish purely national associations from those having national legal status combined with an international character.[77] It was believed that adopting the list of ECOSOC's INGOs could ensure authentic confirmation of the international character and significance of a relevant NGO. Furthermore, it was estimated that limiting the scope of the convention in this way would increase the probability of states acceding to it.[78]

The draft requested states parties to extend benefits to INGOs legally constituted on the territory of an acceding state and having consultative status with ECOSOC (or a UN Specialized Agency). Essentially, the convention established a system by which states undertook to provide entitled INGOs with the same rights enjoyed in the country where they were constituted.[79] Nevertheless, states reserved the power to limit these rights to those granted in their respective jurisdictions 'to the most favored category of similar

[75] And presumably until the development of international organizations establishes conditions in which a more reliable and less objectionable form of international control can be envisaged – see ibid.

[76] For the text of the draft agreement see UIA, op. cit. note 2, App. 4.7, pp. 1–3.

[77] See UIA app. 3.3, op. cit. note 71, p. 7.

[78] See ibid.

[79] The authors of the draft had to decide between two alternatives: either reference to the legal position in the country of origin, or to the country in which the INGO wished to carry on its activities. Obviously, the second solution is more advantageous to INGOs. However, the drafters estimated that the majority of states could not endorse such a convention – see ibid, p. 8.

organizations'.[80] In this way, the suggested status was subject to twofold limitations: on the one hand, limitation by the legal status of associations in the country of origin, and on the other hand, by the treatment given to similar national associations in the country in which the benefits were claimed. Interestingly, the draft provided that the International Court of Justice (ICJ) would adjudicate disputes arising from the convention.[81]

In 1950, the CCNGOs adopted a resolution recommending that INGOs carefully study the draft convention and submit their views to the bureau of the conference.[82] However, the bureau scarcely received any responses. This fact revealed that INGOs were unprepared to cooperate on common problems. Rodgers explained that INGO officials were 'too concerned with the trees of international life to see the forest as a whole', and maintained that since they felt that the convention did not solve particular problems, such as facing individual INGOs on a here-and-now basis, they would be unwilling to devote the time and effort needed to produce an overall solution over time.[83]

In any case, the work of the CCNGOs indicates that the strong emphasis on the arrangements under Article 71 created a situation in which the concept of a uniform international status became largely pointless. The new arrangements supposedly provided a certain internationally recognized *de facto* status that was generally welcomed by leading INGO activists, as well as by diplomats. This development, however, provoked new challenges: first, the need to closely define genuine INGO entities;[84] and second, the need to

---

[80] See UIA app. 4.7, op. cit. note 76, Art. 2. Clearly, it was not considered possible to impose on states an imperative obligation to treat foreign INGOs more favorably than domestic associations. In any case, the draft wished to compensate this situation by maintaining that INGOs shall automatically be included in the *most favored* category of domestic associations – see UIA app. 3.3, ibid, p. 9.

[81] Probably another echo of the 1923 Politis proposal; see UIA app. 4.7, ibid, Art. 9. Here, however, the incorporation of the ICJ as a device for settling disputes arising from the proposed convention was not as unrealistic or Utopian as in the case of Politis' proposal, since it was essentially based on the need to adjudicate on questions of *conflicts of domestic laws* between states.

[82] See Rodgers, op. cit. note 1, p. 130.

[83] ibid, pp. 130–131.

[84] This created tensions within the non-governmental community, since many 'INGOs' were left outside the general discourse, turning from 'INGOs' into mere 'NGOs'.

outline, in detail, the INGOs' specific legal requirements. As we shall see, these challenges remain relevant and unresolved until this very day. Furthermore, the strong link between the consideration of INGOs' international status and that of their acquired UN consultative status turned the already sensitive questions of state-control and IGO-supervision into highly problematic political issues. These concerns, particularly reflected in the involvement of an international diplomatic/quasi-diplomatic/administrative, monitoring/supervising/administering body (the so-called 'international bureau'), will inevitably give rise to considerable tension in the future.

1.6 RESEMBLANCE TO IGOS: THE QUEST FOR FUNCTIONAL LEGITIMACY

Notably, it was the CCNGOs study committee – itself an INGO forum – that decided to avoid the question of recognition to ILP, focusing instead on achieving a practical solution to the problem of conflicts-of-laws.[85] As explained, this was not merely a strategic decision to temporarily waive the preliminary stage of acquiring a uniform status under international law, but a decision to renounce it altogether. Initially, this stage was supposed to reflect a general understanding with regard to INGOs' normative position within the overall composition of the international community. Nevertheless, leading INGO activists, who had seen no progress in this direction for almost half a century,[86] decided not to insist anymore on *formal* consensual recognition under international law which was evidently considered a nuisance. After all, much of the required recognition by states and IGOs had apparently been provided by the very inclusion of Article 71 in the UN Charter. Moreover, activists and jurists had clearly become aware of the fact that a uniform status was meaningless without the actual ability to secure the privileges deriving from it. Therefore, they concluded that the acquired UN status provided sufficient moral and legal basis to demand substantial privileges from states. In this respect, the change in INGOs'

[85] For further explanation of this development see Rodgers, op. cit. note 1, p. 129; Kopelmanas' report, UIA app. 3.3, op. cit. note 71, p. 11.

[86] See, for example, Rodgers, ibid, p. 120.

strategy was not in the nature of a realistic compromise, but rather an expression of a supposedly powerful position.

The background for the self-assured position adopted by leading INGOs at the time is important. The strengthening of the status of IGOs in general, through the adoption of the UN Charter and the creation of the UN system, and especially through the leading precedent delivered by the ICJ in the 1949 *Reparation for Injuries* case that reaffirmed and consolidated IGOs' ILP,[87] raised huge expectations among INGO activists and their academic proponents. These expectations were generated by the conceptual association of INGOs with IGOs, followed by an attempt to translate this underlying notion into practical legal demands. Thus, the writings of Kopelmanas (1949),[88] Rodgers (1958, 1960), Lador-Lederer (1963),[89] and others exposed much intellectual confusion among activists and jurists alike. Rodgers, for example, elaborated on the philosophy underlying his work, stating that,

87 *Reparation for Injuries Suffered in the Service of the United Nations*, Advisory Opinion (1949), ICJ Rep. 1949, p. 174. The ICJ stated that the UN was a subject of international law, and could enforce its rights by bringing international claims. The ruling was applied to embrace other international intergovernmental institutions that have been since accepted as possessing rights and duties of their own and a distinctive, objective ILP, limited by their mandate as implied by their constituent documents, as well as their actual powers and practice. The ICJ thus reaffirmed the existence of several levels of international legal capacity, and defined each degree within the context of the function that each relevant entity fulfills in the international society. This observation still underlies the doctrinal distinction between the general capacity of states and the limited functional legal capacity of other subjects of international law – see Shaw, op. cit. note 24, p. 47, 259–260, 1297–1298; H. Mosler, *Subjects of International Law*, in *Encyclopedia of Public International Law*, Vol. 7, (1984), pp. 444–445; H.G. Schermers, N.M. Blokker, *International Institutional Law – Unity within Diversity*, (1999), pp. 976–982.

88 Kopelmanas remarked that, on the basis of their collaboration in the work of inter-governmental bodies, certain groups among the consultative NGOs considered that they should enjoy *real privileges and immunities modeled on those enjoyed by IGOs*, and observed that there seemed to be no chance of this legally unfounded and politically unrealistic claim being accepted by states – see UIA app. 3.3, op. cit. note 71, p. 11.

89 See J.J. Lador-Lederer, *International Non-Governmental Organizations and Economic Entities: A Study in Autonomous Organization and Jus Gentium*, (1963); see also in R.H. Ben-Ari, *The Normative Position of International Non-Governmental Organizations under International Law – An Analytical Framework* (2012), pp. 49–50, fn. 287 p. 81, fn. 368 p. 99, 101–102.

> Every IGO has at least one counterpart in the INGO world ... There is *a legal difference* between IGOs and INGOs however, which prevents the latter from securing *all of the privileges and immunities* of the former ... it will be clear to the reader that *no hard and fast lines can be drawn between organizations.*

Based on the evident difficulty in differentiating between governmental and non-governmental organizations, Rodgers continued:

> If international organizations are *a recognizable class of political and legal entities* then could they not be subject to unified treatment in scholarly and diplomatic practice? ... *The needs and administration of the two main types of organization, IGOs and INGOs, are [remarkably similar]*. ... Since certain INGOs often carry on work *identical* to that of IGOs it seems reasonable to ask whether the INGOs should not also share some of the special facilities which are given to IGOs. ... *Law demands categories but life continually strains against them.*[90]

In the same spirit, Pickard wrote in 1956:

> The juridical status of the IGO is clear; it derives from a general treaty between governments which is something that international law understands, more or less, and has done something about in terms of privileges, duties, immunities, and the like. *But what of the poor NGOs which are negatively defined as not having this relatively solid legal foundation?*[91]

Apparently, some commentators of the period assumed that the groups of IGOs and INGOs were in fact one, namely, 'international organizations'. For them, the two types of entities shared the same fundamental nature and normative position. The difference between them was merely legalistic, not substantive; dividing lines between them were 'thin', 'imprecise', and 'artificial'. Clearly,

---

90 See Rodgers, op. cit. note 1, *Abstract & Part I/Chapter I*, p. 7, 11, 13–15, 17–20, 22. See also R.S. Rodgers, *Classification System for International Organizations (IGO and INGO): Their Bureaux and Officials, Legal Status, Prerogatives and Immunities, and Special Facilities*, (1958). Rodgers drew upon works of other jurists of the period, such as Jessup, Lande and Lissitzyn, concluding that 'it is not possible to draw too sharp a dividing line between private and public international organizations insofar as the performance of functions in the international community is concerned' – see P.C. Jessup et al., *International Organization*, (1955), p. 32, as quoted in Rodgers, op. cit. note 1, fn. 2, p. 18.

91 B. Pickard, *Greater United Nations*, (1956), p. 69, as quoted in Rodgers, op. cit. note 1 fn. 1, p. 29.

these scholars were strongly encouraged and motivated by the fact that states upgraded the position of IGOs by reason of their crucial role in international affairs. Further, they believed that the inclusion of consultative arrangements in this scheme reflected some level of state recognition of INGOs' contribution to the realization of the common international good. And if this were the case, there was no reason not to assume that INGOs, as well, would have already acquired some level of (implied) legal personality, due to their recognized function within the international community[92] – just like IGOs. As firmly stressed, the logic underlying this notion was that IGOs and INGOs performed similar *functions*. Writers who adopted this approach upheld the *internationality* of IGOs, as a common denominator with INGOs, while ignoring their otherwise dominant multi-governmental consensual quality. For them, the IGO entity was not a delegate representing the common will of the governments composing and authorizing it, but rather a discrete, autonomous entity, representing interests going beyond those of its authors. In this decisive respect, their function resembled that of the INGO.

1.7 DISAPPROVAL OF INTERNATIONAL STATUS: INGOS AS NATIONAL *NGOS*

The new approach was highly challenging to the existing establishment of international law and affairs. Consequently, some commentators could not accept the notion that, on the basis of their

[92] These scholars ignored of course the fact that the ICJ's judgment in the *Reparation for Injuries* case, upholding IGOs functional ILP was based on the logic of IGOs being the delegates of nation-states. The ICJ did not 'create' or 'invent' IGOs' personality, but only declared the personality that was *implied* by the sovereign act of states in establishing collectively an IGO; personality was *the means* necessary to fulfill IGOs' mandated function, and was implied by it. It was *derived* from that of the collectivity of states charging IGOs to act on their behalf, through an international treaty, *on the international* (*in the sense of 'inter-State'*) *level*. This crucial point was either misinterpreted or disregarded by some writers. According to them, it was *the international function* of an IGO – on a *supra-national level* – that was decisive. This attitude has been reiterated numerous times in the discourse on the position of INGOs.

collaboration in the work of inter-governmental bodies, non-governmental consultative organizations could enjoy real exemption from the national restrictions however much the latter hindered their activities. Kopelmanas, for example, found this argument both unrealistic and entirely unfounded in terms of legal theory.[93] Alternatively, he assumed that INGOs could, at most, ask states to grant them some concessions to ameliorate the situation. This was the basis for the practical approach, suggesting that states would limit the right of action of organizations constituted abroad by the extent of the rights they granted to the most favored category of similar domestic associations. As explained above, this approach was founded on the acknowledgement by the host state of the INGO's legal status as a *national* NGO in the registering state. This new trend of placing greater emphasis on *particular administrative and fiscal facilities* will characterize the major proposals of the future by concentrating increasingly on the national, rather than the international, levels. It reflects complete disapproval of the idea of ILP or the need to solve the question of legal recognition.

The 1950 Institute Proposal (Bastid)

In its 1950 Session, the Institute adopted a proposal drafted by S. Bastid for an international convention under the title *Resolution on Granting of International Status to Associations Established by Private Initiative.*[94] According to its preamble, the proposal was based on the recognition that INGOs' legal status 'is not always clearly defined', and therefore, 'their work is being hampered by legal and administrative difficulties'. The proposal applied to *all* INGOs, broadly defined,[95] and not specifically to consultative INGOs. The aim was to grant recognition by contracting states of *a*

---

[93] UIA app. 3.3, op. cit. note 71, p. 11; fn. 88 *supra*.

[94] See UIA, op. cit. note 2, App. 4.8, p. 1; Professor Bastid (Faculty of Law, Paris University), who represented the Institute in the CCNGOs study committee, clearly reacted to its work.

[95] As 'groups of persons or of societies, freely created by private initiative, engaged in some international activity of general interest, without seeking pecuniary profit and without any object of a purely national character' – see UIA app. 4.8, ibid, Art. 2.

set of specific rights explicitly defined in the draft, as *a minimum standard* not to be derogated from. This basically referred to a most-favored-organization clause, which determined that INGOs would receive on the territory of each state party 'the most favorable treatment granted by ordinary law to national associations'.[96] This privilege was to be granted to associations following their application for recognition of 'international status', which could be denied on grounds of activity contrary to public policy, morality or statutory provisions, or because of representatives who appeared to constitute a danger to public policy. Finally, the proposal suggested that disputes should be settled, as a last resort, by the ICJ in conformity with its statute.

The proposal was adopted by the Institute. States, however, never displayed any publicly registered interest in the draft convention.[97] Although it was based on some elements of the CCNGOs proposals, at the heart of the Institute's proposal was the introduction of certain international obligations respecting INGOs by way of adoption of a most-favored-organization provision, *equating INGOs to privileged national NGOs*. Bastid's modest approach, focusing on the national rather than the international level, can be explained by her negative evaluation of previous proposals.[98] Thus, commenting on the Politis initiative, she maintained that his suggestions, which included granting ILP to INGOs, were 'much beyond positive law and had no practical effect'.[99] Furthermore, regarding the old problem of determining which INGOs should benefit from international status, Bastid explained that her draft was designed to leave the states parties full discretion on the matter. Accordingly, she avoided the idea of designation by an international diplomatic body, in explicit contradiction to the much wider approach presented by Politis and his followers. Moreover, it was made clear that the option

[96] Particularly in issues such as transfer of currency, ownership of property, donations, tax exemptions, etc.

[97] Rodgers, op. cit. note 1, p. 136.

[98] Some observers maintained that the proposal did not offer designation of any international prerogative, but simply promoted uniformity in national legislations - see UIA app. 4.8, op. cit. note 94, pp. 5–6.

[99] Quoted by Rodgers, op. cit. note 1, p. 132. For the text of Bastid's *'Report on the Proposal of the Institute of International Law 1950'* – see UIA, op. cit. note 2, App. 3.4.

of international judicial settlement would only prevail between states, leaving no doubt as to the inferior position of INGOs in that context.

1.8 INTERNATIONAL *NGOS: A SOCIO-POLITICAL* NON-*LEGAL PHENOMENON*

The 1950 proposal – in sharp contradistinction to the Institute's earlier proposals – was clearly designed with the objective of tilting the balance to the side of the host state and removing concerns of political reliability. This approach raised numerous questions regarding its actual effectiveness, and provoked meticulous theoretical discussions. On the one hand, in line with his general attitude, Rodgers maintained that the method of equating INGOs to privileged national NGOs was open to serious questioning, unless the organization being compared was an IGO rather than a national NGO.[100] On the other hand, other writers, such as Sir Eric Beckett, were inspired to reconsider the very idea of an international convention regulating the position of INGOs, maintaining that since INGOs were potentially legion in number and since a privileged status was contemplated, only a limited number of organizations could expect to benefit. This necessarily involved machinery for picking and choosing, that 'would in fact be virtually fatal to the whole scheme'.[101]

Sir Eric identified the main freedoms required by INGOs as including the freedom of association, the freedom to propagate their cause, the ability to hold funds and property and to enter into contracts, the freedom of representatives to travel freely, and the freedom to move funds across borders.[102] He maintained that these freedoms could be secured only through the treaty-based or customary international obligations undertaken by the *national* liberal jurisdictions to secure the rights and freedoms of their citizens as well as those of the foreign nationals present in their territory. The typical INGO

[100] He explained that, after all, if an INGO is at all welcome in a country, it would normally secure the terms applicable to favored national NGOs; 'it is precisely because these terms are not satisfactory that a different approach is needed' – see ibid, p. 134.

[101] As quoted in ibid, pp. 135–136.

[102] See ibid, pp. 134–135.

entity was thus regarded as a collective of citizens and foreign nationals and not as an autonomous entity recognized on the supra-national level. Consequently, the status of this collective derived directly from the aggregate rights and freedoms accorded by the national authorities to individuals, whether nationals or foreigners, and not from any independent status acquired by the collective, *per se*. Therefore, there was neither a practical nor a juridical need to internationally regulate the position of INGOs as such.

According to this approach, the *internationality* of INGOs was essentially regarded as a *social* or *political* phenomenon and not as a legal tenet. Recognition under international law was therefore meaningless, as it did not precede, preclude, or otherwise define the socio-political quality of the INGO entity. In other words: legally speaking, '*International* NGOs' did not exist! All that was evident in the international sphere, and within international affairs, was the socio-political impact of *national* NGOs, involved in international spheres of concern. Representing a highly realistic line, jurists such as Beckett, Kopelmanas and Langrod[103] obviously assumed that international legal recognition of the INGO entity, as such, would mean the transformation of the world into a genuine *supra-national* system in which states and INGOs shared the process of setting the normative agenda. This entailed a certain level of surrender of states' sovereignty for the benefit of the group of non-state entities. This was, of course, an altogether different concept from that which had been acknowledged in the case of IGOs, which remained genuinely *international*, as opposed to *supranational*, entities.[104]

Evidently, the heated scholarly debate, as well as the frequent release of conflicting proposals during the 1950s also inspired some

---

103 Langrod, commenting on the 1950 Bastid proposal, wondered: 'is it correct to say that the lack of uniformity in [INGOs'] status may seriously impede their work and place them in a state of 'inferiority'? Or is it on the contrary merely an architectural fault, an asymmetry which is vexing to those who like clear-cut schemes imposed 'from above'?' – see A. Langrod, *'Evaluating the Role of INGOs', International Associations* (UIA, 1955), quoted in Rodgers, ibid, p. 136; see also M. Merle, *'Guerre et Paix'*, (1953), p. 97, in Rodgers, ibid, fn. 1, p. 137.

104 This can explain Sir Eric's recommendation to the Institute to drop the project altogether, or alternatively to circulate a list of INGOs which states would be asked to favor, which was 'the best one can reasonably hope for'– see Rodgers, ibid, p. 136.

states to discuss the issue of the legal position of INGOs. The fact that the matter was taken up by the Hague Conference on Private International Law (HCPIL) indicates, however, that even state officials considered the matter to be primarily one of conflicts-of-laws, as opposed to an initiative suggesting an autonomous international status. In either case, although these discussions raised some expectations within the INGO community,[105] they failed to create a progressive breakthrough.

The 1956 Convention Concerning Recognition of the Legal Personality of Foreign Companies, Associations and Institutions (HCPIL)

According to this convention,[106] legal personality, acquired by an association under the law of the contracting state where its charter seat is located, shall be recognized as a matter of course in the other contracting states.[107] The convention was drafted in broad and vague terms, and failed to provide any definition of the scope of its application in terms of the associations to which rights were extended, or indeed any definition of the term 'legal personality'.[108] Nevertheless, it maintained that recognition of legal personality implied the 'capacity attached thereto by the law under which it has been acquired'. In any case, 'rights not granted by the law of the state of recognition to national organizations of the corresponding type, may be refused'.[109] Where the governing law did not grant personality, the relevant associations 'shall have in other contracting states the legal situation which such law accorded to them, and they shall not have the right to a more favorable legal treatment, even if they satisfy all the conditions which in such states confer the benefit of personality'.[110]

[105] See *List of Problems Hindering INGOs Action* in *The Future of Transnational Associations from the Standpoint of a New World Order, Proceedings of a Symposium* (Geneva, 1976), UIA (1977), App. 4, para. 34 ('International legal status of INGOs').

[106] Available: http://www.hcch.net/index_en.php?act=conventions.listing; UIA, op. cit. note 2, App. 4.9.

[107] See ibid, Art. 1.

[108] See Commentary by L.A. Nypels, in ibid, p. 10, para. 6.

[109] See UIA app. 4.9, ibid, Art. 5.

[110] See ibid, Art. 6. Moreover, rights not accorded to corresponding national entities could be refused.

Finally, the convention suggested that states parties reserve the right to exclude application of its provisions on a unilateral basis on a ground of public policy, however defined by the state.[111] Notably, although it requires a minimum of only five ratifications, the convention has not yet entered into force.

1.9 NON-GOVERNMENTAL NON-*COMMUNITY: WHOSE STATUS?*

In view of the intellectual puzzle prevailing at the time, as well as the failed attempt of states to provide even a limited solution to the problem, it is not surprising that the subsequent 1959 UIA proposal for a *Draft Convention on Facilitating Activity of International NGOs*,[112] which was based on consultations with small-group conferences of INGO officials and interested experts, reflected complete conceptual confusion and a clear loss of any systematic direction.

The 1959 UIA Proposal

The proposal returned to the idea adopted by the UIA almost 50 years earlier, to establish an international INGO agency functioning as an independent registry bureau, which was now modified to suggest the establishment of a quasi-diplomatic bureau of INGO officials nominated in agreement with UNESCO and subject to approval by the UIA.[113] It was believed that the joint representation of associations with indirect intergovernmental control would somehow progressively evolve into an independent supra-national mechanism or a sort of international 'self-government' of INGOs.[114]

As noted in its preamble, the draft convention was based on the recognition that useful work was being carried out by INGOs through supplementary services of consultation and publicity, benefiting IGOs. However, in contrast to IGOs, 'INGOs are still in an uncertain juridical position and their international activities are often impeded

[111] See ibid, Art. 8. See also Commentary, in ibid, p. 8.
[112] UIA, op. cit. note 2, App. 4.10, p. 1.
[113] See Rodgers, op. cit. note 1, p. 137.
[114] See ibid.

by administrative difficulties'. Therefore, the convention aimed at permitting 'their access to more favorable legal status'.[115] The proposal suggested that contracting states provide some *listed benefits* to eligible INGOs, which were then very narrowly defined. States parties and IGOs which maintained consultative relations were to extend lists of recognized INGOs to UNESCO and to the UIA, functioning as an international registrar. An international commission, set up by the UIA, would then verify the conformity of the lists with the conditions established by the draft regarding privileged INGOs, and issue a comprehensive updated list.[116] As for the benefits recognized under the proposed international status, the draft suggested that states parties would grant privileged INGOs *the rights accorded to them in their country of original constitution*. States, however, reserved the right to grant INGOs such privileges afforded under national legislation to the most favored category of national organizations of the same character.[117]

In 1960, UNESCO, to which the proposal was submitted for review,[118] concluded that there was little possibility that states would adopt a convention of this kind.[119] More interesting, however, was the UIA draft's attempt to outline the typical INGO entity in a manner less dependent on the consultative arrangements with IGOs. The UIA draft suggested that *apart from* an international aim and activity, eligible INGOs would have to adduce evidence of representatives belonging to at least six countries, an internationally composed administration and a permanent secretariat, activities recognized by at least one state party or, alternatively, established consultative status with an IGO, and funds derived substantially from more than one country.[120] Clearly, these strict criteria were

115 See Preamble, UIA app. 4.10, op. cit. note 112, pp. 1–2.

116 It was unclear how the lists of states were to be reconciled with that of the UIA commission; it may be assumed that the commission's list was considered superior – see Rodgers, op. cit. note 1, p. 139, 140. The commission was to consist of 15 members holding at least seven different nationalities, nominated by the UIA in agreement with UNESCO. IGOs having official relations with INGOs could send observers.

117 That is 'a most favored organization clause'.

118 See Rodgers, op. cit. note 1, pp. 138–139.

119 See UIA app. 4.10, op. cit. note 112, p. 1; see also Rodgers, ibid, pp. 139–140 & fn. 1.

120 See UIA app. 4.10, ibid, Art. 1.

meant to set a very high standard that could be fulfilled only by very few leading and well-funded INGOs. Apparently, the UIA drafters were acting against the approach reflected in the Institute's 1950 proposal which suggested a very broad definition of eligible INGOs, and which, in fact, left the decision in this regard to the states, thus opening the way for the acquisition of international status by national NGOs with an international aim and activity. In response, the UIA proposal meant to emphasize the 'internationality' of 'genuine' INGOs, as distinct from national NGOs. Indeed, the very need to pursue the difficult exercise of positively defining the international character of INGOs suggests that the competition between leading INGOs and national NGOs, active in similar or related fields and therefore bearing analogous responsibilities, had increased; leading INGOs were aware of the risk of strengthening the status of powerful national NGOs that had also managed to secure a consultative status with ECOSOC.[121] Furthermore, the rivalry *within* the INGO community must have deepened over time, with a growing number of associations competing to impact overlapping areas; the struggles over resources, funding, reputation and recognition had clearly intensified. Another complementary mechanism established by the draft, also reflective of the growing conflicts of interest within the non-governmental community, was that of the awkward 'UIA Commission', decisions of which regarding privileged INGOs were supposed to override those of states and IGOs.

Notwithstanding the great political obstacles which all these mechanisms were expected to create, the inconsistencies of the arrangements as well as their poor articulation introduced many new juridical complications.[122] Consequently, the draft raised many more new and significant questions than it actually answered or clarified.

---

121 See, for example, Rodgers, op. cit. note 1, p. 129.

122 As a matter of definition, the above requirements concerning eligible INGOs did not replace the requirement of 'international activity', but added to it. 'International activity' remained, however, a separate and undefined condition – see UIA app. 4.10, op. cit. note 112, Art. 1(c). Furthermore, significant issues such as the quality and ranking of the INGO representatives, the essence of the 'international' composition of the INGO administration, and the meaning of an 'international' secretariat, all remained completely vague.

1.10 THE TURN TO REGIONALISM: PAN-EUROPEAN INTELLECTUAL ENVIRONMENT

At this point in the evolution of the discourse on the legal status of INGOs, it seemed that the two main approaches, that of a single international status on the one hand and conflict-of-laws on the other hand, had been distinguished, modified and perfected to the greatest possible extent. Proposals that failed to distinguish between the mechanisms deriving from the two approaches or which tried to create compromises between them, produced very confused and complex results. The wider implications of adopting either of the two options were repeatedly reflected in the manner with which the two veteran problems of registration (that is, political control by states or IGOs) and choosing which organizations should enjoy international rewards (that is, how to define the genuine INGO entity) were treated. In any case, one thing became clear: ILP, whether autonomous, functional or limited, was not a matter of positive international law.

That acknowledgement underlined the work of the Council of Europe (CoE), which became deeply involved in the consideration of activity aimed at outlining INGOs' legal status from the early 1980s. This involvement marked a new, significant phase in the ongoing discourse on the international position of INGOs. Evidently, the turn to regionalism was stimulated by scholars who grew rather disillusioned with the possibility of finding satisfactory solutions at the international level, and believed that the intellectual and political European environment would yield more progress. Such was the conclusion of Merle's *Report on INGOs and their Legal Status,*[123] which was submitted to the CoE, and became an important milestone in the chronology of the evolving discourse on the position of INGOs; it is still highly relevant today.

1983 Report on INGOs and their Legal Status (M. Merle)

Recalling that the number of INGOs had grown from several dozen at the beginning of the 20th century to several thousand, Merle

[123] Law Faculty, Paris University; see UIA, op. cit. note 2, App. 3.5; see Appendices, 1.2. The report was presented during a 'Colloquy on the Role of INGOs in Contemporary Society', hosted by the CoE's Parliamentary Assembly.

regarded this sharp increase to be indicative of governments' tolerance towards these entities. However, he observed that at this stage of the evolutionary process, the 'international society movement' was making such strong demands that it was no longer content with tolerance on the part of governments and felt uneasy, confined within the limits of consultative status.[124] Furthermore, there was an inherent conflict between INGOs' international vocation and the national legal status to which they were confined.[125] In this light, there was indeed no avoiding giving INGOs international status, guaranteeing them minimum rights and a degree of freedom of action *vis-à-vis* the various national or international authorities. In any case, previous attempts to propose international conventions in this regard had failed. The main reasons for these failures, according to the report, were: (1) States were disinclined to grant ILP, since it might prejudice their own authority. This instinct for 'self-preservation' was enshrined in the rules of international law, which only allowed states to make rules of law conferring legal capacity on other entities; (2) Even if states could agree to grant international status, the question regarding within what framework and under whose jurisdiction it could be prepared was in itself a major obstacle in view of the various political systems involved, and their opposing perceptions of the role of private enterprise; and (3) States realized that INGOs not only differed in power, size and aim, but also sometimes served to cover up subversive or terrorist activities; the granting of international status could thus threaten internal security.

All in all, the report concluded that the problem had to be looked at 'from the point of view of re-shaping the structure and organization of the international community'; the rise of the 'transnational

---

[124] See ibid, p. 2. Merle adopted a realistic critical approach towards consultative arrangements. He realized that not only was a minority of INGOs granted the status, but also the term was ambiguous, since the status did not confer any right capable of being exercised before any national or international authority, except for the granting IGO; it had a merely limited effect, and could not amount to legal status within the full meaning of the term. In most cases, it was confined to receiving information, without effective participation in consultation; it was granted at the discretion of the IGO and could be withdrawn at any time – see p. 5.

[125] See ibid, pp. 3–4.

private sector' constituted a genuine challenge to the nation-based international community, and 'the spontaneity and variety which are among the most positive attributes of international associations', still constituted 'a handicap *vis-à-vis* the coalition of states and will continue to do so for a long time to come'.[126] The consequent instinctive mistrust on the part of governments could probably, at most, lead to the adoption of an 'outline status application', subject to the full discretion of states.[127] The likelihood of an overall agreement in this context was however practically nil; the task was easier in *regional* frameworks, due to a minimum political consensus among member states.[128]

The same acknowledgements, although arrived at from a different angle, underlined the conclusions put forward by other writers, such as Rodgers, who observed, almost 20 years before Merle, and in view of the complex 1959 UIA proposal, that although a general treaty status could be defined, 'an amelioration of the position of INGOs is not likely to come about through an overall scheme'; attention had to be turned to other more *practical* possibilities, such as *regional* treaties.[129] In this way, it was realized that the regional platform was the only option remaining. And indeed, being conscious of the fact that the head offices of two-thirds of the INGOs were concentrated in the member states of the CoE,[130] and being equally aware of the absence of any international instrument in force aimed at facilitating their activities at an international level,[131] the CoE decided to study the possibility of intergovernmental action at the European level. This decision culminated in the adoption of the 1986 European Convention.

---

126 See '*Conclusion*' in ibid, p. 8.

127 See ibid. Merle maintained that 'even if international status defining the rights and privileges of NGOs were adopted the problem of designation of organizations to benefit from that status would remain unsolved'.

128 See ibid, pp. 3–4.

129 See Rodgers, op. cit. note 1, pp. 16–17, 144. Rodgers admitted that INGOs *were not* generally entities in *legal* theory, unlike *political* theory or *sociology*.

130 See Rechenberg, op. cit. note 45, p. 618; *Explanatory Report on the Convention*, available on: http://conventions.coe.int/treaty/EN/Reports/Html/124.htm, para. 1; see Appendices, 3.2.

131 See Explanatory Report, ibid, para. 3.

The 1986 European Convention on the Recognition of the Legal Personality of International NGOs

This convention reflected one of the more interesting and significant endeavors undertaken to regulate the legal status of INGOs.[132] To date, however, the *de facto* juridical value of the convention is still quite limited. The lessons to be learned from this attempt at regulation, together with the formulations it contains, are nevertheless of considerable importance.

The convention was based on the desire of member states 'to establish *in their mutual relations* rules laying down the conditions for recognition of the legal personality' of INGOs, in order to facilitate their activities *at European level*.[133] According to the convention, 'the legal personality and capacity, *as acquired by an INGO in the Party in which it has its statutory office*,[134] shall be *recognized as of right in the other Parties*'.[135] No special procedure had to be followed to obtain recognition.[136]

As opposed to the UN consultative arrangements, the convention dealt categorically with *international* NGOs.[137] Nevertheless, it was more lenient regarding the scope of territorial activity and it did

---

[132] Eur.T.S. 124, available on: http://conventions.coe.int/treaty/en/Treaties/Html/124.htm; see Appendices, 3.1; total number of ratifications (Jan. 2013): 11. For the standards recommended by the CoE for Member States that have not ratified the convention see *Recommendation CM/Rec(2007)14 of the Committee of Ministers to Member States on the Legal Status of Non-Governmental Organizations in Europe*, Art. 45 ('Foreign NGOs'), available on: http://www.coe.int/t/ngo/Legal_standards_en.asp.

[133] See Preamble to the convention.

[134] As opposed to 'real administrative seat'; see Explanatory Report, op. cit. note 130, paras. 14–15, explaining this choice.

[135] See 1986 Convention, op. cit. note 132, Art. 2.

[136] See Explanatory Report, op. cit. note 130, para. 13. Nevertheless, recognition is subject to domestic qualifications based on 'essential public interests', as well as general restrictions applicable to all foreigners – see paras. 17–18. Specific guarantees are recognized in order to 'counterbalance the effects of the automatic recognition of personality', providing grounds on which, in exceptional cases, a refusal of the recognition can be based – see 1986 Convention, ibid, Art. 4; Explanatory Report, ibid, paras. 23–28.

[137] Four 'fundamental requirements' must be satisfied by eligible INGOs: (1) non-profit-making aim of international utility; (2) establishment by an instrument governed by the internal law of a state party; (3) activities with effect in at least two states; and (4) statutory office in the territory of a state party and the central management and control in the territory of that party or of another state party.

not contain requirements concerning democratic structure.[138] All that considered, the following observations are noteworthy. First, it was felt necessary to conclude the convention because of the perceived ineffectiveness of formerly existing regional consultative status arrangements for INGOs that had already been recognized by the CoE in 1951.[139] Clearly, regional experience had also lowered expectations that the existing global UN arrangements, however appraised and reconstructed, would yield any progressive results in the future. In view of the fact that the CoE was a relatively harmonized legal grouping, characterized by political consensus and mutual recognition between legal systems based on many unifying elements,[140] the regional European experience in this regard became even more instructive. Moreover, the very drafting of the convention was powerful evidence of the abandonment of the instrumental approach towards INGOs, underlining the consultative status arrangements. That tendency was reflected both expressly, in the preamble of the convention which indicated that the ultimate goal of its adoption was the facilitation of INGOs' independent activities, and implicitly,

---

For further analysis, see Explanatory Report, op. cit. note 130, paras. 7–10; Olz, op. cit. note 40, p. 319.

[138] See Olz, ibid, ibid. Interestingly, the French Declaration (Nov. 26, 1999), after noting that the convention is applied differently in the ratifying states, and calling for harmonization of the differing interpretations, provides that, INGOs having 'consultative status with international organizations of the UN system' will be assumed to satisfy the conditions for applying the convention – available on: http://conventions.coe.int/treaty/EN/Declarelist.asp.

[139] See Explanatory Report, op. cit. note 130, para. 2. In 2003, the CoE 'consultative status' was modified into a 'participatory status' – see *Committee of Ministers Resolution Res(2003)8, Participatory Status for INGOs with the Council of Europe,* (Nov. 19, 2003); see Appendices, 3.3. This move was 'an expression of democratic pluralism and an essential element for the further development of a citizens' Europe'. For the rules governing decisions on the granting of participatory status and the benefits involved, see *Rules for Participatory Status for INGOs at the CoE* (annexed to Res. (2003)8). In practice, however, the participatory status does not grant any additional participatory rights – see Rossi, op. cit. note 60, p. 10. The change is therefore 'mainly in nomenclature'. More than 400 INGOs, known collectively as the 'Conference of INGOs of the CoE', obtain the status – see: http://www.coe.int/t/ngo/conf_intro_en.asp (Jan. 2013). For special arrangements between the CoE and *national* NGOs, see *Committee of Ministers Resolution Res(2003)9, Status of Partnership between the Council of Europe and National NGOs (Nov. 19, 2003)*; see Appendices, 3.4.

[140] Explanatory Report, op. cit. note 130, para. 15.

through the formulation of specific arrangements, such as the adoption of the 'statutory office rule', based on the idea of respect for the choice of the INGO concerned.[141] In this, the convention became a manifestation of notions of cooperation and interdependency.[142] Bearing in mind, however, that the convention was explicitly based on the acknowledgment of the absence of any international instrument in force aimed at facilitating the activities of INGOs,[143] the project as a whole had to be understood as providing a temporary substitute in the form of transitional machinery on the regional level. Admittedly, even at this level, the suggested confined legal regime could not compensate for the lack of global solutions.[144]

Whatever the case may be, it must be recognized that the convention was, in fact, a treaty with a very definite objective. As Wiederkehr, who reviewed the convention's backstage deliberations and *travaux préparatoirs*, revealed, the goal was to establish a convention 'limited to indispensable dispositions aimed at improving the legal status of NGOs in the Member States'; it was realized that 'any more global approach would not be allowed', as the Member States 'were in favor of making a gesture towards NGOs but not to give them international legal status, which would require modifications of their fiscal policies or their policies concerning entry of foreigners'.[145] That explained that the content of the convention was indeed 'limited to the consecration of the principle of the recognition by all the Parties of the legal personality obtained in another Party'. Clearly, it was not intended to provide INGOs with any ILP or other similar standing, which required global, rather than regional, arrangements.[146] But the convention did not even go so far as to

---

141 See ibid, para. 14.

142 See, for example, M.-O. Wiederkehr, *La Convention Européene sur la Reconnaissance de la Personnalité Juridique des Organisations Internationales Non-Gouvernementals du 24 Avril 1986, Annuaire Francais de Droit International* (Vol. XXXIII, 1987), p. 749.

143 See Introduction to the Explanatory Report, op. cit. note 130, para. 3.

144 As becomes clear from the *French Declaration* concerning the still differing applications and interpretations of the convention in the ratifying countries – see op. cit. note 138.

145 See Wiederkehr, op. cit. note 142, p. 752, 756 (original text in French); but compare with Olz, op. cit. note 40, p. 325.

146 See as well Malanczuk, op. cit. note 62, p. 91.

recognize the existence of such personality relative to the States Parties.[147] In fact, it only recognized a *national* legal personality, obtained within any State Party, as having equal effect in another State Party. To that extent, it was based on the notion of reciprocity and mutuality, rather than on acquisition of autonomous legal status, independent from national will or regional undertaking.

1.11 IN SEARCH OF POLITICAL SUPPORT: ACTION AT THE SUPRANATIONAL LEVEL

The Merle report, and the preparatory work on the 1986 European Convention, also triggered activity at the European Community (EC) level. As regional arrangements became more supranational in character, they seemed a more fitting framework for carrying on the discourse on the legal status of INGOs. Generally speaking, international and intergovernmental systems are established and designed to fit the interests of nation-states. Indeed, in international legal theory, the individual, or groups of individuals, are the final object of the normative system. However, this is true as long as their relationship with the nation-state is what is involved; the latter is a link that cannot be circumvented, overlooked, or skipped over in the international normative hierarchy. However, in an integrative regional system, such as the EC, the normative logic is different. Within such arrangements, states *transfer* certain sovereign competencies, which are invested in supranational institutions. These, in turn, use their authority for the benefit of *both* the member states and the individuals located within the jurisdictions of the regional system. Thus, the logic underlying the supranational regional system is to bypass the authority of the individual nation-states, in order to create a shared independent and authoritative system that acts in certain areas for the benefit of individuals and citizens *instead* of their national governments. Theoretically, therefore, the regional integrative platform seems much more accessible and attuned to the needs

[147] Compare to B. Cheng, *Introduction to Subjects of International Law,* in M. Bedjaoui (ed.), *International Law: Achievements and Prospects,* (1991), pp. 32–33, considering *quasi-international law* arrangements.

of INGOs, which consider themselves to be genuinely supranational entities – just like the integrative institutions.

The link, however, between integrative regional institutions and INGOs has an even greater significance, going beyond legal theory, deep into the socio-political sphere. INGOs, sharing the supranational integrative vision, play a primary role in the very formation of regional integration.[148] In fact, the main actors in the integration process are those above and below the nation-state. Above the state are the supra-national regional institutions, whereas below the state are interest groups and political parties.[149] As Mattli observed, these interest groups and the supra-national regional institutions complement each other. Thus, the regional institutions promote integration, foster the development of interest groups, cultivate close ties with them and with fellow-technocrats in the national civil services, and 'manipulate both if necessary'; the EC Commission 'forges behind-the-scene working alliances with pressure groups', and as its policy-making role grows, 'interest groups coalesce across national boundaries in their pursuit of community-wide interests'.[150] INGOs and the supra-national regional institutions thus form a partnership to generate and uphold the integrative momentum. Clearly, this partnership leads to mutual support and protection. This bond underlined the motion for a *Resolution on the Role and Administration of Associations and the Law Governing Them in the EC*,[151] submitted, in 1984, to the European Parliament (EP).[152] According to the motion, which was adopted in 1987,[153] an action in favor of associations would enable the Community to better achieve its

---

[148] See W. Mattli, *The Logic of Regional Integration – Europe and Beyond*, (1999), p. 24.

[149] See ibid, p. 28.

[150] See ibid. According to neofunctionalism, the role remained for national governments is 'creatively responsive'. As holders of the ultimate political power, they may either choose to, or feel constrained to, yield to the pressures of converging supranational and sub-national interests – see pp. 28–29.

[151] *Doc. 2–290/84* (European Parliament); see as well UIA, op. cit. note 2, App. 4.13, pp. 1–2.

[152] The motion was also inspired by the extensive preparatory work and debates on the CoE 1986 Convention – see Preamble to the *Resolution on the Non-Profit Making Associations in the European Communities*, UIA, ibid, App. 4.12, p. 2.

[153] *European Parliament*, Vol. 3/87, March 1987, pp. 94–96; see UIA app. 4.12, ibid, p. 1. The motion was referred for review, together with a later motion for a resolution on freedom of assembly and association in the Community. The joint review

fundamental objectives.[154] It was thus meant to lead to the development of a comprehensive Community policy towards associations.

The 1986 EP Resolution on Non-Profit Making Associations in the European Communities

According to its preamble, the resolution was based on the need to provide the necessary means for the exercise of the freedom of association and membership as essential democratic rights. It took note of the size of the 'association movement' within the EC, and assumed that the specific nature of the associations made them 'particularly suitable for promoting the values' on which European integration was based. Consequently, the European institutions were required to pursue the measures laid down by the EC's constituent documents, as well as those available to them to support the establishment of the 1992 Internal Market and the progress of integration, in order to harmonize legislation required for cooperation on the community level. Based on the above, the resolution requested the rapid abolition, throughout the EC, of all of the discriminatory measures based on nationality that affected the right to belong to, form, or administer an association.[155] Moreover, it required the establishment of a system of mutual recognition of associations within the EC member states. This meant the recognition in each state of the same level of legal recognition acquired by an association in the state in which it had its head office.[156] The resolution also required the formulation of a Community-wide statute for associations operating in more than one member state, regulating their specific requirements.[157]

---

produced a '*Report on Non-Profit Making Associations in the European Community*', *European Communities, European Parliament, Report drawn up on behalf of the Committee on Legal Affairs and Citizens' Rights* (Rapporteur: N. Fontaine), Working Documents, Series A, 8 January 1987 (Doc. A 2–196/86); see UIA app. 4.12, ibid, pp. 1–8.

[154] See UIA app. 4.13, op. cit. note 151, p. 1.

[155] With regard to EC Member States citizens; regarding the delicate and complex issue of the definition of the associations forming the subject-matter of the resolution – see generally UIA, op. cit. note 2, App. 3.7.

[156] The Commission was called upon to submit a proposal for an implementing directive in this regard.

[157] Through a Commission's regulation proposal.

During the parliamentary debate on the proposed resolution, it was explained that Europe needed 'inspiration to take a further step towards its destiny as a Community', and nonprofit making associations were 'an opportunity to be taken in this respect'.[158] The same applied to the statement made by the Vice President of the EC Commission, who considered the issue to be 'a political and cultural problem which is of great significance to the Community', taking note of 'the very great importance of the activity of European associations in shaping public opinion to support the development of the Community politically, economically, and culturally'.[159] Indeed, in the sense of the formal activity of the EC, the consideration of the status of INGOs presented a new challenge. It signaled a significant turn in the general discourse on their normative position, reflecting a change of perception: from one which was international to one operating in a regional-federal context.

Nevertheless, the wish to develop a body of 'European Law on Associations' and to establish a single status on the regional level was soon debated against the urgent need to resolve practical questions of conflict-of-laws. This was reflected in the eventual articulation of the 1986 CoE European Convention, as well as in the concluding remarks of the EP's 1986 *Report on Non-Profit-Making Associations in the EC*, which admitted that although the political difficulties facing harmonization and the promotion of associations seemed to be limited, 'the technical complexity of the harmonization measures must not be concealed'.[160] It was made clear that the more justified the Community's right to take action with regard to the associations sector seemed to be, 'the more essential for that action to keep within the limits laid down by the objective of the development of EU'. Accordingly, any action aiming to give

[158] See UIA app. 3.7, op. cit note 155, paras. 108–109 of the Explanatory Statement by the Representative of the European Parliament's Committee on Legal Affairs and Citizen's Rights.

[159] See UIA app. 4.12, op. cit. note 152, p. 6.

[160] See UIA app. 3.7, op. cit. note 155, para. 107. The statement of the Vice President of the EC Commission of the European Communities revealed the same tension, noting that 'the elaboration of proposals to establish a common legal basis for the work of associations in the Community would be an enormous task, since there are so many different traditions' as well as 'very widely differing legal rules' – see UIA app. 4.12, ibid, p. 7.

associations too uniform and specific a status would be contrary not only to the powers of the States but also 'to the spirit of freedom and independence required by the association movement'.[161] Further, the spirit of a limited Community action was clarified by comparing its initiative to that of the CoE, explaining that the CoE's 1986 Convention 'relates to organizations whose international character is already established in at least two States', whereas in the case of the EC action 'it is a matter of facilitating the activities *of a national association, wishing to keep its identity*, in the direction of States other than that in which it has its head office'.[162] This way, despite the relatively supportive intellectual, political, and institutional environment, the initial regional debates already proved to replicate most of the complexities of the international discourse.

1.12 INTERMEDIARY OBSERVATIONS: DISCRETE DOCTRINAL APPROACHES

As can be seen, many important observations may be drawn from the analysis of the significant phases along the sequence of international conferences and forums attempting to secure an international legal status for INGOs. First and foremost, it has been recognized that the overall effort to conclude a multilateral treaty, whether international or regional, can produce one of three legal mechanisms:

(1) A convention creating a *uniform international status* for INGOs that endows them with a (*limited/functional*) *international legal personality*;
(2) A convention establishing a system of *mutual recognition*, that is, one which recognizes the status acquired by the organization in its state of registration;
(3) A convention listing a closed *set of rights and privileges* which signatories – either states or IGOs – take upon themselves to acknowledge for the benefit of INGOs.

These three options, or compromises based on them, which were considered over the years, are based on completely discrete

[161] See UIA app. 3.7, ibid, paras. 64, 66–68.
[162] See ibid, para. 72.

approaches to the question of the legal status of INGOs. The first scheme, in its authentic form, aims at turning INGOs into (limited) *subjects of international law*. The second scheme endorses the jurisdiction of the state of origin, thereby preserving the status of the INGO as a *national NGO*. The third scheme does not deal with the acquisition of status, but rather is based on the acknowledgement of the immediate needs of INGOs, thus resolving specific *conflicts-of-law problems*.[163] Apparently, these variations reflect varying stages of optimism and pessimism in international relations.[164] In any case, as many drafters admit, and as history clearly shows, each stage was built, at least to some extent, on lessons drawn from previous attempts. It is therefore possible to speak about an evolutionary sequence, which may further guide us in the future.

***

We shall now review some of the new and more significant developments against the background of the historical-contextual analysis. Since the 1990's, the rapidly growing body of literature dealing with the role and relevance of INGOs and their perceived impact on international law- and decision-making has triggered much renewed interest in discussing INGOs' status under international law. The invention of new models and notions within the fields of international relations and political science, based essentially on post-modern, neo-liberal perceptions of contemporary 'processes of globalization', have encouraged international lawyers, mostly active in interdisciplinary frameworks, to develop new theoretical and institutional schemes to deal with problems relating to the exercise of unregulated authority outside the state system. The following list of relevant endeavors is therefore inconclusive. However, as will be discussed in the last part of this work, these initiatives are indicative of significant trends in the ongoing normative discourse.

---

[163] Rodgers identifies this last scheme with the endeavor to provide for a type of 'most favored organization' clause – see op. cit. note 1, p. 117–118. In any case, he indicates only two possible treaty-based legal schemes, neglecting the second option mentioned.

[164] ibid, p. 118.

Chapter Two

NEW INITIATIVES AND DEVELOPMENTS

2.1 INGOS ACCOUNTABILITY CHARTER (2006)

The charter initiative was launched in 2003 by leading INGO representatives in light of increasing demands for their greater accountability.[1] In 2006, eleven human rights, environmental, and social development INGOs endorsed the charter,[2] which was later registered as a company limited by guarantee, and owned by its

---

[1] Voluntary NGO mechanisms are of growing relevance. There are currently more than 320 self-regulation initiatives worldwide, which include certification/ accreditation schemes, peer review and learning networks, and collective codes of conduct, ombudsmen mechanisms, and accountability charters – see J. Nelson, *Effecting Change through Accountable Channels*, in B. Lael & C Derek (eds.), *Global Governance 2.0: Can Philanthropists, the Public, and the Poor Make Poverty History?*, (2008), pp. 174–175; D. Hortsch, *The Paradox of Partnership: Amnesty International, Responsible Advocacy, and NGO Accountability, Columbia Human Rights Law Review*, Vol. 42 (2010), p. 119, 128. These should be valued in the context of the current 'strong and consistent trend' for all international actors to accept forms of accountability, based on demands that add up to a 'wide-ranging critique of the perceived immunity enjoyed by many actors in terms of legal, political and other forms of responsibility' – see P. Alston, *Hobbling the Monitors: Should UN Human Rights Monitors be Accountable?, Harvard International Law Journal*, Vol. 52 (2011), pp. 564–565, 605–607. Hortsch explains that it was mainly the success of major INGOs, that increasingly moved away from charity work and toward political and human rights advocacy, in advocacy campaigns, that fed the calls for greater accountability – see ibid, pp. 126–131. Nelson holds that the emergence of the new INGO development player called for an 'ethos and practice of mutual accountability', underlined by questions about INGOs' public responsibility – see ibid, pp. 150–151, 154, 160–161. For further analysis of the 'mutual accountability model' see D.L. Brown, *Multiply Social Action and Mutual Accountability*, in A. Ebrahim & E. Weisband, *Global Accountability and Moral Community*, (2004), as quoted in Nelson, ibid, p. 162; see as well C.H. Udo, *Nongovernmental Organizations and African Governments: Seeking an Effective International Legal Framework in a New Era of Health and Development Aid, Boston College International and Comparative Law Review*, Vol. 31, p. 371.

[2] For the Charter's text see *Charter Website*, on: http://www.ingoaccountabilitycharter.org; see Appendices, 4.1. The 11 founding signatories were Action Aid Int'l, Amnesty Int'l, CIVICUS, Consumers Int'l, Greenpeace Int'l, Oxfam Int'l, Int'l Save the Children, Survival Int'l, Int'l Fed. *Terre des Hommes*, Transparency Int'l, World YWCA – see website (*'charter background'*).

members.[3] By joining the charter, heralded by its founders as the first international, cross-sectoral code of conduct for NGOs[4] and thus an 'unprecedented step', signatory INGOs were deemed to have come together to demonstrate their commitment to transparency, accountability and excellence.[5] This commitment underlined the signatories' endeavor to identify and define shared principles, policies and practices, to encourage communication with stakeholders, and to improve performance and effectiveness.[6] The original initiative was clearly aimed at underscoring the legitimacy of INGOs,[7] and provide them with a certain baseline of reliability and understanding of responsible advocacy.[8] In any case, although it was expected to attract broad-based support, and some even considered it to be a starting point for a 'Global Civil Society Forum'[9] or a system of global NGO self-regulation,[10] to date very few new

---

[3] The *INGO Charter of Accountability Ltd Company (UK)*. The Board of Directors is consisted of representatives from Member Organizations.

[4] See *'NGOs Lead by Example', Oxfam Press Release*, 7 June 2006, available on: http://www.oxfam.org/en/news/pressrelease2006/pr060606_ngo/charter.

[5] Oxfam Press Release, ibid; Charter, op. cit. note 2 ('Charter's Purpose').

[6] See Charter, ibid.

[7] Thus strengthening public confidence in INGOs, in view of 'a growing mistrust and even disillusionment' with the practices of non-state actors, who many believe are failing the public good – see A.S. Thompson, *Laying the Groundwork – Considerations for a Charter for a Proposed Global Civil Society Forum*, in J.W. St. G. Walker, A.S. Thompson (eds.), *Critical Mass: The Emergence of Global Civil Society*, (2008), pp. 213, 214–215, 218; C.R. Kelly, *Financial Crisis and Civil Society, Chicago Journal of International Law*, Vol. 11, (2011), p. 505, 548, regarding the charter as potentially accrediting INGOs to speak on behalf of those whom they claim to represent. The head of CIVICUS, one of the charter's driving forces, noted that, while external negative criticism has helped to fuel the debate, it was important 'not to underestimate the internally generated drive toward accountability' – see K. Naidoo, *Civil Society Accountability: 'Who Guards the Guardians?', Address Delivered at UN Headquarters* (Apr. 3, 2003), quoted in Nelson, op. cit. note 1, p. 171. Indeed, explaining the charter's rationale, the founding organizations declared to have encountered three challenges: (1) the challenge from media, business and governments to be more accountable; (2) the challenge to identify one global cross-sectoral accountability framework; and (3) the challenge to improve their internal accountability – see *Five Years Strategy Document*, available on website, op. cit. note 2, pp. 1–2.

[8] See G.M. Steinberg, A. Herzberg, J. Berman, *Best Practices for Human Rights and Humanitarian NGO Fact Finding*, (2012), pp. 16–17; Hortsch, op. cit. note 1, p. 126.

[9] See Thompson, op. cit. note 7, p. 213, admitting however that such a proposition requires 'a certain leap of faith and a temporary suspension of disbelief' – pp. 213–214.

[10] See I. Rossi, *NGOs in International Law: Has Regulation Come to a Halt?, Institute for International Law* (Leuven University), Working Paper No. 123

member organizations have joined the charter,[11] while three of the founding signatories have chosen to leave it.[12] Nevertheless, in 2011, the charter signatories adopted a 'Five Years Strategy', aimed at establishing the charter until 2015 as the sector's 'overarching accountability framework'; encouraging all leading INGOs to sign; proposing that donors and key stakeholders recognize its reporting system as 'the premier quality assurance mechanism for INGOs'· and encouraging smaller INGOs and larger national ones to use the charter as a basis for their own accountability.[13]

The charter is based on the foundation of some fairly simplistic, broadly-termed declarative statements.[14] These statements outline an inclusive, self-reflexive framework tailored to fit the most fundamental understandings, aims, and modes of operation shared by many of the INGOs that are active today.[15] In this respect, calling it an '*Accountability* Charter' is misleading;[16] at its core, it resembles a

---

(Feb. 2008), p. 16; D. Brakman Reiser, C.R. Kelly, *Linking NGO Accountability and the Legitimacy of Global Governance, Brooklyn Journal of International Law*, Vol. 36 (2011), pp. 1071–1072.

11 See website, op. cit. note 2, ('*charter members*'; last visited: Jan, 2013). Currently, the charter enlists 24 member organizations, and 2 affiliate organizations.

12 See *Report of the Directors, INGO Charter of Accountability Limited (no. 06527022)* (Dec. 31, 2010), *Sayer Vincent Consultants & Auditors*, p. 2 – see website, ibid ('*charter background*'). Many leading INGOs, such as Human Rights Watch (HRW) and *Medecins sans Frontiers*, are not members.

13 See *Five Years Strategy Document*, op. cit. note 7.

14 See as well Hortsch, op. cit. note 1, p. 134.

15 Thompson admits that none of the NGOs that agreed to the charter is likely committing to anything that it was not already doing – op. cit. note 7, pp. 215–216. The charter is consisted of nine core principles: Respect for universal principles; Independence; Responsible advocacy; Effective programs; Non-discrimination; Transparency; Good governance; Ethical fundraising; Professional management. Compare with G.E. Edwards, *Assessing the Effectiveness of Human Rights NGOs from the Birth of the United Nations to the 21st Century: The Attributes of Highly Successful Human Rights NGOs, Michigan State Journal of International Law*, Vol. 18(2), (2010), pp. 165, 193–213, identifying ten common operative characteristics essential for the activity of human rights NGOs.

16 Reviewing the vast literature on INGOs' accountability is well beyond the scope of this work – see generally S. Charnovitz, *Accountability of Non-Governmental Organizations in Global Governance*, in L. Jordan, P. van Tuijl (eds.), *NGO Accountability: Politics, Principles & Innovations*, (2006), pp. 24–30. Clearly, accountability is today's 'fashionable topic' – see S. Zadek, *Collaborative Governance: The New Multilateralism for the Twenty First Century*, in B. Lael, op. cit. note 1, p. 187, 189. Nevertheless, the concept of accountability remains 'relational', and has too often been used in a profligate and wholly imprecise manner – see Hortsch, op. cit.

declaration of common principles and perceptions of an ideologically like-minded group of organizations,[17] rather than a document prescribing progressive, operational channels and techniques of accountability. The opening statements of the voluntary charter define the group of signatories as independent non-profit organizations that work globally and 'can *complement but not replace* the over-arching role and primary responsibility of governments'.[18] Their right to act is based on 'universally recognized freedoms of speech, assembly and association' and on their 'contribution to democratic processes' and the values they seek to promote; their legitimacy is derived from the quality of their work and the recognition and support of their stakeholders.[19] Touching more directly on issues of accountability, the charter commits its signatories to

note 1, p. 128; Alston, op. cit. note 1, pp. 637–638. The term 'accountability' in the context of the charter means, in fact, 'responsible advocacy'. It definitely does not stand for responsibility (and answerability) towards a higher authority – see generally K.P. Kearns, *Managing for Accountability: Preserving the Public Trust in Public and Nonprofit Organizations*, (1996), pp. 7–9. Today, premised on the notion of the individual's self-fulfillment and direct political engagement, accountability, as viewed by many INGO leaders and proponents, is distinguished from (democratic) representation, since INGOs do not consider themselves to derive their legitimacy from necessary interaction with other actors or individuals; therefore, they supposedly do not depend on external appraisal or an agency function, and their advocacy does not trigger the need for external accountability to the community, to the 'system' or to the 'general public', and certainly not to governments. In fact, it is questionable whether any accountability holder exists. Consequently, it is assumed that the debate about external accountability should be 'reconfigured to seek better performance rather than accountability', optimally monitored by other INGOs – see Charnovitz, ibid, pp. 21, 30–38; M. Edwards, *Forward*, in Jordan, ibid, p. VIII-IX; E. Peruzzotti, *Civil Society, Representation and Accountability: Restating Current Debates on the Representativeness and Accountability of Civic Associations*, in Jordan, ibid, pp. 43, 48–50, 55; H. Kovach, *Addressing Accountability at the Global Level: The Challenges Facing International NGOs*, in Jordan, ibid, pp. 196–197, 199; K. Anderson, *What NGO Accountability Means – and Does Not Mean, American Journal of International Law*, Vol. 103 (2009), pp. 175–176.

17 All the organizations that have joined the charter could be found on either the centre or left-of-centre of the political spectrum. Thus, the charter is unlikely to facilitate a forum that accommodates ideological diversity – see Thompson, op. cit note 7, p. 216.

18 The charter acknowledges that INGOs can often address, through 'constructive challenge', issues that governments are 'unable or unwilling' to address on their own.

19 Stakeholders include the people for whom they work, their members, donors, the wider public, and governmental and other organizations.

'openness and honesty' regarding their governance structures, mission, policies and activities.[20] Regarding the delicate issue of ethical funding, the signatories pledge, *inter alia*, to respect the rights of donors which include the right to anonymity, except in cases where the size of the donation might prejudice their independence;[21] funds and donations should be raised while accurately describing the organizations' activities and needs; donations should further the organizations' mission, while internal financial controls should ensure that funds are not misused.

The charter's main (and almost sole) operational provision with immediate practical implications is the reporting requirement.[22] Considered to be 'a flexible accountability tool',[23] this is undoubtedly the initiative's most significant innovation, which has the potential to evolve into a meaningful compliance mechanism. Together with their declared commitment to abide by reporting requirements in the countries where they operate – which in any case is compulsory under national jurisdictions – by signing the charter, all members commit to report annually on their activities and achievements. These reports, which are submitted to the Charter Company's operating bodies,[24] include a description of objectives and outcomes; governance structure and processes; main sources of funding; financial performance; and compliance with the

---

20 Notably, funding is dealt with under a different heading; this is probably the outcome of INGOs' inability to commit to 'openness and honesty' in this regard, due to the sometimes conflicting 'rights of donors', explicitly acknowledged and secured in the charter. This fundamental conflict-of-interest between the general public and INGOs' donors thus remains an alarming issue in the context of INGOs' legitimacy.

21 The size of such a donation remains however unspecified in the charter.

22 See Charter, op. cit. note 2; charter website ('*home*'), op. cit note 2; Steinberg, op. cit. note 8, p. 17, acknowledges that the charter does not contain much information on liability and enforcement, such as setting up reporting mechanisms.

23 See Charter Company Executive Director's note on website ('*home*'), ibid.

24 All members are required to apply the reporting framework of the Global Reporting Initiative's (GRI) NGO Sector Supplement launched in 2010. The GRI produces the world's largest sustainability reporting framework, setting out principles and performance indicators. It developed a standardized reporting supplement accommodating the specific needs of NGOs, supposedly offering the same standard used by commercial organizations – see website, ibid; Report of the Directors, op. cit. note 12, p. 2 ('*Activities in the year*').

charter.[25] The annual reports are reviewed by an Independent Review Panel (IRP), which took up its work in early 2011.[26] The IRP produces feedback evaluation, on which the member organizations may comment before the report, evaluation, and remarks are published on the charter's website. The IRP also reviews complaints made against the charter and its members.[27]

2.2 *GUIDELINES ON INTERNATIONAL HUMAN RIGHTS FACT-FINDING VISITS AND REPORTS (THE* 'LUND-LONDON GUIDELINES') *(2009)*

Launched by the International Bar Association's Human Rights Institute, in conjunction with the Raoul Wallenberg Institute of Human Rights and Humanitarian Law (Lund University, Sweden),[28] the highly articulated set of guidelines was drafted over several years of wide consultations and extensive research by legal and human rights scholars with the collaboration of institutional professionals and INGO activists.[29] The clearly delineated mandate of the initiative was to propose a framework for regulating the fact-finding

[25] See Charter ('Reporting'), op. cit. note 2. The word 'main' qualifying 'sources of funding' appears in the original text.

[26] For members of the IRP, see website, op. cit. note 2 (*'Independent Review Panel'*). Regarding the criteria for the selection of the IRP's members, the process for their nomination, and measures taken to avoid cases of conflict of interests – see website (*'Independent Review Panel – Terms of Reference'*).

[27] See website (*'Independent Review Panel – Complaints Handling Procedure'*), ibid; the review of complaints is a confidential process, not involving the law of any jurisdiction, while the complainant, as well as the entity against which the complaint is made, are not entitled to legal representation.

[28] The project was supported by the British Institute of International and Comparative Law (BIICL), the Clemens Nathan Research Center, and the Consultative Council of Jewish Organizations (CCJO) – see *Guidelines on International Human Rights Fact-Finding Visits and Reports (The Lund-London Guidelines) Inaugurated 01 June, 2009, International Bar Association (IBA) & Raoul Wallenberg Institute of Human Rights and Humanitarian Law*, available on *Guidelines' Website*: http://www.factfindingguidelines.org/; see Appendices, 4.2; *General Note (2004)*, introducing the project, provided by Mr. Alan Stephens (Clemens Nathans Research Centre) who initiated the project, is on file with the author.

[29] See Steinberg, op. cit. note 8, pp. 30–31. For a list of the participants in the various drafting and research stages – see Guidelines, ibid, p. 2. Together with the many scholars who joined the drafting process, there were experts from the ICRC, OAS, ICTY, HR Commission, the CCJO, 'No Peace Without Justice', IBA, BIICL, Int'l Commission of Jurists, and Int'l PEN.

capacities and reports produced by NGOs, and frequently referred to by courts and international tribunals, as well as by governments, organizations and the news media.[30] In this light, the project proposal was based on the acknowledgement that, despite much discussion, no *procedural standards* had been universally accepted for the conduct of fact-finding enquiries and the assessment of reports;[31] it was therefore 'paradoxical that tribunals which in their own proceedings insist on principles of impartiality, and due process, are sometimes prepared to accept the findings of NGOs' fact-finding commissions at their face value'.[32] Accordingly, the project aimed at producing 'an agreed *international standard of good practice*', amounting to a 'system of quality control', intended to improve accuracy, transparency and credibility in the conduct of fact-finding and the compilation of reports.[33] Currently, the guidelines have been endorsed by only 7 (I)NGOs.[34]

Significantly, the guidelines do not involve any consideration of legal status, or any rights or obligations in the legal sense, in the case

---

[30] See General Note, op. cit. note 28, and website (*'about'*), op. cit note 28. On the growing importance of, and complexities involved in NGOs human rights fact-finding reports, see G. Robertson, *Human Rights Fact-Finding: Some Legal and Ethical Dilemmas, University College London Human Rights Review* Vol. 3 (2010), p. 15. Robertson considers the guidelines a significant step in establishing a contemporary look at the ethical and legal dimensions of fact finding. For example of an INGO report based on the guidelines, see *'Zimbabwe: Time for a New Approach', IBA's Human Rights Institute,* (Sep. 2011), on: http://www.osisa.org/sites/default/files/sup_files/ibahri_report_on_zimbabwe.pdf.

[31] See R.C. Blitt, *Who Will Watch the Watchdogs? Human Rights Nongovernmental Organizations and the Case for Regulation, Buffalo Human Rights Law Review*, Vol. 10 (2004), pp. 333–350.

[32] See General Note, op. cit. note 28. Another concern was that errors in reports could open an NGO to liability for libel – see Steinberg, op. cit. note 8, p. 31; Robertson, op. cit. note 30, p. 15, 17, 41–43.

[33] See General Note, ibid; website, op. cit. note 28; Preamble of Guidelines, op. cit. note 28. The guidelines' preamble suggests that 'if a report has been compiled in accordance with these guidelines it indicates that the allegations, observations, and conclusions in it can be reasonably relied upon'.

[34] See website (*'endorsements'*) (Jan. 2013), ibid. The guidelines were intended to be the first step in a series of initiatives, such as the establishment of a comprehensive Fact-Finding Program/Centre for training fact-finders, with the objective of defining the discipline of fact-finding. However, the project seems to have lost momentum – see Steinberg, op. cit. note 8, p. 32. If successful, such an initiative can obviously become the substance of an international diplomatic conference, with the aim of achieving support by governments, and implementation by international tribunals, IGOs and INGOs.

of INGOs. Furthermore, the guidelines do not make any effort to legally define the archetypal non-governmental entity to which they refer. Rather, the project is founded on careful *practical observations* regarding *certain functions*, typically fulfilled by INGOs, and their consequent impact on international (legal) affairs.[35] In this way, the guidelines open by defining the *function* to which they relate, stating that fact-finding means 'a mission or visit mandated by an NGO to ascertain the relevant facts relating to and elucidating a situation of human rights concern'.[36] The guidelines acknowledge the need to respect NGOs' independence and integrity, due to their distinctive position and expertise;[37] the essentiality of their fact-finding and report-writing functions to human rights monitoring is well-recognized, and therefore 'must be, and be seen to be, conducted in a *bona fide* manner'.[38] This approach clearly takes into account the unique features of INGOs, as being self-appointed and officially unaccountable. However, it also recognizes their general need to gain credibility and legitimacy. With that in mind, the guidelines outline a set of procedural methods underlined by several main themes, including the need to enforce objectivity and to eliminate bias.[39]

Virtually all the various stages in the work of an international non-governmental fact-finding mission are carefully covered by

---

[35] On the importance of NGO fact-finding and reporting, see generally Steinberg, ibid, pp. 1–5; Alston notes that assessing the impact of country visits is a neglected dimension of human rights work, and mentions that even the largest of the civil society monitoring groups, Human Rights Watch, has no truly systemized process for evaluating the effectiveness of its project work – see op. cit. note 1, p. 574.

[36] See guidelines, op. cit. note 28, Art.1, under the heading 'Definition of Fact-Finding'; no definition of an 'NGO' follows.

[37] See generally Blitt, who maintains that the need for human rights INGOs independence ought not to trump the need for recognized fact-finding and reporting standards – see op. cit. note 31, p. 339. Compare with the *Code of Conduct for Special Procedures Mandate-Holders of the Human Rights Council, Res. 5/2 (18 June 2007)*, UN GAOR, 62nd Sess., Supp. No. 53, A/62/53, p. 74, aimed at 'defining the standards of ethical behavior and professional conduct that special procedures mandate-holders shall observe' (Art. 1). Note that fact-finding missions and consequent reporting are two of the principal functions performed by independent experts designated under the HRC system of 'Special Procedures' (or 'Special Rapporteurs') – see in particular Art. 11; see Alston, op. cit. note 1, pp. 572–576.

[38] See Preamble of guidelines, op. cit note 28.

[39] See *International Law In Brief, ASIL* (June 12, 2009), available on: www.asil.org.

numerous provisions, in the form of a step-by-step 'easy-to-use' manual, including: instigation of the mission; articulation of its terms of reference; composition of the delegation; activity of interpreters and other persons associated with the mission; pre-visits; working methods; drafting of the report; its translation and publication; and follow-up activity.[40]

2.3 *REPORTS OF THE COMMITTEE ON NON-STATE ACTORS OF THE INTERNATIONAL LAW ASSOCIATION (ILA) (2008, 2010 & 2012)*

Following the 2010 ILA Conference, the newly established ILA Committee on Non State Actors (NSAs) issued its report under the title 'Non-State Actors in International Law: Aims, Approach and Scope

[40] The following outline is intended only to reflect the main provisions focusing more directly on the enforcement of objectivity and the elimination of bias. The most important provisions in this regard concern the nature of the mission, wording of the mandate, and selection of personnel. Thus, the guidelines insist that a fact-finding mission should be considered in light of the NGO's mandate, while evaluating possible negative consequences of undertaking the mission, as well as the work of other organizations with regard to the same human rights situation. The mission's terms of reference should be articulated in light of the NGO's expertise, and cannot reflect any predetermined conclusions. Delegation members must be, and be seen to be, unbiased, having the competence relevant to matters pertaining to the terms of reference. When selecting the members, the NGO may need to consider certain issues of balance and diversity. It should ensure that all members, as well as all other persons associated with the mission act in an independent, unbiased, objective, professional, lawful and ethical manner. In order to achieve a balanced and comprehensive picture of the 'human rights situation' (for the significance of the wording 'situation' in this context, compare with Rule 44(2) of the *International Criminal Court (ICC) Rules of Procedure and Evidence* (Doc. ASP/1/3, pp. 10–107) – see W.A. Schabas, *An Introduction to the International Criminal Court (4th ed.)*, (2011), pp. 84–86), the delegation should endeavor to thoroughly interview all parties; they must make use of all data collection techniques, taking every reasonable measure to verify the objectivity of the information. In presenting its findings, the delegation must base its reports on the information it has gathered, working independently, within its frame of reference. The mission's report must be accurate, drafted objectively, and fairly reflect all of the gathered evidence. Conclusions and recommendations should attempt to outline practical solutions, having been reached by consensus. The reports should be published within a reasonable time frame, following the conclusion of the mission. Finally, the NGO bears overall responsibility for decisions regarding the report's publication and dissemination, and should consider what, if any, media strategy would be most appropriate.

of Project and Legal Issues'.[41] The report outlines the committee's project of evaluating the challenges to international law posed by the proliferation of NSAs in the international political and legal arenas.[42] Notably, the report follows a preliminary brief report in which the committee set out its tentative mandate.[43] Although the committee's mandate has changed considerably during the two years following its initial session, a brief overview of the 2008 preliminary report is significant in highlighting some of the conceptual complexities characterizing contemporary initiatives dealing with the normative position of NSAs in general, and INGOs in particular.[44]

2008 ILA Report

According to the 2008 report, the committee initially agreed to focus its research on issues of international security law,[45] mainly evaluating the legal position of NSAs in armed conflicts.[46] Significantly, the report dealt with 'NSAs' as a distinct, normative group, although it distinguished certain sub-categories, such as NGOs (civil society), being a 'relatively straightforward' example of NSAs relevant to its mandate.[47] Considering the influence and representation of NSAs in international forums, the committee suggested that in a number of IGOs, NSAs – such as NGOs – 'have *limited legal personality*, in that they can act *as observers*'.[48] It also observed that in order for the

---

[41] The *First Report of the Committee on NSAs, ILA* (*The Hague Conference, 2010*) ('ILA 2010 Report') is available on: www.ila-hq.org.

[42] Ibid, p. 1.

[43] See *Preliminary Issues for the International Law Association Conference in Rio de Janeiro, August 2008, NSAs Committee*, ('ILA 2008 Report'), p. 1 – available on: www.ila-hq.org.

[44] Although the ILA reports deal generally with NSAs, the status of INGOs more specifically is focused on in different sections of the reports. Regarding the decision to relate broadly to NSAs – see, generally, R.H. Ben-Ari, *The Normative Position of International Non-Governmental Organizations under International Law – An Analytical Framework* (2012), pp. 3–5, 47–51, 349–350.

[45] See ILA 2008 Report, op. cit. note 43, p. 1.

[46] See ibid, ibid. No reference to the issue of international terrorism is made in this context – see p. 2.

[47] Ibid. Given its focus on security issues, the committee further mentioned humanitarian and relief NGOs, and refrained from limiting itself to dealing with *international* NGOs in particular.

[48] See ibid, p. 3.

binding force of international law to be palatable to NSAs 'as (possible) subjects of international law', international law norms would need to be established through an 'inclusive process'. This required 'a fundamental rethinking' of international law formation, as well as giving NSAs the right to participate in treaty negotiation and adoption, and granting their practice 'some weight' in the determination of norms of customary international law;[49] law could then become transnational rather than international.[50]

2010 ILA Report

The committee's 2010 report presented a more articulate and ambitious outline. It developed a working definition of 'NSAs',[51] which explicitly included INGOs 'with *some form of recognized international legal status*'.[52] Although the committee adhered to its initial focus on NSAs as a broad normative group, it neglected its intention to focus specifically on international security, in order to focus on the legal position of NSAs in general.[53] The declared aim of the committee's project was 'to derive NSAs' legal 'status' or ILP from

---

[49] Compare with T. Muller, *Customary Transnational Law: Attacking the Last Resort of State Sovereignty, Indiana Journal of Global Legal Affairs*, Vol. 15 (1), (2008), p. 19. Muller foresees the possibility of the emergence of 'customary transnational law' that is not limited to the customs of states but is dependent on the customs of the international community at large – see pp. 21–25.

[50] See 2008 ILA Report, op. cit. note 43, p. 3.

[51] Which includes actors that: (1) are not comprised or controlled by states; (2) perform functions in the international arena that have effects on international law; and (3) are internationally, legally recognized entities – see ILA 2010 Report, op. cit. note 41, p. 6.

[52] Including formal accreditation *and informal relations* with UN and UN-related bodies, at UN and non-UN law-making conferences – see ibid, pp. 6–7. The list includes a category of *sui generis* or unique entities, such as the ICRC. For an evaluation of the exceptional status of the ICRC as an INGO see H.H.-K. Rechenberg, *Non-Governmental Organizations*, in *Encyclopedia of Public International Law*, Vol. 3 (1997), p. 617; H. Mosler, *Subjects of International Law*, in *Encyclopedia of Public International Law*, Vol. 7, (1984), p. 455; Y. Dinstein, *The Interaction Between Customary International Law and Treaties, Recueil des Cours – Collected Courses of the Hague Academy of International Law*, Vol. 322(2006), (2007), p. 243, 268.

[53] Admittedly, the initial focus on 'the topical and controversial subject of security' was proposed in view of the need to limit the scope of the committee's work – see 2010 ILA Report, op. cit. note 41, p. 2.

empirical studies',[54] whereas its purpose was to examine the position of NSAs in international law in terms of their rights and obligations.[55] The committee noted that a definition of the legal 'status' which NSAs could develop would be based on their perceived activities and functions. Although this methodology was based on the legacy of the ICJ *Reparation for Injuries* case, the committee declared that its project departed 'from attempts to fit strictly within the international law notion of 'ILP''.[56]

The presumption underlying the committee's proposal was that, as particular NSAs had a special set of rights and obligations within the frameworks of accreditation relating to particular international bodies, they also had a general set of rights and obligations under general international law.[57] A 'related premise' was that some NSAs assumed governance roles traditionally performed by states;[58] accordingly, there could be grounds for attributing to them 'a type of legal 'status' or ILP'.[59] The committee thus adopted a particular '*functional* research methodology *with the state as a point of reference to look at NSAs in contemporary global 'governance'*'.[60] Consequently, the report outlined an analogy of traditional state governance, with functions existing at the international level. These functions, framed as legal issues, included norm-creation;[61]

---

[54] See ibid; the word 'status' appears within single quotes in the original text, clearly meaning something different from 'ILP'.

[55] See ibid, pp. 1–2.

[56] See p. 7.

[57] See p. 2.

[58] See p. 4. The report maintains that in a globalized world, NSAs are performing tasks classically fulfilled by the State. Accordingly, the committee's objective is to identify features of 'governance', to look at what roles NSAs are assuming, and 'to discover any commonalities that may lead to finding a legal status or ILP'.

[59] See ibid.

[60] See pp. 3–4. 'Global governance' is understood in the report to be 'a constantly evolving system comprised of formal and informal institutions, mechanisms, relationships and arrangements among States, their constituent markets, and private organizations, groups and individuals which through collective interests in the global sphere are articulated, rights and obligations established and differences mediated'.

[61] That is, legislation or law-making – see p. 8. The committee recalls in this context that 'some distinguished scholars do not limit the concept of 'international community' to States', and note that some contemporary scholarship suggests that the concepts of 'subjects' of international law and of 'international legal person' today may be changing; NSAs may thus already have a *natural right* to

monitoring compliance[62] and enforcement;[63] and functions such as the provision of 'public goods'.[64] Altogether, this approach acknowledged that 'states are not the only legitimate actors in the international law arena', and involved determination of whether, and which, NSA practice should count.[65] Operatively, the committee's so-called 'qualitative research project'[66] aimed at exploring arrangements existing in substantive areas of international law,[67] based on formal or informal frameworks for NSA accreditation and participation.[68] Significantly, within its investigation, the committee intended to take particular account of states' international law advisers' views on NSA ILP.[69] Apart from that, 'a key question' was how to assess and classify the practice and opinions of NSAs regarding their own position.[70] At the next stage, the committee would perform a normative investigation as to whether it was desirable to close the gap between the reality of NSA participation in global governance and their extant legal status.[71]

---

political participation and a *legitimate expectation* to a general right to participate in international legal discourse – see pp. 9–12.

62 That is, administration or law application.

63 Referring to dispute settlement or adjudication.

64 Based on an analogy to the hypothetical social contract existing between the state and its citizens – see 2010 ILA Report, op. cit. note 41, pp. 4–5.

65 See ibid, p. 12.

66 See p. 5.

67 'Legal arrangements' include treaties, 'soft' law texts, contracts etc., existing, *inter alia*, in the fields of international human rights, humanitarian law, environmental law, criminal law, economic law, etc. 'Rights' may include claims, privilege, powers or immunities, while 'obligations' may derive from treaties, customary international law, contracts, soft law etc. – see ibid, pp. 4–5.

68 See p. 5.

69 Ibid.

70 Ibid. This initial stage of the committee's work involves empirical research responding to the question to what extent has the law already responded to the challenges of NSAs in international law. The drafters acknowledge this to be 'an *objective, definitional and descriptive* research question at the epistemic level of knowledge *where the researcher tries to remain detached and eliminate personal bias*' – see p. 7.

71 See pp. 5–6. This second stage of the committee's work seeks to answer 'more *subjective, interrelated theoretical questions* that require more *qualitative* assessments'. These questions are: 'How do NSAs affect international law-creation, application, adjudication and enforcement?'; 'How does international law affect NSAs?'; and 'How does this reflect upon the concept of ILP?' A forth issue may concern a conceptualization toward a 'transnational law', being a possible respond to the question how should international law deal with NSAs – see p. 7.

The committee touched more directly upon three significant issues regarding the position of INGOs as a distinct group of NSAs. Acknowledging that accountability under international law had become a recurring issue concerning NSAs' legal position in general,[72] the report noted that INGOs did not incur legal liability on the international plain.[73] In any case, in light of 'the services they render for the global public good', the report questioned whether such liability was desirable, and adopted the position that, given the often 'laudable goals of NGOs' actions', one could indeed argue that 'unrecoverable costs caused by their resistance action would have to be anticipated'; INGOs' international legal liability therefore had to be excluded.[74] Considering the issue of immunity, the report recalled that immunities from jurisdiction and enforcement were mainly grounded upon functional considerations.[75] Consequently, following the ICJ's perceived logic in the *Reparation for Injuries*,[76] if the nature of ILP depended upon the needs of the community, then one could query whether granting immunity to certain NSAs might satisfy such needs. It could thus be argued that many NSAs 'should be granted forms of immunity due to their global reach and roles played in contributing to global governance'.[77] Finally, the report dealt squarely with the issue of NSAs' ILP or the drafters' preferred term,[78] legal 'status'. Adopting the view of 'a growing number of scholars' who rejected the positivist doctrine of ILP as having 'no credible reality and no functional purpose', the committee was clearly aware of the far-reaching implications of its normative endeavor in this regard, seeking an answer to the question of,

> ... whether the *de facto* reality of interactions between States and IGOs on the one hand, and various NGOs on the other, forces us

---

[72] See p. 17.
[73] See p. 18.
[74] Ibid, & fn. 95.
[75] See p. 19.
[76] See *Reparation for Injuries Suffered in the Service of the United Nations*, Advisory Opinion (1949), ICJ Rep. 1949, p. 178.
[77] 2010 ILA Report, op. cit. note 41, p. 19.
[78] See, p. 21.

> to *shift our thinking about international law*, and to *the normative question of whether ILP should be re-conceptualized* so that *it recognized various gradations of international law 'status'*.[79]

Once again, the drafters emphasized that their analysis began with 'the opening of the door' in the *Reparation* advisory opinion, in which the ICJ 'took a more open approach than under orthodox doctrine that allows for a changing of who is an international legal person', by making a connection between the doctrine of ILP and the requirements of international life.[80] The report next employed Article 71 of the UN Charter as a starting point for constructing 'a theory of kinds of NSA legal 'status'',[81] regarding the ECOSOC consultative arrangements to be the principal means states employed to formalize the international legal 'status' of NSAs.[82] Further mentioned was the CoE's 1986 European Convention, as the 'best existing example' of states bestowing legal status on NSAs by establishing a treaty 'creating such legal status'.[83] Ultimately, the committee articulated the major normative challenge that characterized the relationship between states and NSAs, which was to 'develop attributes relating to NSAs' legal position, *so that they can become genuine subjects of international law*, and *de jure* participants in international law processes'.[84]

---

[79] See, p. 24 ('Concluding Observations').

[80] See pp. 20–21. The drafters however acknowledge that an IGO's ILP is less than that of States, and that 'NSAs will generally have an even more limited ILP'. States thus remain the "original' full subjects of international law', while all other ILP is derived from States, that decide 'whether or not and the extent to which ILP will be conferred on other international 'actors' or 'participants'' – p. 21.

[81] See pp. 21–22.

[82] The report uses the term 'NSAs' in this regard and not INGOs. It is unclear whether the authors employ these arrangements as a platform or a model for the regulation of the status of NSAs at large; or whether they wish to employ these arrangements as reflecting broad (or customary) acceptance of NSAs by states.

[83] See ILA 2010 Report, op. cit. note 41, p. 22. This contention is peculiar, since, as we have seen, the convention does not do that, and has no intention of doing that; see also pp. 9–10. A misunderstanding is clearly revealed regarding the legal implications of the convention, the intention of its drafters and the historical background leading to its conclusion – see text in chapter one, section 1.10, and fns. 145–147, *supra*.

[84] See ibid, p. 23.

2012 ILA Report

The committee's 2012 report,[85] under the title 'Non-State Actors in International Law: Lawmaking and Participation Rights', provides the first step in implementing the agenda that the committee set itself, addressing NSA activity relevant to norm-creation.[86] It examines NSAs' lawmaking capacity, inquiring whether NSAs, 'like States or IGOs, can *directly* contribute to the creation of international law', as well as NSA *participatory rights*[87] in, and influence on, international legal arrangements 'dominated by States and IGOs' that may produce international legal norms.[88] The report's methodology is expressly based on an 'enlightened' positivist view with an 'ethical premise of a moral imperative', that is a 'universalist' vision which promotes the possibility of a 'public order beyond the state'.[89] This methodology, focused on *dynamics* of actors and participants, follows that of writers who 'emphasize a process-based, dynamic conception of international law', which contradicts, according to the authors of the report, the traditional static perception of international law by international lawyers 'as a mere bundle of rules'.[90]

Indeed, once the authors admit that, essentially, there are no instances of *direct* contribution to international lawmaking by NSAs,

[85] See *Second Report of the Committee on NSAs, ILA* (*Sofia Conference, 2012*) ('ILA 2012 Report') is available on: www.ila-hq.org. The Committee's next report, due 2014, is supposed to focus on NSA obligations, responsibility, and compliance with international law, as well as enforcement and settlement of disputes to which NSAs are parties – see p. 3.

[86] See ibid, p. 2; see fn. 61 *supra*.

[87] Essentially, the authors of the report relate to existing consultative arrangements as establishing '*participatory rights*'. They do not distinguish between the two kinds of arrangements – a distinction that was acknowledged by the Council of Europe when upgrading the CoE's *consultative* status arrangements with INGOs into '*participatory* status arrangements' – see chapter one, fn. 139, *supra*. Furthermore, the report does not explain how, and in what respects, such arrangements can be considered to provide NSAs with 'rights' – see, in this regard, chapter one, under section 1.4, *supra*, as well as Merle's comments in his report, chapter one, under section 1.10, *supra*. This is all the more peculiar in view of the authors' remark that the term 'participation', as used in the report, 'is *not a legal term*' but denotes 'a dynamic of actors taking part in deliberative processes, and in so doing possibly influencing the formation of international rules' – see ibid, pp. 2–3.

[88] See ibid, p. 2.

[89] See ibid, p. 3.

[90] See ibid & fn. 6.

and that they are not considered as 'law-making agencies',[91] most of the report is dedicated to reviewing the *participation* of NSAs. The report considers the participatory roles of NSAs – INGOs in particular – within the many modalities for official participation existing today, mostly within inter-governmental frameworks (UN-related and non-UN IGOs and institutional regimes, as well as dispute-settlement fora), in order to gain a full understanding of their *indirect* influence on international policy- and lawmaking.[92] According to the report, such arrangements developed mechanisms of practical engagement with INGOs, particularly in sharing information and obtaining their specific expertise;[93] they allowed INGOs to initiate intergovernmental lawmaking by states, as well as to contribute to drafting efforts, mainly in the human-based fields of international law;[94] they also allowed INGOs to play an active role in the monitoring and enforcement of some international and regional instruments.[95] In this framework, the drafters return to the UN ECOSOC consultative arrangements as the 'best known and foundational institutional arrangement',[96] which set the example for other specialized agencies and institutional regimes; they further mention the CoE, as the organization which 'has conferred the most far-reaching NGO participatory rights' through the adoption of the 1986 European Convention, and the participatory arrangements with NGOs.[97]

All in all, although the committee discerns a 'participatory revolution' in the case of NSAs,[98] it doubts whether they can be considered to 'even have a general right to access and participation', and points out that there are practical as well as normative limits to the process of NSAs inclusion.[99] One final important and complementary

---

91 See pp. 4–6, 26.

92 See pp. 6–7. The report also mentions other informal channels and arrangements for NSA influence on policy- and lawmaking – see p. 18.

93 See p. 8.

94 See p. 9.

95 See p. 25.

96 See p. 13.

97 See p. 15.

98 Supposedly undergird by the rationales of expertise, democracy/legitimacy, sheer power, and norm effectiveness – see p. 26.

99 See pp. 26–27. The authors nevertheless maintain that 'there may be said to be an *expectation* that NSAs are included in deliberative processes', although they

inquiry that remains unresolved is that of the *actual effectiveness* and *impact* of NSA participation and involvement – empirical research which falls outside the committee's mandate.[100]

***

We shall now move to the last part of this work, in which we will evaluate the significant trends in the contemporary discourse regarding the legal position of INGOs, as reflected in the new initiatives reviewed in the second chapter, against the benchmark derived from the contextual historical analysis of past attempts, and will accordingly suggest some future prospects for the progression of this discourse.

admit that there is no 'magical formula applicable across the board' regarding modalities of participation in the different institutions, regimes and fora that have been found to have arrangements for including NSAs in their decision-making process.

100 Presumably the task of social scientists, rather than lawyers – See p. 27.

Chapter Three

EVALUATION OF NEW DEVELOPMENTS AND CURRENT TRENDS

Taken together, the new initiatives dealing with INGOs' status or the standardization of their activity are a clear indication that there is still much, and apparently growing, interest in these topics. This interest, however, derives from different sources (academia, field activists, international lawyers, etc.) and reflects varying, even contradictory, perceptions of the position of INGOs within the international community and its legal order. Moreover, these initiatives vary with regard to the outcome they are trying to achieve: while the ILA work is taken, first and foremost, as an academic endeavor to outline a certain normative framework, the Lund-London Guidelines provide a practical governance tool; the Accountability Charter is mainly an attempt to establish a platform for the promotion of shared understandings and the invention of common principles and – depending on its future evolvement and broad-based adoption – a self-governing accountability framework. Consequently, these initiatives target different audiences: the ILA reports are mainly addressed to the academic community, whereas the guidelines target NGO activists and state and IGO officials; the charter appeals to INGO representatives as well as to the general public and media. Whatever the case may be, not all of these schemes have taken into account the long history of dealing with similar, related issues. As demonstrated by the following analysis, such an undertaking could yield more realistic, viable, and effective results.

3.1 DOCTRINAL EVOLVEMENT

Much like the early initiatives to propose a formal legal status for INGOs, the 2008/2010 ILA reports straightforwardly raised the question of ILP (or otherwise legal 'status') under international law. In that respect, it could definitely be said that after 100 years, we had returned to the departure points of the early Institute proposals of von Bar and Politis. It is therefore all the more noteworthy that these reports completely ignored the evolution of attempts to deal with the quest for ILP and their consequent results and conclusions. It may be recalled that the initial interest in the normative position of INGOs derived from the problem of ILP and related topics, such as public registration and order. The quest for personality, regarded as advantageous for INGOs, was invoked and pursued by scholars who were INGO activists and who worked under the mandate of INGO forums.[1] This quest was based on the assumption that the development of INGOs was beneficial to the interests of the 'international community', and that consequently, they should be at liberty not to be tied exclusively to a certain state by reason of their nature or goals. However, this initial quest for a *uniform universal status*, based on a highly optimistic and autonomous view of the position of the INGO community, came under much scrutiny, mainly as a result of the unresolved problems of registration, control and order, which the ILA reports completely overlooked. The adoption of the consultative status arrangements, under Article 71 of the UN Charter, further emphasized the difficulties regarding the definition of a genuine INGO entity and its specific legal requirements, matters which remain unresolved even today[2]. Nevertheless, together with the ICJ's judgment in the *Reparation for Injuries* case, renewed discussions about the legal status of INGOs were underlined by the assumption of INGOs' functional resemblance to IGOs. Consequently, the general debate was drastically modified, theoretically as well as practically, to focus on *securing recognition abroad, on the basis of the personality in the state of incorporation* (i.e. 'mutual recognition'). This change in doctrinal focus, based on the need to simplify *rules of conflicts-of-law*, was again the initiative of INGO activists who wished to lift national restrictions on their operations. Later, based on the realization that the assumption of INGOs resemblance to IGOs was politically unrealistic and legally unfounded, a third

[1] Keane observes that the decision in Brussels in 1910 to found the UIA, attended by 132 INGOs and 13 governments, was an important symbol of an emergent 'collective self-awareness among NGOs of their moral influence and power potential' – see J. Keane, *Global Civil Society?*, (2003), p. 47.

[2] See R.H. Ben-Ari, *The Normative Position of International Non-Governmental Organizations under International Law – An Analytical Framework* (2012), pp. 47–51.

doctrinal approach was initiated, based on the notion of *'a most favored national association clause'*, upholding the status of the INGO entity as a national NGO in the registering state. This approach, *based exclusively on the national rather than the international level*, focused on *particular administrative and fiscal facilities*. This reflected complete repudiation of the original idea of ILP or the need to solve the question of legal recognition. The ILA reports nevertheless attempted to revive this normative discussion, this time based on notions of 'global governance' and interdependence, borrowing heavily from the fields of political science and international relations. Indeed, the notion of the establishment of a 'Global Civil Society',[3] although not explicitly mentioned in the reports, clearly underlined the ILA drafters' fundamental premise that NSAs assumed governance roles traditionally performed by states, which led them to adopt a functional methodology with the state as a point of reference to look at NSAs in global governance.[4]

Status Follows Function

As we saw, the basic perception that status should follow function is not new, and had underlined the initial attempts to outline a status for INGOs. Ultimately, however, this notion was not implemented within the confines of ILP, despite the fact that this was the exact logic underlying the acquisition of personality in the case of IGOs (as agents of their member states). After all, the development of the consultative status arrangements throughout the years as well as the

---

[3] The literature on the notion of global civil society – the precise meaning of which is far from being resolved – is vast indeed. On 'global civil society' implying the need for a 'new democratic thinking', openly challenging previous notions based on monistic presumptions, in particular the nation-state – see Keane, op. cit. note 1, p. XI, 2, 22, 36; R. Falk, *The Changing Role of Global Civil Society*, in G. Baker, D. Chandler (eds.), *Global Civil Society: Contested Futures*, (2005), p. 69; T.O. Corry, *Global Civil Society and Its Discontents, Voluntas*, (2006), Vol. 17, pp. 303–324.

[4] Particularly the discussion of competition for the provision of 'public goods', based on an analogy to the social contract existing between the state and its citizens, is based on constructivist neo-liberal international relations theory – see S. Ahmed, D. Potter, *NGOs in International Politics*, (2006), pp. 241–244. For a discussion of the application of the post-modern notions of 'globalization', 'global governance', and 'global civil society' to the ongoing discourse on the normative position of INGOs, see Ben-Ari, op. cit. note 2, pp. 163–261, 314–332.

adoption of the CoE's 1986 European Convention, were exactly the outcome of the determination that solutions regarding INGOs' status could not evolve through the adoption of a formal personality scheme under international law. Ignoring this evolutionary sequence, the drafters of the 2010 ILA report drew on these very arrangements to argue that INGOs should obtain certain rights and obligations that would reflect on their acquisition of ILP. Not surprisingly, in that same vein, the drafters returned to the *Reparation* case to jurisprudentially back up their functional claim for INGOs' status. However, being aware of the fact that the application of the *Reparation* precedent was highly controversial and legally problematic in the case of NSAs other than IGOs,[5] they chose to depart in this regard 'from attempts to fit strictly within the notion of ILP', and to adopt the innovative scheme of 'international legal *status*' which the ILA report, however, could not clearly define.

Apparently, this formulation echoes some contemporary writings.[6] Lindblom, for example, based on her standpoint that the fundamental legal concepts of international law – also those related to its actors – adapt to rather than direct developments of the legal system, and in view of the adoption of new instruments and practices which allow for INGOs' interaction with states and IGOs, concludes that 'the international legal *status* of INGOs is equivalent to the sum of those rules and practices'.[7] Unlike the concept of ILP of INGOs,

---

5 See, for example, C.H. Udo, *Nongovernmental Organizations and African Governments: Seeking an Effective International Legal Framework in a New Era of Health and Development Aid, Boston College International and Comparative Law Review*, Vol. 31, pp. 380–381, 385–387; Ben-Ari, ibid, pp. 308–309. See as well UN Doc. A/CN.4/532, *First Report on Responsibility of International Organizations* (by G. Gaja), *International Law Commission*, 55th Sess. (March 26, 2003), p. 9, para. 16.

6 See B. Maragia, *Almost There: Another Way of Conceptualizing and Explaining NGOs' Quest for Legitimacy in Global Affairs, Non-State Actors and International Law*, Vol. 2, (2002), p. 301–332, who argues that NGOs have acquired some measure of legal personality or so called 'quasi or implicit ILP'– p. 332; P.-M. Dupuy, *Conclusion: Return on the Legal Status of NGOs and on the Methodological Problems which Arise for Legal Scholarship*, in P.-M. Dupuy & L. Vierucci (eds.), *NGOs in International Law – Efficiency in Flexibility?*, (2008), pp. 204–215.

7 See A.K. Lindblom, *Non-governmental Organizations in International Law*, (2005), p. 1 (italics added). Compare with Rechenberg, chapter one, fns. 62–63, *supra*, and Politis' proposal, chapter one, fn. 12, *supra*. Lindblom finds significance in the fact that INGO participation has become a common component of many (UN) conferences, which provide examples of practices 'which have evolved to a

which is 'possibly something partly different' and 'not particularly helpful in relation to NGOs', the concept of international legal *status*, according to Lindblom, openly admits that the specific content of this status may vary according to the circumstances; it should be broadly defined, as encompassing all kinds of rules which refer explicitly to an entity or which can be used by the entity for acting on the international scene; it is 'a neutral concept', meaning only that an entity has 'some sort of status in some respect', which needed to be specified for each particular entity.[8] Underlying this argument, however much disguised by dichotomies such as 'international legal *status*' as supposedly distinguished from ILP, are the same assumptions that had inspired earlier writers who wished to establish a functional approach to the question of INGOs' ILP. This approach builds upon a particular appraisal of the position of INGOs within the international community *vis-à-vis* states and IGOs (i.e. their partnership with, or resemblance to, IGOs, and even states[9]). It is based on the understanding that INGOs' expanding functions may indicate broad acceptance on the part of states, which underlines an acknowledgment of a certain level of personality evolving as a customary rule. Indeed, as our contextual historical investigation reveals, this methodology is deeply rooted in legal texts written in the late 1950s and early 1960s. These texts were the outcome of a mistaken, and therefore misleading, reading of the normative

point where the participation of INGOs have become a general rule rather than the individual instances' – see p. 9. Lindblom echoes P. Willetts, *From 'Consultative Arrangements' to 'Partnership': The Changing Status of NGOs in Diplomacy at the UN, Global Governance*, Vol. 6, (2000), p. 205 – see in J.E. Nijman, *The Concept of International Legal Personality: An Inquiry into the History and Theory of International Law*, (2004), pp. 404–405 & fn. 175.

[8] Lindblom believes that, when taken together, the different rights and practices which are afforded on all or categories of INGOs under international and regional treaties express a degree of general acceptance of INGOs as international actors, which has reached a degree where it should be considered relevant for their ILP. Consequently, 'all INGOs are *potential* for ILP of a general character'; a customary ILP for the most respected organizations might thus possibly develop – see ibid, pp. 6–8, 10.

[9] See discussion in this chapter, section 4.2, *infra*; see for example, J.E. Alvarez, *International Organizations: Then and Now, American Journal of International Law*, Vol. 100, (2006), p. 324, 333, 335.

developments at that time, such as the incorporation of Article 71 into the UN Charter and the relevance of the *Reparation* judgment, and were rejected by subsequent practice. In this respect, it is difficult to see how the ILA scheme, as reflected in its 2010 report, could become a progressive stage in the evolvement of the discourse on the normative position of INGOs. It seems that, more than innovating, it repeated earlier stages of the discourse. The onus is thus heavy on the ILA drafters' shoulders to explain how, in view of continuous rejection by states, as well as the growing complexity of the unresolved problems of registration, control and order,[10] the discussion of ILP in the case of INGOs is still relevant today.

Restrictive Functionalism vs. Democratic Pluralism

One may further argue that the ILA scheme is not intellectually sound, since it argues a normative scheme based on a *pluralist belief in democratic policy-making*, on the basis of existing arrangements that reflect *functionalist appeals* (such as the consultative arrangements and the 1986 European Convention). These theoretical frameworks are contradictory. As Willetts explains in a similar context,[11] most of the existing INGO institutional arrangements are based on functionalist ideas applied to governance systems (the UN in particular), strongly emphasizing the ability of experts to maximize welfare and depoliticize decision-making.[12] The ILA scheme's eventual goal is, however, based on notions of fairness and democratic pluralism.[13] As such, the 2008 tentative report acknowledged the

[10] Particularly in view of the growing number of INGOs, and the lack of an agreed definition of the *international* non-governmental entity. Nowadays, these problems also present major obstacles to the development of the existing consultative arrangements.

[11] P. Willetts, *The Cardoso Report on the UN and Civil Society: Functionalism, Global Corporatism or Global Democracy?*, *Journal of Global Governance*, Vol. 12 (2006), pp. 305–324; available on: http://www.staff.city.ac.uk/p.willetts/PUBS/GG-2006.HTM (references follow the online version).

[12] Also reflecting (neo)corporatist desire to involve the affected interests. This appeal is comparable to functionalism in that it has been described as a system of functional representation, although it differs in acknowledging that different interests may be in conflict with each other, and in recognizing that governments are the focal point for the political resolution of such conflicts – see Willetts, ibid, pp. 6–8.

[13] The report's ideas regarding INGOs' accountability and immunity should be evaluated in this context.

need for international law norms to be made through an inclusive process, which might 'a fundamental rethinking of international law formation', giving NSAs weight in the determination of norms. The 2010 report further acknowledged that NSAs were treated primarily as objects of regulation while behaving in practice as *de facto* participants; the challenge was, therefore, to develop attributes relating to their legal position, so that they could become 'genuine subjects of international law'. The drafters further noted the need to determine whether it was possible to acknowledge that states were not the only legitimate actors, a normative endeavor which required us to 'shift our thinking about international law', and to re-conceptualize ILP. The problem is, as Willetts explains, that a belief in democratic pluralism involves the assertion of principles that are incompatible with functionalism, which, by definition, is not inclusive, but aims at restricting participation to experts and the more competent and relevant actors.[14] Possibly, that also explains why, throughout the years, as the historical sequence clearly shows, the early appeals for the acknowledgment of INGOs' uniform universal status, based on pluralistic democratic appeals reflecting transnational worldviews, had to be withdrawn to allow for the adoption of functionalist arrangements. That was also acknowledged by INGO activists themselves, who, on many occasions, advocated the restricted participation of only certain groups of (I)NGOs. It is therefore difficult to see how the drafters of the ILA reports plan to base their broad, normative democratic-pluralistic scheme on the foundation of existing arrangements that essentially reflect functionalistic notions. Indeed, this intellectual leap may have been the reason behind the need to discuss international legal 'status' instead of ILP – which is, after all, one of the most fundamental institutions of the existing international legal order, based on selective functionalist perceptions.

Functional Legitimacy and Self-Governance

The Lund-London Guidelines and the Accountability Charter are not normative schemes; at least, not in the strict juristic sense.

---

14 See Willetts, op. cit. note 11, pp. 10–11.

Unlike the ILA project, they do not endeavor to give new or alternative meaning to existing arrangements. They do not involve consideration of any (international) legal status in the case of INGOs that might compete with, contradict, or replace such arrangements; but endeavor to complement them by providing more practical governance tools and frameworks that are tailored to fit INGOs' perceived functions, when taken at face value. They acknowledge the significance of INGOs' unique contributions to human development in certain fields; they nevertheless recognize the complexities and difficulties involved in such activity and determine to establish mechanisms that will assist in confronting them. Both of these initiatives focus on issues reflecting INGOs' legitimacy on the socio-political level, rather than on the legal-normative level. In this respect, they are clearly responsive to the recent trend to question the accountability of all NSAs, and INGOs in particular.[15] They are further aware that IGOs and their member states prefer not to impose accountability mechanisms on INGOs outside of the national legal sphere,[16] but tend instead to encourage self-governance and self-organizing processes, in response to deficiencies in existing arrangements.[17] This is clearly in line with the evolvement of the ongoing discourse about INGOs position, showing that issues bearing direct effect on the formal legal status of these organizations are channeled to the national, rather than the international authorities. In large part, this is the outcome of the fact that INGOs have always been reluctant to resolve the question of registration, selection and order through an

[15] See generally chapter two, fns. 1, 7, 16, *supra*.

[16] Thus leaving INGOs to establish their own accountability mechanisms on the international level – see I. Rossi, *NGOs in International Law: Has Regulation Come to a Halt?, Institute for International Law* (Leuven University), Working Paper No. 123 (Feb. 2008), p. 12.

[17] See ibid, pp. 11, 14–15; the UN and the CoE have been reluctant to take steps to expand NGO participation or to encourage their regulation at the international level, but rather prefer, even with respect to the issue of accountability, to make NGOs more efficient by encouraging them to better organize themselves. See also the *Report of the Panel of Eminent Persons on United Nations-Civil Society Relations* (the *'Cardoso Report'*), UN Doc. A/58/817 (June 11, 2004), p. 11; *'United Nations: The Relationship between Member States and Civil Society, Including NGOs', Report to the President of the 60th General Assembly* (*by Ambassadors J.L. Løvald* (*Norway*) *& R.I. Jenie* (*Indonesia*)), July 2005, p. 7.

international mechanism that might have given states and IGOs decision-making power and control over their internal matters and activities, as well as the parallel reluctance of states to consider making arrangements that would eventually lead to an articulation of some degree of ILP for INGOs.

To a certain extent, the Accountability Charter revives the old idea of INGOs' self-governance through an 'International Bureau'. Since its current charter version is disconnected from any consideration of official status, such a loose, self-governing body does not pose any normative or political threat to states and IGOs, and can be relatively easily promoted among their officials. Moreover, depending on the evolvement of its reporting mechanism, as well as on its broad adoption and ability to generate sincere commitment on the part of its members, the charter can become a mechanism that complements and facilitates the work of existing IGOs' accreditation procedures. The Lund-London Guidelines, if adopted by inter-governmental bodies and state-officials as well as the NGO community, can, quite similarly, become a model for self-regulating codes-of-conduct evolving on a sectoral basis. This can certainly complement existing, and less successful, inter-governmental codes such as the Code of Conduct for Special Procedures Mandate-Holders[18] and facilitate the work of inter-governmental bodies that cooperate extensively with INGOs, such as the Human Rights Council and the ICC, as well as national and international courts and tribunals that consider their reports. Eventually, these initiatives – the charter and the guidelines – can even complement each other. Sector-based codes-of-conduct using the model of the guidelines, and tailored to fit the functions of INGOs in specific areas (humanitarian assistance, development aid, environmental protection, etc.), could become major factors in the overall assessment of INGOs' transparency and good governance, facilitated by the reporting procedure of the charter. This would probably encourage further compliance on the part of INGOs using these codes-of-conduct.

All in all, if broadly adopted and seriously implemented, these initiatives could reflect a significant trend in the evolutionary

---

[18] See in chapter two, fn. 37, *supra*.

progression of the discourse on the normative position of INGOs, based on the detachment of questions of accountability and legitimacy from those of status. This may be the most realistic and practical way to deepen the involvement of INGOs in global governance, making them more efficient, meaningful and trustworthy, without altering their current legal status.

3.2 RESEMBLANCE TO IGOS

As the contextual historical investigation clearly indicates, many scholars and activists in the past established their positions on the basis of a conceptual and practical correlation between INGOs and IGOs; the writings of some jurists of the period[19] clearly indicated the notion that INGOs' functions not only complemented but resembled those of IGOs. Consequent documents and writings have upheld the notion of a derived formal status for INGOs, based on their perceived international functions and collaboration in the work of inter-governmental bodies. This strategy was initially meant to bypass the old, difficult questions of public registration, order and selection, and to gain exemptions from national restrictions. Nevertheless, flawed as this doctrinal foundation is, these hurdles remain unresolved in practice and theory, and therefore continue to be highly alarming.

Normative Legitimacy and Complex Organizational Reality

Resemblance to IGOs clearly underlined the claim for legitimacy. It served several authors to anchor INGOs' *normative* legitimacy by showing that their relevance had become as essential for the international community as that of IGOs. As explained in the case of IGOs, their normative legitimacy was acknowledged under international law by the attainment of their (limited/functional/implied) ILP, which, in turn, paved the way for the development of the body of international institutional law, upholding IGOs' *regulatory* legitimacy. In the case of INGOs, this strategy was unsuccessful.

[19] Kopelmanas in 1949; Pickard in 1956; and especially Rodgers in 1960 and Lador-Lederer in 1963.

The ILA 2010 report, however, adopted the same logic, but went a step further to claim resemblance to, and therefore competition with, *states*. Underlined by the notions of global governance and the idea of an autonomous global civil society, this claim was based on contemporary neo-liberal calls for the rethinking of the concept of legitimacy and its disconnection with the nation-state.[20]

As Ossewaarde, Nijhof and Heyse explain, this claim for INGOs' *normative* legitimacy entails the generalized perception that their actions are desirable within their institutional environment and that, INGOs, in particular, are in the position to put the themes of an endangered world on the global agenda, often against the resistance of national authorities and international organizations.[21] INGOs, positioned in competition with, or resemblance to, states, thus embody the idea that the human interest, rather than the nation-state, is the legitimating principle in a global order.[22] On the basis of this normative legitimacy claim, the ILA report proposes to establish an intuitive scheme for INGOs' *regulatory* legitimacy under international law, which concerns the questions regarding who bears the right to intervene in local or international affairs, to break the sovereignty principle, and how this right can be justified.[23] This entails that international rules and doctrines (such as ILP, international liability and immunities in the case of the report) have to correspond with INGOs' missions and norms, together with public recognition of INGOs' moral entitlement to influence international legislators. But as much as this scheme proved to be impossible to implement in the past, so it remains today.

Ossewaarde et al. acknowledge that normative legitimacy is not enough in the case of INGOs. Organizational reality and the fact that the social forces that shape INGO legitimacy patterns are different from those of (inter)governmental institutions (i.e. they are not legitimized through electoral systems and are not necessarily

---

20 See R. Ossewaarde, A. Nijhof, L. Heyse, *Dynamics of NGO Legitimacy: How Organizing Betrays Core Missions of INGOs, Public Administration and Development Journal*, Vol. 28 (2008), p. 42, 43. See as well Ahmed, op. cit. note 4, pp. 243–244; this chapter, fn. 3, *supra*.

21 See Ossewaarde, ibid, p. 43.

22 See pp. 43–44.

23 See p. 44.

democratic[24]) mean that INGOs are in need of further *regulatory* legitimacy, *cognitive* legitimacy and *output* legitimacy. In other words, their normative legitimacy must be institutionalized and organized in order to show how they strive for the achievement of the laudable goals that supposedly underlie their normative legitimacy.[25] *Cognitive* legitimacy derives from the ongoing ability to prove that technical expertise and intellectual knowledge are constantly used to effectuate the organization's stated mission, thus serving the human interest;[26] *output* legitimacy refers to organizational professionalization, requiring an INGO to show how it actually achieves its objectives by being accountable to its stakeholders through transparent decision-making and communication structures.[27] The problem is that INGOs are at a crossroads between their stated mission and their quest for legitimacy; the contradictory demands that follow from their global objectives and the organizational necessity to communicate actual performance create a complex state of affairs. Thus, the need to organize their motives through professional monitoring and accountability mechanisms requires a technical expertise that typically characterizes the processes of an organization, instead of humanity at large. In this way, the more that is demanded from an INGO as an organization (that is, in terms of regulatory, cognitive and output legitimacy), the less the organization's ideal is stamped (in terms of its normative legitimacy).[28] There are, therefore, inherent increased tensions between the four sources of INGO legitimacy.[29] Consequently, INGOs' potentially favorable position to gain normative legitimacy, depending primarily on congruence between values as the basis for mobilizing human and

---

24 See also Willetts, op. cit. note 11, who notes the unique problem of democracy at the global level, being the absence of accountability through global elections. He considers the suggestion made by some INGOs to remedy this 'democratic deficit' by direct elections to a (UN) 'Peoples Assembly' to be not politically feasible in the foreseeable future – p. 9.

25 See Ossewaarde, op. cit. note 20, p. 51.

26 Ibid, p. 44.

27 Depending on the incorporation of technical and managerial expertise, the technical provision of objective evidence through evaluation research and monitoring systems – see ibid, p. 45.

28 See p. 51.

29 See p. 43.

financial resources, is obstructed by increased pressure for accountability, effectiveness and transparency. Indeed, we saw how, in the past, many initiatives based on broad normative legitimacy claims, upholding INGOs' position as global actors resembling IGOs, had to be withdrawn in the face of complex organizational requirements. The fact that solutions could not have been articulated for the problems of selection, registration and order – nor for the composition of an 'International Bureau' and the definition of the INGO entity and its basic requirements – repeatedly frustrated these initiatives. It is likely that this is also the reason why the ILA report tends to totally dismiss questions regarding INGOs' accountability and (international) liability, in view of the 'services they render for the global public good' and the 'often laudable goals of their actions'.[30]

Modest Normative Claims and Organizational Legitimacy Schemes

The guidelines and the charter, on the other hand, focus on issues of INGOs' *cognitive* and *output* legitimacy, and therefore refrain from making any preliminary *normative* legitimacy claims based on the positioning of INGOs resembling, or competing with, states or IGOs. The very opening statements of the charter thus make clear that the group of INGOs signatories, although working globally, can '*complement but not replace*' the over-arching role and responsibility of governments; the signatories declare their legitimacy to derive from the quality of their work and achievements – an *output* legitimacy claim, and the recognition and support of their stakeholders – a *cognitive* legitimacy claim, and therefore they seek to uphold these legitimacy claims through the promotion of transparency and accountability. Their *regulatory* legitimacy is primarily grounded in universally recognized freedoms of speech, assembly and association, processed through the declared commitment to abide by reporting requirements on the *national* level, and potentially, through the charter's reporting mechanism. Quite similarly, the guidelines' *normative* legitimacy claim is based on recognition of the significant role and expertise of INGOs in the provision of a certain function

[30] While arguing, for the very same reasons, a claim for granting them forms of immunity.

(fact-finding and reporting). They thus seek to legitimize the *activity* and not the organization performing the activity. The guidelines' opening provision therefore defines the *function*, and not the INGO entity or its position, *vis-à-vis* other entities. The rest of the guidelines are dedicated to the issues of the nature of INGO missions, the wording of their mandates and the selection of personnel – that is, *cognitive* legitimacy issues, as well as the practical production and conclusion of the fact-finding report, its publication etc., which are *outcome* legitimacy issues.

3.3 TENSIONS WITHIN THE NON-GOVERNMENTAL COMMUNITY

Many authors still relate to the non-governmental community as a single coherent body or a distinct regime, with sub-units presumably sharing common features and similar goals. The growing use of network models and notions upholding the establishment of a 'global civil society' in the last decade have clearly deepened this tendency by giving the impression that INGOs have already become the building blocks of a comprehensive, well-connected structure.[31] However, proposals and reports of INGO forums, which endeavored to outline positively the typical INGO entity, especially following the adoption of the consultative arrangements with ECOSOC, revealed considerable competition and disagreement within the INGO community. This feature of the non-governmental world worsened over

[31] Clearly, the frequent use of the 'network' metaphor to describe the web of INGOs as interacting within a 'Global Civil Society' reflects a certain normative conception – see A. Herod, M.W. Wright, '*Introduction*', in A. Herod & M.W. Wright (eds.), *Geographies of Power: Placing Scale*, (2002), pp. 7–9. See also H. Leitner, C. Pavlik, E. Sheppard, *Networks, Governance, and the Politics of Scale: Inter-Urban Networks and the European Union*, in Herod, ibid, pp. 274–299; H. Anheier & H. Katz, *Network Approaches to Global Civil Society*, in H. Anheier, M. Glasius & M. Kaldor, *Global Civil Society Yearbook 2004–2005*, p. 206; R.B.J. Walker, *After the Globe, Before the World*, (2010), pp. 8–9. Notably, already in 1976, a UIA symposium acknowledged that INGOs lacked an 'INGO identity', and did not conceive of themselves as a well-defined group with common concerns and consequently had little basis for collective action – see *List of Problems Hindering INGOs Action* in *The Future of Transnational Associations from the Standpoint of a New World Order, Proceedings of a Symposium* (Geneva, 1976), UIA (1977), App. 4, para. 34 ('International legal status of INGOs').

time, with growing numbers of associations competing for limited sources of funding and impacting overlapping areas. Furthermore, proposals regarding the legal status of INGOs exposed significant resentment on the part of 'genuinely composed' INGOs with an international staff towards national NGOs aspiring to a mere international goal. Thus, debates over the requirement of 'international activity' and 'international composition' exposed growing conflicts of interest between INGOs and national NGOs, as well as within the INGO community itself. These features of the non-governmental world further emphasized the old problems of registration, selection, and control.

The ILA 2010 report ignores this issue altogether. This is not surprising, given that it deals with 'NSAs' as a broad, normative group. The decision of the drafters to adopt such a wide perspective is indeed peculiar. It is probably the outcome of a strong influence by international relations theories focusing on the role of international institutions and transnational actors.[32] In any case, it clearly promises many definitional and conceptual complexities down the road, as various unrelated entities are gathered under the umbrella term 'NSAs', which is one reason for the confusion surrounding this usage.[33] The drafters' initial taxonomy of non-state entities under its mandate does not seem to suggest any solution in this regard, and leaves the ILA NSAs Committee with an unreasonably wide spectrum of entities to deal with, having no more in common than the fact that they are 'non-state'. Reading the report, however, one immediately gets the impression that despite its declared intention to deal with NSAs at large, it mainly focuses on (I)NGOs' arrangements. It may thus be expected that in subsequent reports, particularly in view of the committee's stated mission to deduce normative

32 See Ben-Ari, op. cit. note 2, pp. 3–5.

33 See F. Grunfeld, *The UN and Non-State Actors: Legitimacy and Compliance*, in T.C. van Boven, C. Flinterman, F. Grunfeld, R. Hut (eds.), *The Legitimacy of the UN: Towards an Enhanced Legal Status of Non-State Actors*, *Netherlands Institute of Human Rights*, SIM special, No. 19, (1997), p. 11, 14; see as well T.C. van Boven, *Non-State Actors: Introductory Comments*, in van Boven et al., ibid., p. 3, 5–6. See also B. Reinalda, B. Arts, M. Noortmann, *Non-State Actors in International Relations: Do They Matter?*, in Arts et al., op. cit. note 5; and B. Reinalda, *Private in Form, Public in Purpose: NGOs in International Relations Theory*, in ibid, p. 13.

conclusions from existing arrangements, it will have to be more precise and explicit in this regard, and will probably be required to either narrow its mandate or split the project into several sub-categories, in accordance with more realistically defined research priorities. If that is the case, it will be more difficult to ignore the fact that today, we still do not have a definition of the 'internationality' requirement of *international* NGOs.[34] In view of the data regarding the burgeoning growth in the number of INGOs, and the apparent phenomenon of '*sans frontiérisme*', describing *national* NGOs' calculated turn to international activity and formation as *international* NGOs,[35] it will no longer be possible to ignore the implications of this aspect within any normative evaluation of INGOs' status.

The charter initiative raises some difficult questions in this regard. The articulation of some of its specific declaratory provisions and mechanisms and the process bringing about its adoption are reflective of the existing, deepening tensions within the non-governmental community. Despite its title – '*International* NGOs Accountability Charter' – it contains no definition of the 'internationality' requirement which presumably underlies its self-selection membership. Nevertheless, judging by its founding and current membership, the charter seems to be evolving as a highly selective membership framework, reserved for, and tailored to fit the interests and characteristics of the few prominent and well-funded INGOs.[36] The charter's 'Five Years Strategy' is also indicative, in this respect, stating that its primary aims are to sign on all *leading international* NGOs, while *smaller international* organizations and *larger national* ones will use it as a basis for their own accountability, probably without actually signing it. In view of the above and the facts that

---

[34] See Ben-Ari, op. cit. note 2, pp. 47–51.

[35] See J. Siméant, *What is Going Global? The Internationalization of French NGOs 'Without Borders'*, *Review of International Political Economy*, Vol. 12, No. 5, (2005), 851, 853.

[36] Thompson notes that the agreement of the signatories to raise funds without assistance from governments is a luxury that is generally reserved for only the largest, most well-established international NGOs with extensive and elaborate fundraising strategies – see A.S. Thompson, *Laying the Groundwork – Considerations for a Charter for a Proposed Global Civil Society Forum*, in J.W. St. G. Walker, A.S. Thompson (eds.), *Critical Mass: The Emergence of Global Civil Society*, (2008), p. 219.

the charter's Secretariat is owned by six of its founding and leading signatories,[37] and that major INGOs have not joined, while three of its founding signatories have already left, it may be argued that this initiative could not overcome the tensions within the non-governmental community and might actually have deepened them. Thompson further remarks that although the charter spans a wide range of related but independent actors, what unites the organizations that have signed it is an ideological like-mindedness.[38] Thus, the charter's members can be found on either the centre or left-of-centre of the political spectrum. As a consequence of being unable to accommodate political, ideological and organizational diversity, the charter could become highly divisive. Certainly, all this would diminish the normative as well as the practical value of this initiative.

The guidelines, on the other hand, bypass these organizational and political hurdles by sticking strictly to function-related matters and adopting a highly professional standpoint with regard to (I)NGOs' activity. The fact that the guidelines' starting point is the acknowledgement of fact-finding and reporting as unique non-governmental functions, as opposed to focusing on the identity or position of the entities that take on these functions, is highly significant in this regard. This may also be the reason behind the fact that although the guidelines' title mentions '*International* Human Rights Fact-Finding Visits and Reports', its preamble and various provisions simply relate to 'NGOs' as opposed to INGOs. The guidelines can therefore potentially be adopted by a wide spectrum of organizations, connected by their unique function, and not by their ideological tendencies, socio-political affiliations or organizational features.

3.4 AUTHORS OF INITIATIVES

The historical survey suggests that all of the significant initiatives, proposals and reports regarding the legal status of INGOs were the

37 See *Charter Website* (*'reporting and reviewing'/'charter background'*), on: http://www.ingoaccountabilitycharter.org.

38 See Thompson, op. cit. note 36, p. 216.

outcome of the work of (European) academic scholars, most of whom were law professors. Some were also INGO activists. However, the lack of any significant contribution by diplomats, other state officials or even field activists is relevant.[39]

By and large, the ILA reports are an academic theoretical initiative. Some of the ILA NSAs Committee members are international relations and political science theorists. None of its members are INGO activists. The authors of the charter initiative, on the other hand, are all INGO activists. In that respect, the charter initiative is unique and refreshing, and may indeed reflect a progressive evolution in the discourse regarding INGO normative position. The fact that some leading INGO officials and activists have decided to come together to initiate a forum, based exclusively on their shared understandings and mutual commitment, may point to their disappointment in the ability of academics and state representatives to acknowledge the genuine needs and concerns of INGOs.

Most interesting and innovative in this regard are the guidelines. They are the product of a private initiative on the part of several international legal experts. The guidelines' drafting committees uniquely combined legal scholars, INGO field activists, and international lawyers and practitioners from both inter-governmental and non-governmental professional organizations, with strong emphasis on practical experience. Undoubtedly, this unique combination of experts and practitioners facilitated an outcome which may broadly appeal to, and speak the language of, state officials, (I)NGO activists, international civil servants and various institutional professionals at the same time.

3.5 INGOS' DISINTEREST

It is highly significant that, in general, members of the INGO community have shown considerable indifference towards the recurring attempts to achieve formal recognition for their legal status.

[39] Compare with C. Tomuschat, *Obligations Arising for States Against Their Will, Recueil des Cours – Collected Courses of the Hague Academy of International Law*, Vol. 241(IV) (1993), p. 195, 236, who finds much significance in the fact that 'international community' is not an invention by academics but by state-representatives.

Although most of the important proposals were indeed initiated by INGO forums, the INGO community, as a whole, has almost completely ignored these attempts. Very few proposals have earned any serious consideration or have even been mentioned by INGO officials. Thus, nearly 40 years after the establishment of the UIA in 1910, it was only the adoption of the UN Charter, establishing consultative arrangements with ECOSOC, that created sufficient momentum for further consideration to be given by the newly appointed CCNGOs. Nevertheless, despite explicit requests, even the CCNGOs' proposals failed to achieve adequate discussion or support from consultative status INGOs. Evidently, even with their impressive capacity for networking, lobbying, and media manipulation, INGO activists were simply reluctant to invest their resources or to cooperate on this matter, and demonstrated an interest only in solving specific problems on an occasional basis. Issues of INGOs' normative status remained, for the most part, the concern of a few individual legal and socio-political scholars.

There is hardly any reason to believe, therefore, that INGO activists and officials will cooperate with, support, or be interested in, the ILA initiative, which as we saw, resembles in many aspects past attempts to formalize the status of INGOs. As has been revealed many times in the past, and was even openly admitted by INGO leading academic proponents, INGOs are generally not interested in acquiring formal legal recognition, since many of them use methods that 'would not be acceptable from an entity enjoying formal ILP'.[40] Almost needless to say, the same disinterest goes for most government officials, primarily because of their fear of strengthening groups suspected of political disloyalty and support for terrorism. In this regard, the ILA drafters' declared intention to receive the views of states' international law advisers on NSAs' ILP, as well as the opinions of NSAs themselves regarding their position under international law, is highly significant and indeed crucial; if such an inquiry were to be carried out seriously, systematically and objectively, it could become the major contribution of the ILA initiative to the

[40] Such as Crawford and Rodley - see N. Rodley, *Human Rights NGOs: Rights and Obligations (Present Status and Perspectives), SIM 19 Special*, p. 62 & fn. 34. See as well Ahmed, op. cit. note 4, pp. 244–250.

ongoing discourse on the normative position of INGOs under international law.

The charter initiative is also revealing in this regard. Evidently, when INGOs *are* interested, they can find ways to create the momentum and settings required to express and advance their interests. The fact that the charter does not involve any consideration or promotion of the acquisition of a formal legal status under international law is a clear indication on the part of some leading INGOs that such a development is indeed unwarranted. If anything, the charter is another clear signal that the INGO community still regards the political and social arenas to be the proper platforms for the evaluation of their activities, as opposed to the legal arena. Obviously, translation of their involvement and performance in global governance into strictly defined international rights and obligations is considered by them to be counterproductive.

The drafters of the guidelines were undoubtedly aware of the sensitivity of INGOs towards potentially restrictive legal mechanisms and took into account the fact that there was hardly any possibility that INGOs would abide by a formal international accountability framework set out by states or IGOs. They therefore appealed to INGOs' need to uphold their public reputation and proficiency, as opposed to any formal status, in order to maintain their political and professional legitimacy. In that respect, the guidelines, as a 'soft law', non-formal code-of-conduct, mirror the same concerns as those underlying the formation of the self-governing reporting mechanism of the charter.

3.6 EUROPEAN FOCUS

Failing on the international level, scholars in the past sought support in the regional European arena. Theoretically, the normative regional platform seemed more accessible and attuned to the needs of INGOs. Nevertheless, despite the relatively encouraging institutional and political atmosphere, the initial regional debates almost immediately began to replicate the complexities of the international discourse. Again, the aspiration to establish a single status on the regional level was debated in the light of an urgent need to resolve practical questions of conflicts-of-laws. Current initiatives, however, seem to indicate that it is still difficult to develop the discourse on the normative position of INGOs outside the intellectual environment of Western Europe.[41] It is remarkable, in this regard, that the ILA NSAs Committee is characterized by a strong West-European academic membership.[42] Furthermore, all the charter's founding signatories, as well as most of their head officials, are European, while North-American-based or other INGOs still do not form part of this initiative. It is only the guidelines' Steering Committee that has managed to unite a group of experts and professionals behind the guidelines' project, that cannot be characterized as being, intellectually, European-oriented.

---

[41] For further analysis of the differing Pan-European vs. American intellectual atmospheres, and their influence on the vision of global governance and the discourse on the normative position of INGOs – see Ben-Ari, op. cit note 2, pp. 261–276.

[42] The committee is currently (2012) chaired by M. Noortmann (Netherlands), with C. Ryngaert (Belgium) as Rapporteur. Other members include some 30 scholars, most of whom are of European background (others are from Australia, Brazil, Canada, Hong-Kong, Israel, Japan, Korea, South-Africa, USA).

Chapter Four

CONCLUSIONS AND FUTURE PROSPECTS

Evidently, the historical path, followed in the attempt to secure a certain status for INGOs under international law, has taken many twists and turns. Numerous obstacles have arisen, while hardly any solutions have been found. This work does not purport to point to any solutions to these hurdles. However, it does endeavor to provide essential background and points of context that are vital to any future evaluation of the complex matters involved in the consideration of INGOs' normative position by state officials, international civil servants, scholars, or INGO activists.

One of the maladies of INGO-related scholarship, as Charnovitz observed, is a tendency to presume novelty in practices that have been going on for decades.[1] This is clearly the case with regard to the scholarly debate about the legal status of INGOs. As has been explained, almost every stage in the long sequence of juridical developments dealing with the matter has been built on lessons drawn from previous attempts. Consequently, writers who avoid the conclusions and observations that have been based on an historical contextual inquiry revive old assumptions, which have long been rejected, or repeat debates that have long since been discussed and concluded. Moreover, by upholding and prolonging old theoretical inconsistencies, some writers channel the discourse away from current, authentic, and difficult issues, which require prompt resolution. In fact, as we have seen, most of these issues are not new. They have been raised and dealt with since the very first initiatives, and have had a bearing on the attempts to outline an official legal status ever since, without any real success at resolving them. The problems of order, registration, confirmation and selection of organizations, that were initially reflected in the debates regarding the composition and *modus operandi* of an 'International Bureau',

---

[1] See S. Charnovitz, *Nongovernmental Organizations and International Law*, *American Journal of International Law*, Vol. 100 (2006), p. 350.

gained significance over time. In subsequent years, they reappeared in the form of issues regarding the definition of INGOs, and more recently, their responsibility and accountability. Proven to be politically and legally insoluble hurdles, these matters repeatedly thwarted the initiatives to suggest a framework for the attainment of formal legal status for INGOs. They further revealed the extent to which the underlying views of certain INGO forums and enthusiastic academic proponents conflicted with those of states and IGOs in relation to the composition of the international community. Thus, it was generally acknowledged that the problems relating to the legal status of INGOs had to be examined from the point of view of reshaping the structure and organization of the international community, and that the rise of the 'transnational private sector', characterized by spontaneity and variety, constituted a genuine challenge to the firm association of nation-states.

Today, against the background of the heated discussions about the future of 'governance',[2] renewed interest in INGOs' legal position is mainly motivated by two contradictory interests. The first, and less ordinary, is generated by the general quest for greater accountability and liability of international actors.[3] In this regard, international status may arguably assist in confining the burgeoning growth in the number of INGOs and in monitoring and scrutinizing their activities, thereby improving their proficiency and responsible advocacy. The second interest derives from the growing involvement of INGOs in international governance, which is frequently hailed as being beneficial to the 'international community as a

---

[2] See H. Holmén, M. Jirström, *'Look Who's Talking!' Second Thoughts about NGOs as Representing Civil Society, Journal of Asian and African Studies*, Vol. 44(4), (2009), p. 429, 430.; K. Anderson, *Global Governance: The Problematic Legitimacy Relationship between Global Civil Society and the United Nations, Washington College of Law Research Paper No. 2008–71*, p. 20–21, who explains that the terminological shift from 'global government' to 'governance' originates in the invention of a new theory of political globalization in the 1990's, that enables the UN to exercise 'governance' without being 'government' in view of the reluctance of states to surrender their sovereignty.

[3] Consider Gaja's discussion of INGOs' status in UN Doc. A/CN.4/532, *First Report on Responsibility of International Organizations* (by G. Gaja), *International Law Commission*, 55th Sess. (March 26, 2003), pp. 7–9, paras. 14, 16–17, and governments' comments, p. 12, para. 21 & fn. 59.

whole', suggesting significant humanitarian and democratic alternatives to existing channels of socio-political representation.[4] In this context, legal status is supposedly required to facilitate INGOs' cross-border activities by the provision of rights, privileges and immunities. This quest is occasionally based on a call for the establishment of a fairer international legal order[5], one that would reflect the position and relevance of all significant international actors, including INGOs, thereby legitimizing their voice and ensuring their participation. The first motive of greater accountability is clearly disadvantageous for INGOs, while the latter interest, of official participation by right, raises growing concerns with states and IGOs. This way, the two most relevant actors – states and INGOs – remain, as they always have been, generally disinterested, having much more to lose than to gain from the acquisition of a formal status by INGOs.

In the current 'age of INGOs'[6] and 'processes of globalization', some international lawyers are encouraged by the hasty invention of models and notions that endeavor to explain the complexities of 'global interdependence'.[7] Being dissatisfied with the fact that

---

[4] See Holmén, op. cit. note 2, pp. 429–430.

[5] See D.M. Johnston, *World Constitutionalism in the Theory of International Law*, in R. SJ. Macdonald, D.M. Johnston, *Towards World Constitutionalism – Issues in the Legal Ordering of the World Community*, (2005), pp. 3–4, 7–9; J.E. Nijman, *The Concept of International Legal Personality: An Inquiry into the History and Theory of International Law*, (2004), pp. 410–411, 414–419; D. Grieg, *International Community, Interdependence, and All That ... Rhetorical Correctness?*, in G. Kreijen (ed.), *State, Sovereignty and International Governance*, (2002), p. 522; T.M. Franck, *Fairness in International Law and Institutions*, (1995), p. 480, 484; R.H. Ben-Ari, *The Normative Position of International Non-Governmental Organizations under International Law – An Analytical Framework* (2012), pp. 314–323.

[6] See Holmén, op. cit. note 2, p. 429.

[7] Indeed, the term 'global civil society', that scholars and laymen alike now take for granted, was publicly used for the first time just in 1991 – see T.O. Corry, *Global Civil Society and Its Discontents, Voluntas*, (2006), Vol. 17, p. 303; J. Keane, *Global Civil Society?*, (2003), pp. 1–2; Anderson, op. cit. note 2, pp. 17–27. Moreover, 15 years ago, when Charnovitz published his seminal work reviewing two centuries of INGOs' participation, he upheld the notion that INGOs could promote peace by the merit of their ideas, and by facilitating global social cohesion through the creation of an international networks community – S. Charnovitz, *Two Centuries of Participation: NGOs and International Governance, Michigan Journal of International Law*, Vol. 18 (1997), pp. 265, 284–286. Nevertheless, less than 10 years later, he admitted that measuring INGOs' success had become more and more complicated, and that 'today, overwhelming NGO support for the international rule of law can no longer

INGOs do not fit neatly into existing legal rubrics and doctrines, these scholars might be anxious to apply new concepts, borrowed heavily from the fields of political theory, political economy and, in particular, international relations,[8] in order to suggest transformative initiatives – or downright normative revolutions – that would officially incorporate the INGO actor into the international legal order. In most cases, this quest is based on a very optimistic view of an angelic community of INGOs, collegially networking to achieve laudable goals and rendering morally merited services for the global public good.[9] This view rests on the assumptions that INGOs' involvement makes international decision-making fairer and more effective, that INGOs are representative and do not act out of self-interest, and that – unlike governments, inter-governmental institutions and their officials – they are civilized, in agreement and immune to corruption.[10] However, these assumptions are far from being empirically verified, and are therefore still based more on belief than on knowledge.[11] Furthermore, even the meaning of ideas and notions that provide intellectual backing for these assumptions – such as 'international governance', 'global civil society', and de-territorializing 'processes of globalization', frequently employed as paradigmatic tools in the formation of analytical frameworks for the consideration of INGOs' position, is unresolved, bearing varying interpretations; certainly, these concepts do not portray an intellectually coherent picture or represent any straightforward truisms.[12]

INGO's legitimacy must therefore be earned on an individual, case-by-case basis. It cannot be assumed *a priori* due the existence

be assumed' – Charnovitz (2006), op. cit. note 1, p. 348. All this is indicative of the rapidly evolving theories, as well as the changing perceptions regarding INGOs' involvement in world affairs and institutions, within a very short period of two decades.

8 Mainly focused on sketching the appropriate position and interrelations of political actors – see Nijman, op. cit. note 5, pp. 387–389; Ben-Ari, op. cit. note 5, p. 319; A.M. Slaughter, *International Law in a World of Liberal States, European Journal of International Law*, Vol. 6, (1995), p. 503, 505, 506–508.

9 See, for example, *First Report of the Committee on NSAs, ILA (The Hague Conference, 2010)* ('ILA 2010 Report'), available on: www.ila-hq.org, p. 18.

10 See Holmén, op. cit. note 2, p. 430.

11 Ibid, p. 431.

12 For an analysis of these notions – see Ben-Ari, op. cit. note 5, pp. 181–260.

of a networking, representative '*Global* Civil *Society*', which, beyond an intellectual construct for conveying legitimacy,[13] does not exist in the form of a cross-border, cross-sectoral, overarching unity that promotes international relations and the rule of law.[14] Certainly, such a notion and related assumptions cannot feature any serious normative scheme for the articulation of INGOs' ILP or even 'status'. Furthermore, as was realized from the very earliest initiatives towards a formal status for INGOs and as has become more and more apparent in the last few decades, by and large, INGOs should be valued as political, self-interested, occasionally very powerful actors.[15] Leading INGOs, which initially based their participation on

---

[13] See Anderson, op. cit. note 2, p. 31; D. Chandler, *Constructing Global Civil Society: Morality and Power in International Relations*, (2004), p. 1, 18; G. Baker, D. Chandler, *Global Civil Society and the Future of World Politics: Introduction*, in G. Baker, D. Chandler (eds.), *Global Civil Society: Contested Futures*, (2005), p. 1, 7; D. Josselin, W. Wallace, *Non-State Actors in World Politics: A Framework*, in D. Josselin, W. Wallace, *Non-State Actors in World Politics*, (2001), p. 12; A. Colas, *Global Civil Society: Analytical Category or Normative Concept?*, in Baker, ibid, p. 17, 18; H. Anheier, M. Glasius, M. Kaldor, *Introducing Global Civil Society*, in H. Anheier, M. Glasius, M. Kaldor (eds.), *Global Civil Society Yearbook 2001*, pp. 16–17. Keane notes that global civil society necessarily bears an elusive, ideal-type quality – see op. cit. note 7, p. 7, while Falk describes it as a 'mental construct' – see R. Falk, *The Changing Role of Global Civil Society*, in Baker, ibid, p. 70.

[14] See Anderson, ibid, p. 38; Holmén, op. cit. note 2, pp. 434–440.

[15] See Anderson, ibid, p. 29, who notes the change in INGOs' strategy, backing away from their 'extravagant claims to represent peoples and populations'. See also G.E. Edwards, *Assessing the Effectiveness of Human Rights NGOs from the Birth of the United Nations to the 21st Century: The Attributes of Highly Successful Human Rights NGOs, Michigan State Journal of International Law*, Vol. 18(2), (2010), maintaining that INGOs 'do not have to be representative to be legitimate' – p. VIII-IX. Notably, in 1976, a UIA symposium acknowledged INGOs' political ineffectiveness as one of the main problems hindering their action. The symposium acknowledged INGOs' failure to think and act politically and to acknowledge that the purpose of their relationships with governments and IGOs 'is to exchange influence'. INGOs were therefore encouraged to become aware to governmental assessment of their position 'in terms of the importance of the political constituency they represented', and concluded that 'INGOs can only be effective by relating to governments and IGOs politically' – see *List of Problems Hindering INGOs Action* in *The Future of Transnational Associations from the Standpoint of a New World Order, Proceedings of a Symposium* (Geneva, 1976), UIA (1977), App. 4, para. 34 ('International legal status of INGOs'). Clearly, this situation has changed since then. See also, generally, L. Polman, *The Crisis Caravan – What's Wrong with Humanitarian Aid?*, (2010); C. Magone, M. Neuman, F. Weissman, *Humanitarian Negotiations Revealed: The MSF Experience*, (2012); G.W. Jenkins, *Nongovernmental Organizations and the Forces against Them: Lessons of the Anti-NGO Movement, Brooklyn Journal of International Law*, Vol. 37(2), (2012), p. 459.

the provision of certain expertise and proficiency, recurrently prioritize issues such as campaigning and advocacy instead of relief and charity.[16] Furthermore, many INGOs have become political allies of certain political parties, states, and IGOs – even going against their own member states.[17] Some are accused of not denouncing violence,[18] or even supporting terrorism.[19] International lawyers must therefore realize that INGOs can be either 'good' or 'bad'; they can potentially facilitate international cooperation and the rule of law, but they can also obstruct them. These acknowledgements, simple though fundamental, underline initiatives such as the Lund-London Guidelines. Moreover, they are indirectly endorsed by leading INGOs themselves, when seeking to establish frameworks such as the Accountability Charter.

As the historical contextual inquiry shows, ILP in the case of INGOs is highly theoretical, not to say irrelevant; it is politically unattainable, and legally implausible.[20] Until the problems of

---

[16] See Holmén, op. cit. note 2, p. 431.

[17] See Anderson, op. cit. note 2, pp. 14–16; Holmén, ibid, pp. 441–442.

[18] See G. Delanty, *Cosmopolitanism and Violence – The Limits of Global Civil Society, European Journal of Social Theory*, Vol. 4, (2001), pp. 41–52. Keane warns that global civil society provides convenient hideouts for gangsters, war criminals, arms traders and terrorists; global terrorism in particular threatens 'every corner of global civil society, including its local networked components', operating 'like a deadly enemy from within its entrails' – see Keane, op. cit. note 7, pp. 12–13, 146–148, 150–152, 156.

[19] See F.B. Adamson, *International Terrorism, Nonstate Actors, and Political Mobilization: A Perspective from International Relations*, in T.J. Biersteker, P.J. Spiro, C.L. Sriram, V. Raffo, *International Law and International Relations: Bridging Theory and Practice* (2007); M. Albrow, H. Anheier, *Violence and the Possibility of Global Civility*, in H. Anheier, M. Glasius, M. Kaldor, *Global Civil Society Yearbook 2006–2007*, p. 1; E. Aydinli, J.N. Rosenau, *Globalization, Security and the Nation-State: Paradigms in Transition* (2005); C. Coker, *Globalization and Insecurity in the Twenty-First Century: NATO and the Management of Risk, Adelphi Paper* 345 (2004). See also *January 1996 CIA Report on 'International Islamic NGOs and Links to Terrorism'*, as mentioned in E.F. Kohlman, *The Role of Islamic Charities in International Terrorist Recruitment and Financing, Danish Institute for International Studies*, Working Paper no. 2006/7, pp. 1–2 & fn. 3; *'9/11 Commission Report', Final Report of the National Commission on Terrorist Attacks Upon the United States*, July 22, 2004, pp. 169–171, available on: http://www.govinfo.library.unt.edu/911/report/index.htm.

[20] See as well Charnovitz (2006), op. cit. note 1, pp. 356–357; Compare with P.-M. Dupuy, *Conclusion: Return on the Legal Status of NGOs and on the Methodological Problems which Arise for Legal Scholarship*, in P.-M. Dupuy & L. Vierucci (eds.), *NGOs in International Law – Efficiency in Flexibility?*, (2008), pp. 208–210.

international registration, selection and order are squarely addressed and resolved[21] – clearly an unrealistic prospect – it will be impossible to consider any implied/functional personality. In view of the wildly growing numbers of INGOs, their conflicting interests and competition on both the international and national levels, the fact that there is yet no common definition for the 'internationality' requirement of the *international* non-governmental entity, and the growing mistrust of states – there is hardly any reason to believe that initiatives that continue to deal head-on with INGOs' ILP (or otherwise official 'status'), while ignoring the many theoretical and institutional difficult issues involved, will gain more success than in the past. On the other hand, initiatives such as the guidelines and, to a lesser extent, the charter, seem to be more adaptable to the lessons learned from the sequence of past attempts to regulate the legal position of INGOs. These initiatives, based on the detachment of questions of role, function and relevance from formal legal status, seem to complement each other, as well as the existing international mechanisms. Further, they are harmonized, and potentially add to national mechanisms and domestic legislation. In this way, they can provide viable channels for the progression of an ongoing discourse on INGOs' position under international law. Consequently, they may prove to be the most practical frameworks – or the most that can be expected – for confronting the complexities incurred by the growing involvement of unregulated INGOs in international governance.

Greater focus should accordingly be directed into researching the genuine and essential legal needs of INGOs working across borders, on a carefully defined functional and sectoral basis, and balancing them against the major concerns of states regarding these activities. This endeavor would probably lead to the definition of the *international* non-governmental entity in a way that would, first and foremost, facilitate the work of existing consultative frameworks, and confine the uncontrolled growth in INGO numbers, which clearly points to a lack of efficiency and a tremendous waste of resources

21 See as well Holmén, op. cit. note 2, pointing at the urgent need for selection of organizations – p. 442.

and funding. As far as international legal theory is concerned – based on past experience, it might, after all, not be such a good idea to start a revolution that would turn international law into transnational law, regulating the international legal status for INGOs. Such a process would probably require a more solid foundation than the current spontaneous invention of new models and notions, or the stretch of scholarly imagination.

BIBLIOGRAPHY

BOOKS & ARTICLES

Adamson F.B., *International Terrorism, Nonstate Actors, and Political Mobilization: A Perspective from International Relations*, in Biersteker T.J., Spiro P.J, Sriram C.L., Raffo V., *International Law and International Relations: Bridging Theory and Practice*, (Routledge), (2007), p. 79.

Ahmed S., Potter D., *NGOs in International Politics*, (2006).

Albrow M., Anheier H., *Violence and the Possibility of Global Civility*, in Anheier H., Glasius M., Kaldor M., *Global Civil Society Yearbook 2006–2007*, p. 1.

Alvarez J.E., *International Organizations: Then and Now, American Journal of International Law*, Vol. 100, (2006), p. 324.

Anderson K., *Global Governance: The Problematic Legitimacy Relationship between Global Civil Society and the United Nations*, American University Washington College of Law, *Research Paper Series*, Working Paper on Ethics of Global Philanthropy, Paper No. 2008–71 (Draft of October 14, 2008), (electronic copy available at: http://ssrn.com/abstract=1265839).

——, *What NGO Accountability Means – and Does Not Mean, American Journal of International Law*, Vol. 103, (2009), p. 170.

Alston P., *Hobbling the Monitors: Should UN Human Rights Monitors be Accountable?, Harvard International Law Journal*, Vol. 52 (2011), p. 564.

Anheier H., Glasius M., Kaldor M., *Introducing Global Civil Society*, in Anheier H., Glasius M., Kaldor M. (eds.), *Global Civil Society Yearbook 2001*, p. 3.

—— & Katz H., *Mapping Global Civil Society*, in Anheier H., Glasius M., Kaldor M. (eds.), *Global Civil Society Yearbook 2003*, p. 241.

Arts B., Noortmann M., Reinalda B. (eds.), *Non-State Actors in International Relations*, (2001).

Aston J.D., *The United Nations Committee on Non-Governmental Organizations: Guarding the Entrance to a Politically Divided House, European Journal of International Law*, Vol. 12, (2001), p. 943.

Aydinli E., Rosenau J.N., *Globalization, Security and the Nation-State: Paradigms in Transition*, (State University of New York Press), (2005).

Baker G. & Chandler D., *Introduction: Global Civil Society and the Future of World Politics*, in Baker G., Chandler D. (eds.), *Global Civil Society: Contested Futures*, (Routledge), (2005), p. 1.

Ben-Ari R.H., *The Normative Position of International Non-Governmental Organizations under International Law – An Analytical Framework* (Martinus Nijhoff/Brill), (2012).

Blitt R.C., *'Who Will Watch the Watchdogs?': Human Rights Nongovernmental Organizations and the Case for Regulation, Buffalo Human Rights Law Review*, Vol. 10, (2004), p. 261.

van Boven T.C., *Non-State Actors: Introductory Comments*, in *The Legitimacy of the UN: Towards an Enhanced Legal Status of Non-State Actors, SIM special, No. 19*, (Netherlands Institute of Human Rights), (1997), p. 1.

Brakman Reiser D., Kelly C.R., *Linking NGO Accountability and the Legitimacy of Global Governance, Brooklyn Journal of International Law*, Vol. 36 (2011), p. 1011.

Brown D.L., *Multiply Social Action and Mutual Responsibility*, in Ebrahim A., Weisband E., *Global Accountability and Moral Community*, (2004).

Chandler D., *Constructing Global Civil Society: Morality and Power in International Relations*, (Palgrave), (2004).

Charnovitz S., *Two Centuries of Participation: NGOs and International Governance*, *Michigan Journal of International Law*, Vol. 18, (1997), p. 183.

——, *Accountability of Non-Governmental Organizations in Global Governance*, in Jordan L., van Tuijl P. (eds.), *NGO Accountability: Politics, Principles & Innovations*, (Earthscan), (2006), p. 21.

——, *Nongovernmental Organizations and International Law*, *American Journal of International Law*, Vol. 100, (2006), p. 348.

Cheng B., *Introduction to Subjects of International Law*, in Bedjaoui M. (gen. ed.), *International Law: Achievements and Prospects* (UNESCO), (1991), p. 23.

Coker C., *Globalization and Insecurity in the Twenty-first Century: NATO and the Management of Risk, Adelphi Paper 345*, (Routledge), (2004).

Colas A., *Global Civil Society – Analytical Category or Normative Concept?*, in Baker G., Chandler D., *Global Civil Society: Contested Futures*, (Routledge), (2005), p. 17.

Corry T.O., *Global Civil Society and its Discontents*, *Voluntas*, Vol. 17, (2006), p. 303.

Delanty G., *Cosmopolitanism and Violence – The Limits of Global Civil Society*, *European Journal of Social Theory*, Vol. 4, (2001), p. 41.

Dinstein Y., *The Interaction between Customary International Law and Treaties*, *Recueil des Cours – Collected Courses of the Hague Academy of International Law*, Vol. 322, (2006), (Martinus Nijhoff Publishers), (2007), p. 243.

Dupuy P.-M., *Conclusion: Return on the Legal Status of NGOs and on the Methodological Problems which Arise for Legal Scholarship*, in Dupuy P.-M., Vierucci L. (eds.), *NGOs in International Law – Efficiency in Flexibility?*, (Edward Elgar), (2008), pp. 204–215.

Edwards G.E., *Assessing the Effectiveness of Human Rights NGOs from the Birth of the United Nations to the 21st Century: The Attributes of Highly Successful Human Rights NGOs*, *Michigan State Journal of International Law*, Vol. 18(2), (2010), p. 165.

Edwards M., *Foreword*, in Jordan L., van Tuijl P. (eds.), *NGO Accountability: Politics, Principles & Innovations*, (Earthscan), (2006), p. vii.

Falk R., *The Changing Role of Global Civil Society*, in Baker G., Chandler D. (eds.), *Global Civil Society: Contested Futures*, (Routledge), (2005), p. 69.

Franck T.M., *Fairness in International Law and Institutions*, (Clarendon Press), (1995).

Grieg D., *International Community, Interdependence, and All That ... Rhetorical Correctness?*, in Kreijen G. (ed. in chief), *State, Sovereignty, and International Governance*, (Oxford), (2002), p. 521.

Grunfeld F., *The UN and Non-State Actors: Legitimacy and Compliance*, in van Boven T.C., Flinterman C., Grunfeld F., Hut R. (eds.), *The Legitimacy of the UN: Towards an Enhanced Legal Status of Non-State Actors, SIM special, No. 19*, (Netherlands Institute of Human Rights), (1997), p. 11.

Herod A., Wright M.W., *Placing Scale: An Introduction*, in A. Herod A., Wright M.W. (eds.), *Geographies of Power: Placing Scale*, (Blackwell), (2002), p. 1.

Higgott R.A., Underhill R.D., Bieler A. (eds.), *Non-State Actors and Authority in the Global System*, (2000).

Holmén H., Jirström M., *'Look Who's Talking!' Second Thoughts about NGOs as Representing Civil Society*, *Journal of Asian and African Studies*, Vol. 44(4), (2009), p. 249.

Hortsch D., *The Paradox of Partnership: Amnesty International, Responsible Advocacy, and NGO Accountability*, *Columbia Human Rights Law Review*, Vol. 42 (2010), p. 199.

The International Law Association Australian Branch, *The International Status of Human Rights Non-governmental Organizations*, (1978).

Jessup P.C. et al., *International Organization* (New York, Carnegie Endowment for International Peace), (1955).

Jenkins G.W., *Nongovernmental Organizations and the Forces against Them: Lessons of the Anti-NGO Movement*, *Brooklyn Journal of International Law*, Vol. 37(2), (2012), p. 459.

Johnston D.M., *World Constitutionalism in the Theory of International Law*, in Macdonald R. SJ., Johnston D.M., *Towards World Constitutionalism – Issues in the Legal Ordering of the World Community*, (Martinus Nijhoff Publishers), (2005), p. 3.

Josselin D., Wallace W., *Non-State Actors in World Politics: A Framework*, in D. Josselin D., Wallace W., *Non-State Actors in World Politics*, (Palgrave), (2001), p. 1.

Keane J., *Global Civil Society?*, (Cambridge University Press), (2003).

Kearns K.P., *Managing for Accountability: Preserving the Public Trust in Public and Nonprofit Organizations*, (1996).

Kelly C.R., *Financial Crisis and Civil Society*, *Chicago Journal of International Law*, Vol. 11, (2011), p. 505.

Kohlman E.F., *The Role of Islamic Charities in International Terrorist Recruitment and Financing*, *Danish Institute for International Studies*, Working Paper no. 2006/7.

Kovach H., *Addressing Accountability at the Global Level: The Challenges Facing International NGOs*, in Jordan L, van Tuijl P. (eds.), *NGO Accountability: Politics, Principles & Innovations*, (Earthscan), (2006), p. 195.

Kreijen G. (ed.), *State, Sovereignty and International Governance*, (2002).

Lador-Lederer J.J., *International Non-Governmental Organizations and Economic Entities: A Study in Autonomous Organization and Jus Gentium*, (AW. Sythoff, Leyden), (1963).

Lagoni R., *Article 71*, in Simma B. (ed.), *The Charter of the United Nations: A Commentary* (Oxford University Press), (1994), p. 904.

Langrod A., *Evaluating the Role of INGOs*, *International Associations*, (The Union of International Associations Publications), (August Issue, 1955).

Leitner H., Pavlik C., Sheppard E., *Networks, Governance, and the Politics of Scale: Inter-Urban Networks and the European Union*, in Herod A., Wright M.W. (eds.), *Geographies of Power: Placing Scale*, (Blackwell), (2002), p. 274.

Lindblom A.K., *Non-governmental Organizations in International Law*, (Cambridge University Press), (2005).

Malanczuk P., *Akehurst's Modern Introduction to International Law*, 7th rev. ed., (1997).

Magone C., Neuman M., Weissman F. (eds.), *Humanitarian Negotiations Revealed: The MSF Experience*, (2012).

Maragia B., *Almost There: Another Way of Conceptualizing and Explaining NGOs' Quest for Legitimacy in Global Affairs*, *Non-State Actors and International Law*, Vol. 2, (2002), p. 301.

Mattli W., *The Logic of Regional Integration – Europe and Beyond*, (Cambridge University Press), (1999).

Merle M., *Guerre et Paix*, (1953).

Mosler H., *Subjects of International Law*, in *Encyclopedia of Public International Law*, Vol. 7, (1984), p. 442.

Muller T., *Customary Transnational Law: Attacking the Last Resort of State Sovereignty, Indiana Journal of Global Legal Studies*, Vol. 15(1), (2008), p. 19.
Nelson J., *Effecting Change through Accountable Channels*, in Lael B., Derek C. (eds.), *Global Governance 2.0: Can Philanthropists, the Public, and the Poor Make Poverty History?*, (2008), p. 174.
Nijman J.E., *The Concept of International Legal Personality: An Inquiry into the History and Theory of International Law*, (2004).
Nye J., *Soft Power: The Means to Success in World Politics*, (2004).
Olz M.A., *Non-Governmental Organizations in Regional Human Rights Systems, Columbia Human Rights Law Review*, Vol. 28, No. 1, (1997), p. 307.
Ossewaarde R., Nijhof A., Heyse L., *Dynamics of NGO Legitimacy: How Organizing Betrays Core Missions of INGOs, Public Administration and Development Journal*, Vol. 28 (2008), p. 42.
Otto D., *Nongovernmental Organizations in the United Nations System: The Emerging Role of International Civil Society, Human Rights Quarterly*, Vol. 18, (1996), p. 107.
Peruzzotti E., *Civil Society, Representation and Accountability: Restating Current Debates on the Representativeness and Accountability of Civic Associations*, in Jordan L., van Tuijl P. (eds.), *NGO Accountability: Politics, Principles & Innovations*, (Earthscan), (2006), p. 43.
Pickard B., *The Greater United Nations*, (New York, Carnegie Endowment for International Peace), (1956).
Polman L., *The Crisis Caravan – What's Wrong with Humanitarian Aid?*, (2010).
Rechenberg H.H.-K., *Non Governmental Organizations*, in *Encyclopedia of Public International Law*, Vol. 3, (1997), p. 612.
Reinalda B., Arts B., Noortmann M., *Non State Actors in International Relations: Do They Matter?*, in Arts B., Noortmann M., Reinalda B. (eds.), *Non-State Actors in International Relations, Non-State Actors in International Law, Politics and Governance Series*, (Ashgate), (2001), p. 1.
Reydams L., *Universal Jurisdiction: International and Municipal Legal Perspectives*, (Oxford), (2003).
Robertson G., *Human Rights Fact-Finding: Some Legal and Ethical Dilemmas, University College London Human Rights Review*, Vol. 3 (2010), p. 15.
Rodgers R.S., *Classification System for International Organizations (IGO and INGO): Their Bureaux and Officials, Legal Status, Prerogatives and Immunities, and Special Facilities*, (1958).
——, *Facilitation Problems of International Associations: The Legal, Fiscal and Administrative Facilities of International Non-Governmental Organizations – An International and Comparative Law, Organization, and Policy Study*, (Union of International Associations), (1960).
Rodley N.S., *Human Rights NGOs: Rights and Obligations (Present Status and Perspectives)*, in van Boven T.C., Flinterman C., Grunfeld F., Hut R. (eds.), *The Legitimacy of the UN: Towards an Enhanced Legal Status of Non-State Actors, SIM special, No. 19*, (Netherlands Institute of Human Rights), (1997), p. 41.
Rossi I., *NGOs in International Law: Has Regulation Come to a Halt?, Institute for International Law (Leuven University)*, Working Paper No. 123 (Feb. 2008).
Schabas W.A., *An Introduction to the International Criminal Court*, (4th ed.), (2011).
Schermers H.G., Blokker N.M., *International Institutional Law: Unity within Diversity*, 3rd rev. ed., (1999).
Shaw M.N., *International Law*, 6th ed., (2008).
Siméant J., *What is Going Global? The Internationalization of French NGOs 'Without Borders', Review of International Political Economy*, Vol. 12, No. 5 (2005), p. 851.

Slaughter A.-M., *International Law in a World of Liberal States, European Journal of International Law*, Vol. 6, (1995), p. 503.

Steinberg G.M., Herzberg A., Berman J., *Best Practices for Human Rights and Humanitarian NGO Fact Finding*, (Martinus Nijhoff), (2012).

Thompson A.S., *Laying the Groundwork – Considerations for a Charter for a Proposed Global Civil Society Forum*, in Walker J.W. St.G, Thompson A.S. (eds.), *Critical Mass: The Emergence of Global Civil Society*, (2008), p. 213.

Tomuschat C., *Obligations Arising for States Against Their Will, Recueil des Cours – Collected Courses of the Hague Academy of International Law*, Vol. 241(IV) (1993), p. 195.

Udo C.H., *Nongovernmental Organizations and African Governments: Seeking an Effective International Legal Framework in a New Era of Health and Development Aid, Boston College International and Comparative Law Review*, Vol. 31, p. 371.

Union of International Associations, *The Future of Transnational Associations from the Standpoint of a New World Order, Proceedings of a Symposium (Geneva, 1976)*, (1977).

——, *Yearbook of International Organizations – Guide to Global and Civil Society Networks 2009/2010*, Edition 46, Vol. 1B (Organizations descriptions and cross-references), (K.G. Saur), (2009).

Vabulas F.A., *What is a Seat on the ECOSOC NGO Committee Worth? Exploring the State Motivations and Benefits of Granting UN Access to NGOs, American Political Science Association 2011 Annual Meeting Paper*, available at SSRN: http://ssrn.com/abstract=1900279.

Walker R.J.B., *After the Globe, Before the World*, (Routledge), (2010).

Wiederkehr M.-O., *La Convention Européene sur la Reconnaissance de la Personnalité Juridique des Organisations Internationales Non-Gouvernementales du 24 Avril 1986, Annuaire Francais de Droit International*, Vol. XXXIII, (1987), p. 749.

Willetts P., *From 'Consultative Arrangements' to 'Partnership': The Changing Status of NGOs in Diplomacy at the UN, Journal of Global Governance*, Vol. 6 (2000), p. 205.

——, *The Cardoso Report on the UN and Civil Society: Functionalism, Global Corporatism or Global Democracy?, Journal of Global Governance*, Vol. 12 (2006), p. 305.

Zadek S., *Collaborative Governance: The New Multilateralism for the Twenty First Century*, in Lael B., Derek C. (eds.), *Global Governance 2.0: Can Philanthropists, the Public, and the Poor Make Poverty History?*, (2008), p. 187.

CONVENTIONS, CASES, REPORTS & DOCUMENTS

Convention Concerning Recognition of the Legal Personality of Foreign Companies, Associations, and Institutions 1956 (Hague Conference on Private International Law) available on: http://www.hcch.net/index_en.php?act=conventions.listing.

The European Convention on the Recognition of the Legal Personality of International Non-Governmental Organizations of 24.IV.1986, Eur.T.S. 124, available on: http://www.conventions.coe.int/treaty/en/Treaties/Html/124.htm.

Reparation for Injuries Suffered in the Service of the United Nations Advisory Opinion (1949), I.C.J. Rep. 1949, p. 174.

Draft International Convention on International Associations, Follow-up to the 1st World Congress of International Associations (1910), available on: http://www.uia.org/legal/home.php.

von Bar L., *Draft Convention on the Legal Status of International Associations & Comment*, Institute of International Law, (Christiana Session, 1912), available on: http://www.uia.org/legal/home.php.

van Overbergh C., *Draft Convention on International Associations, Report to the 2nd World Congress of International Associations*, (Brussels, Ghent, 1913), available on: http://www.uia.org/legal/home.php.

Politis N., *Draft Convention Relating to the Legal Position of International Associations*, Institute of International Law, (Brussels, 1923), available on: http://www.uia.org/legal/home.php.

Niboyet J.P. & Kopelmanas L., *'Granting of International Juridical Personality to Consultative NGOs', Report to the Study Committee on Legal Status*, The Conference of Non-Governmental Consultative Organizations, (Geneva, 1 March 1949), available on: http://www.uia.org/legal/home.php.

Habicht H. & Kopelmanas L., *Report of the Study Committee on Legal Status,* The Conference of Non-Governmental Consultative Organizations, (Geneva, 1 June 1949), MNGO/7/49, available on: http://www.uia.org/legal/home.php.

Bastid S., *'Perspectives d'un Statut International pour les Organisations Internationales Non-Gouvernementales', Report on the Proposal of the Institute of International Law,* The 44th Session of the Institute of International Law (Bath, 1950), available on: http://www.uia.org/legal/home.php.

——, *Resolution on Granting of International Status to Associations Established by Private Initiative*, Institute of International Law, (49th Session, Bath, September 1950), available on: http://www.uia.org/legal/home.php.

Nyples L.A., *Draft Convention Concerning Recognition of the Legal Personality of Foreign Companies, Associations, and Foundations*, The Hague Conference on Private International Law, (The Hague, 1951), available on: http://www.uia.org/legal/home.php.

Speeckaert G.P., *Draft Convention on Facilitating Activity of International NGOs*, The Union of International Associations, (11 July 1959), available on: http://www.uia.org/legal/home.php.

Arrangements for Consultation with NGOs, ECOSOC Res. 1296 (XLIV), 23.5.68, ESCOR (XLIV), Supp. No. 1.

Report of the Council Committee on NGOs, ECOSOC, UN Doc. E/5257/Add.1, April 9, 1973.

Merle M., *Report on International Non-Governmental Organizations and their Legal Status, Colloquy on the Role of International Non-Governmental Organizations (NGOs) in Contemporary Society*, The Parliamentary Assembly of the Council of Europe, (Strasbourg, February 1983), available on: http://www.uia.org/legal/home.php.

Project de Reglement du Conseil Portant Creation de l'Association Europeenne, Preliminary Draft, Motion by MEP L. Eyraud, (November 1984), available on: http://www.uia.org/legal/home.php.

Smith D., *Legal Status of International Non-Governmental Organizations in Europe*, Explanatory Memorandum concerning the Draft European Convention on Recognition of the Legal Personality of International Non-Governmental Organizations, Legal Affairs Committee of the Parliamentary Assembly of the Council of Europe (1985), Council of Europe Doc. 5381.J (26 March 1985), available on: http://www.uia.org/legal/home.php.

Regulation (EEC) No. 2317/85 of 25 July 1985 on the European Economic Interest Grouping (EEIG), available on: http://www.uia.org/legal/home.php.

Explanatory Report on the European Convention on the Recognition of the Legal Personality of International Non-Governmental Organizations of 24.IV.

1986; Eur.T.S. 124, available on: http://conventions.coe.int/treaty/EN/Reports/Html/124.htm.

Fontaine N., *Report on Non-Profit Making Associations in the European Community*, Explanatory Statement, Committee on Legal Affairs and Citizens' Rights of the European Parliament, (17 December, 1986), European Communities, European Parliament, Working Documents, Series A, 8 January 1987, Doc. A 2-196/86, available on: http://www.uia.org/legal/home.php.

Resolution on Non-Profit-Making Associations in the European Communities, European Parliament, Texts adopted by the European Parliament, Vol. 3/87, March 1987, p.p. 94–96, available on: http://www.uia.org/legal/home.php.

Debates of the European Parliament, 12.3.87, No 2-350, p.p. 236–237, 239–240.

Report of the Secretary General, UN ESCOR, Open-Ended Working Group on the Review of Arrangements for Consultations with Non-Governmental Organizations, 1st Sess., Provo Agenda Item 3, UN Doc. E/AC.70/1994/5, (1994).

CIA Report on 'International Islamic NGOs and Links to Terrorism', January 1996.

International Criminal Court (ICC) Rules of Procedure and Evidence, Doc. ASP/1/3, pp. 10–107.

Naidoo K., *Civil Society Accountability: 'Who Guards the Guardians?', Address Delivered at the UN Headquarters (Apr. 3, 2003)*.

Committee of Ministers Resolution Res(2003)8, Participatory Status for INGOs with the Council of Europe (Nov. 19, 2003).

Committee of Ministers, Resolution Res(2003)9 on Status of Partnership between the Council of Europe and National Non-Governmental Organisations (Nov. 19, 2003).

First Report on Responsibility of International Organizations (by G. Gaja), *International Law Commission*, 55th Sess. (March 26, 2003), UN Doc. A/CN.4/532.

Report of the Panel of Eminent Persons on United Nations-Civil Society Relations (the 'Cardoso Report'), UN Doc. A/58/817 (June 11, 2004).

'9/11 Commission Report', Final Report of the National Commission on Terrorist Attacks Upon the United States, July 22, 2004, available on: http://www.govinfo.library.unt.edu/911/report/index.htm.

Report of the Secretary General in Response to the Report of the Panel of Eminent Persons on United Nations-Civil Society Relations, UN Doc. A/59/354 (Sep. 13, 2004).

Guidelines for Fact-Finding with Respect to Alleged Breaches of Human Rights, General Note on the Joint Project of the International Bar Association (IBA), the Clemens Nathan Research Centre (CNRC), and the Raoul Wallenberg Institute at Lund University (Sweden), (2004), (on file with the author).

'United Nations: The Relationship between Member States and Civil Society, Including NGOs', Report to the President of the 60th General Assembly (by Ambassadors J.L. Løvald (Norway) & R.I. Jenie (Indonesia)), July 2005.

International Non Governmental Organizations' Accountability Charter 2006, available on: http://www.ingoaccountabilitycharter.org/.

'NGOs Lead by Example', Oxfam Press Release, (7 June 2006), available on: http://www.oxfam.org/en/news/pressrelease2006/pr060606_ngo/charter.

Code of Conduct for Special Procedures Mandate-Holders of the Human Rights Council, Res. 5/2 (18 June 2007), UN GAOR, 62nd Sess., Supp. No. 53, A/62/53.

Recommendation CM/Rec(2007)14 of the Committee of Ministers to Member States on the Legal Status of Non-Governmental Organizations in Europe, available on: http://www.coe.int/t/ngo/Legal_standards_en.asp.

Preliminary Issues for the International Law Association Conference in Rio de Janeiro, August 2008, Non-State Actors Committee, International Law Association, available on: http://www.ila-hq.org/.

'Non-State Actors in International Law: Aims, Approach and Scope of Project and Legal Issues', First Report of the Committee on Non-State Actors, International Law Association (The Hague Conference, 2010), available on: www.ila-hq.org.

'Non-State Actors in International Law: Lawmaking and Participation Rights', Second Report of the Committee on Non-State Actors, International Law Association (Sofia Conference, 2012), available on: www.ila-hq.org.

United States Congress, House of Representative Res. 1361, (September 23rd, 2008), available on: http://www.ngo-monitor.org/digest_info.php?id=2091.

Guidelines on International Human Rights Fact-Finding Visits and Reports (The Lund London Guidelines), June 2009, International Bar Association (IBA) & The Raoul Wallenberg Institute of Human Rights and Humanitarian Law at Lund University (Sweden), available on: http://www.factfindingguidelines.org/.

International Law in Brief, American Society of International Law, (June 12, 2009), available on: www.asil.org.

Report of the Directors, INGO Charter of Accountability Limited (no. 06527022) (Dec. 31, 2010), Sayer Vincent Consultants & Auditors.

Report on 'Zimbabwe: Time for a New Approach', International Bar Association's Human Rights Institute, (Sep. 2011), available on: http://www.osisa.org/sites/default/files/sup_files/ibahri_report_on_zimbabwe.pdf.

APPENDICES

APPENDICES[1]

1. Reports on International Status of INGOs
   - 1.1 'The Legal Status of International Non-Governmental Organizations', Conference of Non-Governmental Consultative Organizations, Study Committee on Legal Status, Report by L. Kopelmanas (Geneva, 1949)
   - 1.2 'International Non-Governmental Organizations and their Legal Status', Report by M. Merle (Strasburg, 1983)
2. UN Consultative Arrangements
   - 2.1 Economic and Social Council Resolution 1296(XLIV) on Arrangements for Consultation with Non-Governmental Organizations
   - 2.2 Economic and Social Council Resolution 1996/31 on Consultative Relationship between the United Nations and Non-Governmental Organizations
3. Regional Arrangements (Council of Europe)
   - 3.1 European Convention on the Recognition of the Legal Personality of International Non-Governmental Organizations (1986)
   - 3.2 European Convention on the Recognition of the Legal Personality of International Non-Governmental Organizations (1986) – Explanatory Report
   - 3.3 Council of Europe, Committee of Ministers, Resolution Res(2003)8 on Participatory Status for International Non-Governmental Organisations with the Council of Europe
   - 3.4 Council of Europe, Committee of Ministers, Resolution Res(2003)9 on Status of Partnership between the Council of Europe and National Non-Governmental Organisations
4. New Initiatives
   - 4.1 International Non-Governmental Organizations Accountability Charter (2006)
   - 4.2 Guidelines on International Human Rights Fact-Finding Visits and Reports (The Lund-London Guidelines) (2009)

---

[1] Unless otherwise indicated, all italics in the text are the author's.

Appendix One

REPORTS ON INTERNATIONAL STATES OF INGOS

1.1 'THE LEGAL STATUS OF INTERNATIONAL NON-GOVERNMENTAL ORGANIZATIONS', CONFERENCE OF NON-GOVERNMENTAL CONSULTATIVE ORGANIZATIONS, STUDY COMMITTEE ON LEGAL STATUS, REPORT BY L. KOPELMANAS[1] (GENEVA, 1949)

In a report to the representatives of non-governmental consultative organizations it would be superfluous to emphasize the fact that non-profit-making international associations are becoming increasingly important in the various fields of international life. Nor can there be any doubt that this is so. Since the end of the last century, increasingly numerous and powerful private groups with objectives other than profit and extending to several countries, or even to the whole of international society, have been formed and are continually being formed in all branches of disinterested human activity, whether charitable or scientific institutions or societies for the defence of professional interests. The value of the contribution that such groups can make to progress in international relations has been clearly recognized by many governments. *This attitude of governments with regard to non-governmental international organizations has been most strongly expressed in Article 71 of the United Nations Charter,* which permits the general international organization established at San Francisco to associate non-governmental international organizations with the work of international economic and social co-operation on a consultative basis.

As in many other spheres of international law, positive legal practice on this point has remained far behind the development of events. *In spite of the continually increasing social importance of non-profit-making international associations, it has not so far been possible to endow them with a juridical standing appropriate to their particular private requirements.* The result is that their work is subjected to considerable difficulties, some of a specific and permanent nature arising from the lack of a formal legal status, others caused by the general obstacles place in the way of the development of

[1] Director of Research at the National Scientific Research Center, Paris; Deputy Rapporteur of the CCNGOs Study Committee on Legal Status.

international relations by the present world structure which, it may be hoped, is only temporary.

The lack of suitable legal status affects the work of non-profit-making international associations insofar as it may hinder them in the performance of the everyday legal acts necessary for the accomplishment of the work they have undertaken. Any international association may be called upon, at some time in its existence, to receive gifts and bequests, to collect contributions, to enter into contracts, to make legal provision for the disposal and administration of its property, to use its property for the attainment of the purposes for which it was created, to defend its rights or be a party to legal proceedings etc., all this in all the countries to which its work extends. *In law, therefore, the problem is to give international associations the capacity to have rights and obligations* and thus enable them to carry on their work.

In positive law, the capacity to possess rights does not automatically belong to all private groups of whatever nature. In principle private social organizations only become juridical persons if they are qualified or recognized as such under the legal system to which they are subject. In order to acquire legal capacity, non-profit-making national associations must be constituted in accordance with the regulations in force in the country in which they propose to carry on their work. The laws of that country will define the extent of the capacity granted to non-profit-making associations and will determine the particular provisions that they must observe in their operation. Moreover, it is understood that national associations must respect the legal provisions applicable, in the country to which they belong, to all persons entitled to rights and that they are also subject to all administrative and judicial regulations designed to ensure maintenance of public order and the enforcement of law.

It is clear that the capacity granted to non-profit-making domestic associations only has undisputed legal effect in the countries in which they were constituted. *It is true that certain countries recognize associations constituted abroad as being entitled to rights; but this is a voluntary concession which each country is free to grant or not and which, when granted, it may withdraw at any time. The practice in this respect is extremely varied.* Certain countries grant no rights to foreign associations, others make recognition subject to individual authorization and yet others give general recognition, but of varying scope. The rights accorded to foreign associations may in fact only comprise the right of being a party to an action at law in respect of legal questions arising abroad, or the right of making certain contracts, or the right of carrying on social activities, the latter right being, of course, exercised subject to local legislation. While granting foreign associations legal capacity on their territory, some countries only grant them the rights they enjoy in their country of origin. Others, on the contrary, after establishing that a foreign association has juridical personality in the country where it was constituted, class it, as regards status within their territory, with their domestic associations, even if such status includes rights refused by the country of origin to the association in question. In view of the multiplicity of national solutions, which may be further aggravated by the freedom left to each country to change its attitude regarding this problem, the legal situation of domestic associations which are obliged to defend their rights or to act abroad, is ill-defined and unstable. But that is the legal system which must now be applied to non-profit-making international organizations. *As there is at present no international procedure for constituting private groups, if the non-profit-making international associations wish to acquire legal capacity they have no alternative but to place themselves under a national legal system and to constitute themselves in conformity with the legislative provisions of the legal system they have chosen,* either because of the facilities and advantages that may be offered them by such national law on non-profit-making associations, or because of the geographical centre of their interests or because of the needs and material conveniences of their establishment. *From the formal point of view, non-profit-making international associations agreeing to place themselves under a specific national regime become, in the view of their adopted country, truly national associations, while in the other countries in which their purposes oblige them to operate, they are legally regarded as foreign associations.*

But if the uncertainty of their legal position is only a minor inconvenience to ordinary foreign associations, since purely domestic bodies are only called upon to act abroad in exceptional circumstances, international associations whose sphere of activities extends, by definition, to several countries, if not to the whole of international society, cannot in the long run be satisfied with any solution that does not assure them legal capacity and the right to pursue their social aims in all countries with which they are concerned. Consequently, in order to avoid the difficulties of dependence on a single legal system, which might limit their opportunities for international action, international associations may be tempted to adopt the form of national associations in each country in which they wish to be able to act. But the cure would be worse than the disease, for the international associations would thus be transformed into a series of national associations, between which all connection might finally disappear. A less dangerous solution for the international aspect might be that of international associations on the federal plan; legal and social action under legal systems other than that under which the international association itself was constituted could be carried on, when necessary, by the national associations which belonged to the federation. But there are international associations which are not organized on a federal basis, and among international federations of domestic associations there are many which cannot allow legal action affecting the work of the federation to be taken by national members. Such a practice might well result in a shifting of the federal balance to the detriment of the federation's powers.

If international associations are to be able to perform their social functions in a satisfactory manner, it therefore appears essential to seek a revision of their existing legal status under ordinary law, so that they may be able to operate in all countries to which their objectives extend. *Some particularly large associations may possibly hope to obtain from States legal privileges which would actually meet all their practical needs for international operation. But this can only apply to very few international associations* and even then political changes may cause the withdrawal of benefits previously granted. In any case *the practical needs of the vast majority of international associations can only be fully satisfied by a system which bases their legal capacity and right to act in the countries to which their work may extend, on an imperative rule of international law, not on an optional concession by States. There are two ways of achieving this result. The most radical solution would be to free international associations from all formal ties with a particular national legal system. In this case their juridical personality would derive from registration with an international body.* This formality evidently could not directly confer rights on international associations under the national laws governing their work, because the capacity to possess rights can only be granted by individual national law so far as that law is concerned. But *by signing an international convention, the different States are free to give abstract recognition, under their own law, of the capacity to possess rights, with all the consequences they may wish to derive therefrom, to international associations constituted in accordance with an international registration procedure. In order to be effective, international procedure for constituting non-profit-making international associations should be supplemented by a convention giving some degree of legal capacity under the domestic laws of contracting States, and possibly the right to carry on their social work, to associations constituted directly on the international level, in accordance with procedure which should, moreover, be determined in the convention itself. The other alternative would be of such a convention to be based on the formal dependence of international associations on a national legal system. This second scheme would retain the obligation now imposed on international associations aspiring to perform legal acts, of being constituted in conformity with the provisions of a specific State's law. Under the terms of an international convention, the contracting States would nevertheless undertake to grant to international associations constituted in accordance with the domestic law of another contracting party, the rights necessary for the performance of their work.*

The system based on international registration of international associations has undeniable advantages. The necessity for placing international associations under a national legal system seems difficult to reconcile with their international character. Being obliged to operate under national law, the association could not avoid being dominated by national influences and traditions. The human factor, the possible predominance in its work of members who were nationals of the country by whose legal system it was governed, would also tend to impair the international character of the association. In addition to this, many persons who would be willing to join an international association or to contribute to it, would hesitate to join a group constituted under foreign law. Moreover, political rivalry between States might result in the refusal of certain countries to admit on their territory international associations connected with a country of whose system and policy they disapprove; this danger could be avoided if the international associations could be directly governed by international law.

The truth of these considerations led a certain number of organizations to prefer the absence of any legal status to dependence on an international legal system. But those international associations, and they are many, which are continually called upon to perform the current legal acts of everyday life, cannot afford the luxury, even for the sake of their international integrity, of remaining "itinerant" associations with no legal status. Thus it can easily be understood that *the creation of international procedure for constituting international associations has always been one of the main demands of the international associations themselves.* This was the objective of such efforts as the work of the Congress of International Associations in 1910 and 1913, the draft submitted in 1912 to the Institute of International Law by von Bar, the two draft conventions on the legal status of international associations based on the report of Nicolas Politis, the draft of the Institute of International Law in 1923 and the draft of the International Chamber of Commerce in 1928.

Up to the present, none of these attempts has led to any practical results. All have suffered from a failure to appreciate the real factors involved. The structure they established was based on the system of confirmation. This means that associations wishing to enjoy international status need only obtain registration by depositing their statutes with an international administrative body specially created for this purpose. The international body is obliged to accept all applications for registration, and may only refuse on the grounds that an application is not in the proper form. *Thus any international association could get itself included in the international register*, provided only that its statutes were drafted in conformity with the provisions of the Convention establishing this register; *this would even apply to associations which were not sufficiently important or useful to deserve special international protection, whose activities might endanger international law and order or public order in different countries, or which were not even truly international.*

This solution is obviously unacceptable. The registration of international associations actually involves very important legal consequences. The draft Convention establishing it also includes an undertaking by Contracting States to grant registered international associations legal capacity and the right to act on their territory. But it would be impossible to obtain such concessions from States for the benefit of all associations applying for registration. No Government would undertake such an obligation without being assured that its benefits would only be enjoyed by international associations giving proper guarantees of their importance, usefulness and legitimate purposes. A choice based on these principles should be made from associations wishing to enjoy international status, and as it has not been provided for in the registration procedure as contemplated in the above mentioned draft Convention, it will have to be made at a later stage.

Politis was well aware of this necessity. That is why the drafts based on his work provide that during a period of four months after Contracting States have been notified of registration, each State retains the right to refuse admittance to its territory to any registered association whose composition or purposes it considers incompatible with law and order. But in order to avoid sanctioning mere arbitrary action by States, the draft of the Institute of International Law gave the registered associations the right to appeal to the Permanent Court of International Justice against refusal by Contracting States. This was going far beyond the present scope of international law, and perhaps in a direction that is hardly desirable, even from the point of view of private interests, as has been well shown by the experience of various joint arbitration tribunals set up after the first World War. Such a solution was soon found to be impracticable. The draft of the International Chamber of Commerce abandons it, by maintaining without any international control, the right of States to refuse the benefits of the Convention on their territory to registered associations whose purposes, or the character of whose leading officers, they consider a danger to law and order in their respective countries. But each country thus remains absolutely free to decide whether or not legal capacity should be granted on its territory to an international association. As under common law, the capacity of international associations to possess rights is here derived, in the last analysis, from a concession by the territorial State, without any effective international obligation being imposed on States.

Thus the systems based on automatic registration of international associations necessarily lead to an impasse. Either the States are permitted to make a free choice, insofar as they are concerned, of registered associations, which shall enjoy the advantages of the Convention – a solution which offers no real security to the associations themselves; or an attempt is made to subject the decisions of States on this matter to international jurisdiction – a solution which the States cannot accept. There is only one way out of the difficulty. The system must be reversed, and discrimination between associations seeking international legal status must be introduced at the beginning of the international registration procedure. The international body responsible for registering international associations should no longer give effect to all applications. It should examine them thoroughly and be instructed to refuse to register associations which it considers to be of no value or perhaps even detrimental to the development of international relations, and only to accept those whose international usefulness it can vouch for. Only on this condition can States be justifiably required to surrender the right to choose the registered associations for themselves, and to give general recognition, on their territory, to the legal capacity required by all associations granted the benefits of registration by the competent international body.

This solution is not only designed to take account of the distrust with which States regard international associations. It also fulfils the requirements of the legal structure of modern societies. The attachment of private groups to a legal system is not a mere formality. It involves real integration of the group in the social life of the system to which it belongs and subjection to the laws and administrative and judicial controls of the legal system concerned. *If it is desired to free international associations from the bonds which now attach them to national legal systems, it is not sufficient to attach them formally to the international legal system, leaving them entirely free from any real subjection to a higher social order of a governmental nature. In this case it is essential to replace the control now exercised over the existence and activities of international associations by the domestic legislation to which they are subjected, by an equivalent control by international law.* But here domestic legal systems have two different procedures, which may, moreover, be combined. Either the groups wishing to constitute themselves on the territory of a State will be subjected to prior examination and will only be able to acquire rights by individual authorization, or the States will surrender the right to prior examination and give general authorization to non-profit-making associations freely to constitute themselves, because they are certain of being able to control their activities by the general procedures applicable to all legal acts performed on their territory. But this second possibility does not at present exist under international law, which has no general organs of control. Consequently *if it is desired effectively to subject international associations to international law, there is no alternative but to make their constitution dependent on prior examination and authorization by a special international body, extending this examination to supervision of the associations' activities, exercised by the same international body, in order to ensure that the activities of the authorized association in fact remain in conformity with the conditions under which authorization was granted.*

Such an important task could certainly not be entrusted to a subordinate administrative committee, as provided for in the previous draft conventions on the legal status of international associations. *Only an important political body would carry sufficient weight with States for its decisions on the qualifications of international associations to enjoy international legal status to be accepted by the contracting parties as undeniable authority for the entitlement to rights, under their respective legal systems, of associations authorized to constitute themselves internationally*. Within the existing structure of positive international organization, it is undoubtedly the principal organs of the United Nations which best satisfy this requirement. Of these organs, the Economic and Social Council is already responsible, under Article 71 of the United Nations Charter, for arranging consultations with non-profit-making international associations, which the Charter designates as non-governmental international organizations. Hence it would appear reasonable to make the Economic and Social Council responsible for examining applications for the registration by these non-governmental organizations, for selecting those which should be granted the benefits of international status and for supervising the activities of non-governmental organizations enjoying international status.

This was the basis of the draft on the international status of non-governmental organizations which the writer of this report, by agreement with Professor J.P. Nyboyet, submitted to the Study Committee on the legal status of non-governmental international organizations, set up by the Conference of Non-Governmental Consultative Organizations. This draft ... had two purposes. First, it attempted to define the conditions in which the economic and Social Council would judge the applications of non-governmental organizations for international legal status and supervise the activities of organizations whose applications were approved. Secondly, it attempted to define the scope of the legal status to be conferred, under the legislation of contracting States, on non-governmental organizations authorized by the Economic and Social Council, in order that these organizations should really be in a position to fulfill their social aims. Between these two equally necessary aspects of the international status of non-governmental organizations, our draft was designed to achieve co-ordination based on the idea that States would only agree to grant non-governmental international organizations sufficient rights on their territory, without being able to withdraw this concession individually, if they could have confidence in the Economic and Social Council's use of its powers of authorization and supervision, under the procedure for international constitution of non-governmental organizations. Insofar as the proposed method was intended to stabilize and strengthen the legal position of non-governmental international organizations, it inevitably had to emphasize the necessary right of inspection by the Economic and Social Council of the operation of organizations wishing to acquire and retain the benefits of international legal status.

The Study Committee, however, considered that most non-governmental organizations would be opposed to such far-reaching intervention in their internal affairs by the Economic and Social Council. In order to allow for this traditional attachment of non-governmental organizations to the principles of freedom and independence, it might perhaps be possible to reduce the proposed controls on this or that particular point. The draft on international status submitted to the Study Committee, which was mainly designed to point out the various problems presented by the organization of the international control required to establish an effective legal status for non-governmental international organizations, does indeed leave a certain latitude for discussion on the possible solutions of specific problems. But *as to the actual necessity for effective control, there can be no concession on this point unless the result is to be either an international régime for non-governmental organizations that is left to the discretionary powers of States and consequently offers no real guarantee to the organizations; or a régime that is impossible in practice, because it provides no real link with any social structure.* And *whatever may be the methods of international control, they will always appear more onerous than the corresponding obligations devolving upon non-governmental organizations under certain domestic legislations; for since internal systems have general means of controlling all legal acts performed on their territory, they can afford to be more liberal in their supervision of non-profit-making associations than the international legal system, which in view of its general organization would be obliged to stress the specific measures for controlling the non-governmental organizations granted the benefits of international status.*

In these circumstances, it is perfectly natural that non-governmental international organizations should resign themselves to the practical disadvantages of attachment to a domestic legal system, rather than accept a régime which would result in restriction of their freedom of action. Moreover, it may be doubted whether the organs of the United Nations are yet in a position to exercise effective control of the activities of non-governmental organizations. Consequently, the Committee decided that *until the development of international institutions establishes conditions in which a more reliable and less objectionable form of international control can be envisaged, the sole basis of the system should, for the present, be the formal attachment of non-governmental international organizations to the national legal system of their choice, though every effort should be made to obtain, by an international convention, recognition on the territory of all contracting parties of the legal status acquired by a non-governmental international organization under the legislation of any State party to the convention. ...*

But it was not considered possible to apply [this solution] to all non-profit-making international associations. However precise a definition may be given to the concept of 'association' or 'non-governmental international organization', it is inevitable that the international character of a private group must first of all depend on the intentions of its founders, as expressed in the statutes of the group. Hence, if an international convention grants certain advantages to associations having domestic legal status, but international in their purposes and character, it would be only too tempting and actually very easy for the directors of a purely domestic association to draft the statutes of their group in such a way as to make it appear international, and to claim the benefits of the convention. But States which had in theory adopted a convention granting legal status under the domestic legislation of all contracting parties to international associations constituted in accordance with the national laws of any one contracting party, could not allow the rights granted by the convention to a well-defined class of domestic associations to be extended, by means of a subterfuge, to all foreign associations. *A convention of this kind must therefore include not only an abstract list of the characteristics required by an association if it is to be regarded as international under the terms of the convention; it must also designate the authority which will be competent, on the basis of the general definition, to decide, in a given case, whether an association claiming the benefits of the convention fulfils the required conditions.*

Such competence could not be granted to any of the States concerned; neither to the State on whose territory an association claiming to be international invokes the convention concerning this class of private groups, nor to the association's country of origin. In the first case, the only result would be to deprive the convention of all its force as soon as it was possible for States to withdraw all concessions generally granted by declaring that such and such an association could not be regarded as international. In the second case the status granted to an association in its country of origin could not be imposed on foreign States. Thus provision should be made for an international decision in cases of dispute, and it would certainly be easier not only to have such a decision in real disputes, which is a complicated and uncertain solution, but to introduce it in the form of *prior distinction between purely national associations, and those having national legal status but an international character, the benefits of the convention being granted only to associations expressly included in the second category by an international body.*

The preparation of the list of associations having domestic legal status and regarded as international for the purposes of a Convention granting legal status to such associations on the territory of all contracting States would not, moreover, require the creation of a new international body or even the introduction of special procedure. For this purpose *it would be possible to make use of the distinction already established between international and domestic non-governmental organizations by the Economic and Social Council, as part of its functions under Article 71 of the United Nations Charter.* There is a further reason for using the list of international non-governmental organizations having consultative status with the Economic and Social Council to determine the scope of a Convention on the general legal status of non-profit-making international associations. Indeed, *the choice of the Economic and Social Council ensures not only authentic confirmation of the international character of non-governmental organizations included in the international category, but also an appreciation of the importance and usefulness of the contribution they can make to the work of international economic and social co-operation.* This limitation of the scope of the Convention to be concluded to non-governmental organizations which have been authentically declared by one of the principal organs of the United Nations to be of international public utility undoubtedly makes it more probable that a large number of States will accede to the Convention. The same argument may be applied to non-governmental organizations which, in their international capacity, have obtained consultative or similar status with one of the specialized agencies of the United Nations. It would thus be justifiable to include them among the non-governmental organizations coming within the scope of the Convention granting international recognition of their domestic legal status, without there being any danger of thereby weakening its effect or of reducing the number of acceding States.

This was the solution finally agreed on by the Study Committee on the legal status of international non-governmental organizations and embodied in the Preliminary Draft Agreement designed to facilitate the work of these organizations, which it prepared in accordance with the terms of reference given to it by the Conference of Non-Governmental Consultative Organizations. The ... Draft in fact stipulates that the proposed Agreement shall apply to non-profit-making associations which fulfill the following conditions:

(a) that they shall have been constituted in the territory of one of the acceding States and in conformity with its laws; and
(b) that they shall have been granted consultative status with the economic and Social Council or an equivalent status with one or other of the Specialized Agencies.

... for the reasons given above, [the authors of the Draft] did not think they could ask States for too extensive undertakings which could not be defined exactly in advance. Thus the application of the legal system provided for in the Agreement to associations not coming under [these conditions], is left to the discretion of acceding States, whereas non-governmental organizations defined by the terms of this provision are entitled to it by virtue of an international obligation.

In determining the legal system to be instituted by the Agreement, the authors of the Draft had two alternatives. They could define it with reference to the legal position of non-profit-making national associations in the country of origin of the non-governmental organization coming under the Agreement, or in the country in which that organization wished to perform legal acts or carry on its social activities, by guaranteeing the organizations coming under the Agreement a minimum of rights which they would enjoy on the territory of all acceding States, whatever the regime applied to national associations in the country of origin or the country in which they wished to claim the benefits of the Agreement.

The second solution seems obviously more advantageous for non-governmental organizations. It would certainly facilitate the performance of their work in all countries bound by the Agreement, because it would enable them everywhere to acquire the rights essential for that purpose, such as those of being a party to legal proceedings, making contracts, possessing movable or immovable property and receiving gifts and bequests under certain conditions. This status could be extended in countries which grant national associations more favourable treatment than the minimum international status guaranteed to non-governmental organizations coming under the Agreement. In the opposite case, however, when the domestic treatment of non-profit making associations remains below this minimum international standard, non-governmental organizations entitled to the benefits of the Agreement would enjoy rights expressly conferred as a result of their international status, even if national associations in the country in which they intended to exercise them did not enjoy such full capacity. Thus in certain circumstances the system might oblige States to grant international associations constituted on their territory a more liberal regime than they accord to their own national associations, or to treat those having the legal status of foreign associations more favourably than national private groups. It is hardly probable that the majority of States would agree to endorse such an arrangement. The advantages of the status granted would therefore have to be bought at the cost of reducing the extent of the Agreement's acceptance which, in the end, would be contrary to the real interests of non-governmental organizations. *Consequently, the Study Committee preferred not to claim, in principle, for non-governmental organizations coming under the Agreement, other rights than those enjoyed by non-profit making national associations under the laws of acceding States.*

Under this system, non-governmental organizations coming under the Agreement would have exactly the same status in their country of origin as all other associations constituted under the laws of that country. And as the legal status of non-governmental organizations in other countries acceding to the Agreement would be based on recognition of their national legal status, they would have no claim in those countries to more rights than they possessed in their country of origin. But their legal status in countries acceding to the Agreement, other than the country in which they were constituted, might be inferior to their original legal status. This would be the case, for instance, when the country in which they claim application of the Agreement does not grant certain rights, which they enjoy in their country of origin, to non-profit making national associations; for their status in the different countries acceding to the Agreement must be determined on the basis of domestic treatment. *Thus, the international status of non-governmental organizations coming under the Agreement would be subject to a twofold limitation. On the one hand it would be limited by the legal status of non-profit making associations in the organization's country of origin, and on the other, by the treatment given to similar national associations by the country in which the benefits of international status were claimed.*

Such is the broad outline of the system embodied in ... [the] Draft Agreement. But the authors of the Draft did not wish to produce a solution that might deprive international associations of advantages now actually granted to them under the laws of certain countries. There are, indeed, countries which, for purposes of legal status, place foreign associations on their territory on exactly the same basis as domestic associations, without being deterred by the consideration that complete equality may give the foreign association certain rights which it does not enjoy in its country of origin. Moreover, it may happen that the legal capacity of a non-profit making association, under the laws of the country where it was constituted, is fully recognized under certain foreign legal systems which do not, however, consider that they need grant their domestic associations such extensive rights. The ... Draft, while based on the principle of two-fold limitation of the international status of non-governmental organizations, both by the legislation of their country of origin and by that of the country in which they operate, nevertheless attempts to reserve to acceding States, or those that may accede in the future, the right to grant to organizations ..., if they so desire, more extensive rights than would be required by strict application of the general principle embodied in the Agreement.

Thus ... the Draft takes as a basis for the international regime for organizations benefiting under the Agreement, the legal status they enjoy in the country in which they were constituted. Nevertheless, acceding States retain the right to limit this status, on their territory, to the rights they grant to the most favoured category of similar organizations. Here the permissive form is intentionally used so as not to exclude the possibility of maintaining the original legal status of non-governmental organizations, even under the laws of acceding States which grant their domestic associations a less favourable status. But as it was not considered possible to impose on States an imperative obligation to treat non-governmental organizations constituted abroad more favourably, in certain circumstances, than domestic associations, acceding States are permitted, on their territory ... to reduce the original status of non-governmental organizations constituted abroad to the status they themselves grant to their domestic associations, if the former is more favourable. It is, however, stipulated that this domestic status, which would then constitute one of the upper limits of the status enjoyed by non-governmental organizations constituted abroad on the territory of a State applying the powers granted under ... the Draft, must be equivalent to that of the most favoured category of domestic association. This provision is designed for countries in which there are several different regimes for non-profit-making associations. The Draft Agreement provides that non-governmental organizations ... shall, in acceding countries other than the country in which they were constituted, be automatically included in the most favoured category of domestic associations, even if the latter must obtain an individual decision by the competent authorities in order to be included in this category. The Study Committee considered this inclusion fully justified because it would benefit organizations already authentically declared to be of international public utility by the

Economic and Social Council or by one of the Specialized Agencies of the United Nations.

It should also be observed that the formula in ... [the] Draft is sufficiently wide to include, under the international status of organizations ..., not only legal capacity but also the right to carry on social activities. Here again, each acceding country may limit the right of action of organizations constituted abroad by the extent of the rights it grants to the most favoured category of similar domestic associations. Acceding States can naturally extend the legal status of non-governmental organizations as established by the foregoing provisions. This additional right of acceding States is expressly affirmed in [the Draft]. At first sight, this provision might appear to be a mere truism. But it had to be inserted in order to allow States which, while according foreign associations the benefit of domestic treatment, are even prepared to grant them rights they would not possess under their original status, to maintain this attitude favouring the activities of non-governmental organizations. ...

Certain States will regard ... the Draft as an attempt to codify positive customary law. Nevertheless, its adoption would represent some progress as compared with the present situation. If it appears probable that the Agreement designed to facilitate the work of non-governmental organizations is most likely to be adopted by States which even without being bound by the ratification of an international convention already voluntarily practice the policies it embodies, it may be allowed, without being too optimistic, that certain States now hostile or merely reserved in their attitude to international associations, may be persuaded to show more understanding towards non-governmental organizations when they are requested to make concessions to only a limited number of organizations, the importance and moral qualities of which have, moreover, been guaranteed by the granting of consultative status with the economic and Social Council or one of the Specialized Agencies of the United Nations. The Agreement's chances of success will naturally be still further increased if its adoption is recommended to States by a resolution of the United Nations General Assembly.

And even as regards States which already grant extensive rights on their territory to associations constituted abroad, accession to an international agreement that transforms their present voluntary practice into fulfillment of an international obligation, would be of undeniable practical value to organizations coming under this agreement. Accession would make it impossible for States to withdraw the status granted to international associations unless they denounced the Agreement. Thus the international legal position or organizations coming under the Agreement would have acquired a stability which is now totally lacking. It would still be necessary to prevent this stability from being entirely destroyed by too frequent denunciations. Hence the authors of the Draft Agreement attempted to give the organizations in question certain guarantees in the event of denunciation of the Agreement by a contracting State. This is the purpose of [the provision] ..., which makes denunciation subject to six months' notice. During the period of notice, organizations would have the right to liquidate their property in the country entering the denunciation and freely to export all their funds. The effects of denunciations, in so far as they were detrimental to non-governmental organizations which settle in the country relying on the status established by the international Agreement, could thus be palliated to a considerable extent. Once the period of notice had expired, organizations which had not taken this opportunity would have only themselves to blame, and would be subject to ordinary law. Even then, denunciation would have no retroactive effect. Acts performed by organizations coming under the Agreement before the expiry of the period of notice, would remain valid and if such acts subsequently gave rise to disputes, the organizations in question would still be entitled to have recourse to the Courts of the State which had denounced the Agreement.

These provisions, and especially the freedom left to organizations coming under the Agreement to export their funds during the period of notice of denunciation without being bound by exchange restrictions, certainly appear more burdensome to the sovereignty of States than most of the other solutions proposed by the Study Committee. It is possible, therefore, that States will be opposed to them. But if they could not be included in the Agreement, this international instrument would lose much of its value for non-governmental consultative organizations. In practice, it would do little to improve their present position, so that it might legitimately be asked whether negotiation of an agreement of this nature would still answer a real need. In these circumstances it would be the non-governmental consultative organization's first duty towards themselves to use all the moral influence at their disposal to try to persuade States to adopt the clauses governing the right of denunciation.

... all other provisions of the Draft, ... are concerned with the *problems raised by the increasing number of difficulties now affecting all human relations that extend across frontiers. At the time when the drafts based on the Politis report were prepared, that aspect of the matter could be ignored. Now it appears much more serious than the specific problem of the legal status of international associations.* Domestic obstacles to the international movement of property and persons are now such that international associations, whose operation is indissolubly bound up with the international circulation of currency, goods, ideas and persons, are literally threatened with suffocation. If, as the United Nations Charter seems to indicate, there is a real desire to make full use of the assistance that non-governmental consultative organizations can render in the organization of international society, then a remedy for this situation is urgently required.

This raises a series of specific problems defined by the real difficulties encountered by non-governmental organizations in their international activities. These include difficulties affecting the issue of passports, visas and foreign exchange for official journeys by the directors and representatives of international non-governmental organizations. A further major problem is raised by exchange restrictions preventing the transfer from one country to another, and sometimes the local use, of the funds of organizations allocated to cover their operating expenses and finance their social work. There are also restrictions on the employment of foreign labour and the difficulties and expense of sending publications and documents. On all these points, measures should be devised to enable non-governmental organizations to continue operating internationally in spite of the legal, economic and social isolationism now practiced by most nations of the world.

On the basis of their collaboration in the work of inter-governmental bodies, certain groups among the non-governmental consultative organizations consider that they should enjoy real exemption from the domestic restrictions that hinder their activities. This would mean claiming for non-governmental organizations real privileges and immunities modeled on those enjoyed by inter-governmental bodies. There seems no chance of this claim being accepted by the States. Moreover, it is entirely unfounded. In law, privileges and immunities can only protect the exercise of State powers. Thus there can be no question of granting them to non-governmental organizations. Non-governmental organizations doing international work could at the most emphasize the particular difficulty they encounter, by the very nature of their international activities, under the various domestic, legal and administrative restrictions and ask States to grant them some relaxation of the administrative regulations which now make the accomplishment of their task almost impossible. And even by this more modest request it would be difficult to obtain any important concessions from States, unless they had some guarantee that the benefits would only be enjoyed by a limited number of non-governmental organizations which were of undoubted international utility and could be trusted not to abuse them. Here again, it would therefore be advisable to define precisely the class of non-governmental organizations to be granted the benefits of measures designed to facilitate their international relations, which are at present hampered by domestic, legal and administrative obstacles.

This was the basis on which the Study Committee prepared the provisions of the Draft relating to difficulties experienced by non-governmental organizations, as a result of the present general domestic obstacles to progress in international relations. All these provisions apply to non-governmental organizations coming under ... the Draft, that is to organizations having consultative status with the Economic and Social Council or a similar status with one of the United Nations specialized agencies. The text of these provisions is not designed to exempt the organizations in question from domestic restrictions but, with regard to the specific points mentioned above on which it appeared essential to facilitate the work of international non-governmental organizations, it attempts to arrange domestic regulations so as to permit international transactions on the scale that is essential if non-governmental organizations are to accomplish their international task. In view of the complexity and diversity of domestic regulations in this field, it was not considered possible to produce precise technical solutions covering all these points calculated to remove all difficulties that might arise and which in any case could not be provided against in advance. For this reason the Study Committee preferred to insert in the Draft, for each class of problems raised by restrictions on private international relations, an undertaking by States to grant organizations coming under the Agreement the most favourable treatment within the general scope of their domestic regulations. If acceding States faithfully fulfill this undertaking – and are not all international obligations subject to such a reservation? – that will be sufficient to facilitate the international operation of non-governmental organizations to a considerable extent.

A more precise technical solution, independent of, and supplementing the provisions of the Agreement, might have been found for *the problem of transferring funds, which now weighs heaviest on international non-governmental organizations.* But the solution of this problem would require a very deep technical study, for which only the most general data can be indicated here. When considering the international distribution of funds belonging to non-governmental organizations, it may easily be concluded that transfer of such funds from one country to another as required by each organization, can be carried out by clearing on the total funds in different countries belonging to international non-governmental organizations. But this concession to non-governmental organizations might lead to evasion of domestic exchange regulations, so that States could not agree to it unless they had sufficient guarantee of proper control and that, to be effective, would have to cover each individual clearing operation. It would have to be shown that each such operation really concerned funds belonging to non-governmental organizations granted clearing facilities, that the purpose of the operation was to satisfy needs really arising from the statutory activities of these organizations, and that the use of the funds obtained by the operation was in conformity with the purpose for which clearing privileges were claimed. It would therefore be necessary to establish special clearing machinery to provide such control.

An ingenious proposal on these lines was made to the Study Committee by Mr. W. Harvey Moore. His proposal was to form an international company of which non-governmental consultative organizations could become members and which would have juridical personality on the territory of all countries acceding to the convention instituting it. This company would administer, as an international trust, the property entrusted to it by members and could thus automatically carry out international clearing operations. But on closer examination the proposal did not appear acceptable either to non-governmental organizations or to States. Non-governmental organizations could not agree to the administration of their property by the proposed fund, which would undoubtedly amount to control of their internal operation by a small private organization. And States would certainly not have sufficient guarantees if exchange operations were controlled by the very body that administered the property affected by the clearing operations. In addition to this, the legal form of a trust would be hard to establish in countries which do not recognize this institution. For these reasons the Study Committee did not feel that it could adopt Mr. Harvey Moore's proposal.

It is evident that the need for controlling clearing operations cannot be satisfied unless the operations are supervised by an inter-governmental body, or at least made part of an inter-State exchange control system. This determines the choice of the body that might be made responsible, in the present circumstances, for carrying out and supervising the international transfer of funds belonging to non-governmental organizations through clearing between the Bank for International Settlements and the International Monetary Fund. The precise conditions and technical procedure for such an international arrangement for transfer of funds belonging to non-governmental organizations through the Fund or the Bank, would have to be determined by negotiation with these two bodies. ... Before deciding their attitude on this or that technical solution, non-governmental organizations should realize that any real control of their international financial transactions will necessarily entail extensive control of their activities. Consequently, it will be for them to decide, first of all, whether they are prepared to surrender what may be an important part of their internal autonomy in order to obtain advantages for the international transfer of their funds, or whether they prefer to retain their autonomy of operation at the cost of continued financial difficulties.

1.2 'INTERNATIONAL NON-GOVERNMENTAL ORGANIZATIONS AND THEIR LEGAL STATUS', REPORT BY M. MERLE[2] *(STRASBURG, 1983)*

Introduction

It would be difficult to imagine an intellectually more stimulating subject than the one proposed here for our study. It has its roots in a long and varied history and leads on to the most topical and concrete problems of world structure and organization. *Our task is no less than to identify the future foundations and principles of the relations, in international life, between private enterprise and the action of public authorities in the form of states and intergovernmental organizations. But however fascinating the subject of the debate may be, any solution to the problem is, as it always was, extremely difficult to find, not only because it implies a network of technical procedures very hard to conceive and equally hard to implement and coordinate, but above all because any change in the existing legal structures has political implications*, whether we like it or not, which cannot be overlooked by any of the parties concerned.

It will be a good thing to recall certain well-known facts in order to determine more accurately the dimensions of this question. To judge by certain examples such as the religious orders, or the trade leagues linking the large medieval cities, the private sector frequently preceded the public sector in international activity. But from the 16th century, with the appearance and growing strength of modern European states, the nature of the problem was to change radically. Where a political authority invokes sovereignty to justify the exercise of exclusive powers over all persons living in or entering the territory it claims to control, the network of private transnational relations is obviously threatened. But as the claims of sovereign states were still less extensive than their means of action, people and ideas continued to circulate across frontiers. ... despite gradual reinforcement of state power, considerable room remained for private enterprise. In the 19th century neither the Holy Alliance nor the Concert of Europe managed to

[2] Professor at the Law Faculty, Paris University; the report was presented to the *Colloquy on the Role of International Non-Governmental Organizations in Contemporary Society* (Strasbourg, February 1983), organized under the auspices of the Parliamentary Assembly of the Council of Europe. See M. Merle, *Le Rôle des ONG dans la Société Contemporaine, Associations Transnationales*, Vol. 35 (1983), 1 (English version in *Transnational Associations*, Vol. 38 (1986), 3, pp. 133–136).

stifle the spread of liberal movements across frontiers, the emergence of international workers' movements or the appearance of humanitarian organizations (ex. the Red Cross).

Today in a strange way both these traditional tendencies have become stronger. *On the one hand, the nation state has become a universal model of society and now occupies all the living space available. The surface of the earth is therefore more compartmentalized than ever before in the course of history. Intergovernmental organizations provide the ideal means of dialogue or confrontation between sovereign states. On the other hand, the tendency to form international associations has, since the beginning of the century, grown at unprecedented speed* as shown by the statistics of the Union of International Associations. There were a few dozen NGOs at the beginning of the century and today in 1987 there are several thousands. This proliferation may be put down to a number of factors which we could sum up under the heading *'the shrinking world'* – breathtaking progress in communications in every field, speeding-up of international exchange of all kinds, increased inter-penetration of activities, blurring of the former sharp distinction between home and abroad through the number and complexity of interrelated activities.

The increase in the number of NGOs would in itself suffice to show that governments have at least shown tolerance towards them. But *a new form of co-operation between the 'public sector' in international society was introduced with the creation of 'consultative status', inaugurated by Article 71 of the United Nations Charter and adopted in similar forms by numerous other intergovernmental organizations.*

So, considerable progress has been made in our field over the last half century. But the process of evolution is always characterized by stoppages and difficult passages. The international association movement is today making such strong demands that it is no longer content with tolerance on the part of governments and feels uneasy, confined within the limits of *'consultative status'*. At both levels of activity *NGOs remain subject to constraints which hamper the freedom of movement to which they aspire. It remains to be seen whether the granting of genuine international status would truly help lighten these constraints.*

NGOs and the States

Under present public international law only states are able to occupy and administer the inhabitable parts of the earth's surface. Thus intergovernmental organizations are obliged, if they wish to occupy a given point on the globe, to make *'headquarters agreements'* with the government on whose territory they have chosen to settle. As they have no territorial basis NGOs are bound, in order to function, to take refuge in the territory of one of some 160 states which control the earth's surface. As a result they are subject to the regulations and jurisdiction of the authorities which agree to have them. *A major contradiction at once emerges between an NGO's international vocation, which is its raison d'être, and the national legal status in which it is confined.*

It would require a huge inventory and encyclopedic knowledge to describe and compare the various kinds of legislation which the 160 countries of the world apply to NGOs. Even on the assumption that a great many countries give little attention to the question of associations and bestow their favours above all on *'private'* organizations whose real purpose is to mould and indoctrinate the population according to the instructions of the powers-that-be, the list of states in which the problem of the status of NGOs truly arises is too lengthy to allow of systematic comparison, especially in a short report of this kind. A typology will help here.

In practice there are only *three possible solutions to the problem of the national status of NGOs*:

The discriminatory system whereby the establishment and operation of NGOs is made subject to conditions more restrictive than those applied to national associations. Until 1981 this was the French solution since, under the terms of a decree of 1939 (issued in the climate of growing peril in Europe), associations deemed to be *"foreign"* on account of the composition of their governing bodies, could not be created without prior authorization and could be dissolved by a simple administrative decision. However, this retrograde, vexatious legislation was applied in a liberal manner. The best proof is the fact that France has always been, and still is the country with the highest number of NGO headquarters. This remark is not intended to justify the situation but it does show – and it would be quite wrong of us to forget this fact here or elsewhere – that there can often be a wide gap between law and reality.

Application of the general law This is the system whereby NGOs are purely and simply assimilated in status to national associations as regards both the conditions of formation and dissolution and the rules under which they operate. This is, in my experience, the situation in countries with a liberal tradition; it is the situation now in France since the Act of 9 October 1981 repealed the legislative Decree of 1939. Thus an NGO may now be created and form an association on French territory simply by means of a '*declaration* published in the Official Gazette (Journal Officiel)'. Once declared the NGO enjoys the same rights as any other association set up in France by French nationals.

Abolition of the discriminatory system does, quite clearly, constitute progress. But is does not solve the problems facing NGOs – far from it. Although based on liberal principles, French legislation on associations contains a whole series of restrictions which turn NGOs into second-class legal entities in comparison with commercial companies or trade unions. The same is true in most countries. Thus the principle of assimilation subjects the NGOs to the same restrictions as all the national associations with which their lot is bound up.

But the most serious drawback to this arrangement is that it does not meet the specific requirements of NGOs which have to do, essentially, with their relations with individual members or sections beyond the frontiers. For example the introduction of rigorous exchange control has no effect on the running of a French anglers association but can paralyze the financing and thus the activities of an international NGO.

Preferential status This is the system set up in the well known Belgian Act of 25 October 1919 which still serves as a reference point in this question. With the aim of encouraging the establishment of NGOs in Belgium territory the Act recognizes them as corporations even when they are composed of non-Belgian nationals, provided that one of their directors is a Belgian national. Its provisions are more flexible than those of French legislation concerning property rights and donations. But nonetheless prior authorization is required and fairly strict requirements are imposed concerning the drafting of the statutes.

In fact the most audacious provision of Belgian legislation concerns recognized rights in Belgian territory, of international associations with headquarters in another country. This measure which has no parallel in other legislations, has the advantage of conferring rights on an extraterritorial private entity. If a similar measure were adopted by the legislation of other countries it would effectively solve many problems and open the way to multilateral 'transnationality', without there being any need to introduce an international status worked out by all the governments.

But the fact is that the Belgian example has not been followed and it seems unlikely that it will be in the near future. The unilateral granting of preferential status, even if combined with facilities to NGOs established in other countries, solves only part of the problem of the functioning of NGOs. In the most developed version (the Belgian Act) national legislation can go so far as to recognize, within the national territory, the validity of activities whose origin is outside their frontiers but it cannot and will never be able, without the consent of foreign states, to control those same activities beyond the limits of national territory.

But *the problem raised by the existence and functioning of NGOs is precisely how to escape the constraints of the legislation of the host state and how to find in one form or another, the legal means of gaining recognition and respect for the specific nature of their activities.* Unless we can hope for a sudden unanimous conversion of all states throughout the world to the position adopted by Article 8 of the Belgian Act recourse to national legislation will remain ineffective. The hypothesis of a sudden conversion of that kind is the more improbable as *apart from the major obstacle of territorial sovereignty, account must be taken of the factors of state interest, public order and the defence of economic interests. It is these considerations which also explain, as we shall see below, the reticence of governments with regard to the preparation of an international status for NGOs.*

NGOs and IGOs

This question has already been commented on so abundantly that one hesitates to deal with it in a few lines. But an explanation of the situation is both feasible and necessary.

The granting of *'consultative status'* to a great many NGOs by the UN, its specialized institutions and several regional organizations, obviously constitutes considerable progress as compared to the situation at the time of the League of Nations. Although commentaries on the question are too often not supported by statistics and factual research defining the extent of the phenomena, *there is little doubt that the consultation machinery and, especially, practical co-operation in the field have resulted in an unprecedented dialogue between governments acting collectively and vast sectors representing numerous currents of opinion throughout the world.*

But while we may take note of this progress *we can still cast a critical eye on the limits of the evolution that has been taking place* around us over the last 36 years or more.

(a) *'Consultative status'* is at present *granted only to a minority of NGOs* (approximately 600 of the 4,000 listed by the UIA).[3] The majority are thus excluded and cannot enjoy the advantages of this status.
(b) The term *'consultative status'* is ambiguous, to say the least. It simply governs relationships between a given IGO and a given NGO and *does*

[3] Data mentioned in the original report. Currently, there are nearly 4000 organizations obtaining ECOSOC consultative status, out of approximately 40,000 organizations listed with the UIA.

not confer any right on an NGO capable of being exercised before any other national or international authority. The fact of belonging to that category of privileged bodies does provide a kind of badge of respectability and leaders of NGOs are jealously devoted to the granting and maintaining of such status, but *access to consultation has only limited effects and under no circumstances can it amount to legal status in the full meaning of the term.*

(c) The three levels of consultation which have been introduced in most IGOs establish a new *form of discrimination among NGOs.* In fact most of them are *confined to a role of recipient of information from the IGO and are legally powerless to take any effective part in consultation.*

(d) *'Consultative status'* is *'granted' at the discretion of IGOs and may be withdrawn on the same basis.* We may refer here to incidents that occurred in the Economic and Social Council at the end of the 60s or in UNESCO in the 70s in order to show the tendency of IGOs to demand a sort of ideological conformity on the part of their *'consultants'*. Insofar as the question involved is observance of the statutes of the IGO, conformity may be a legitimate requirement; but this is less the case when it is imposed, in individual cases, by temporary majorities *in connection with political disputes between member states.* If tendencies of this sort were to predominate in future the very basis of co-operation between NGOs and IGOs would be threatened and NGOs would be simply left with a choice between withdrawal from the consultative system or complicity in manoeuvres in contradiction with their own aims.

For these various reasons the *'consultative status'* offered and controlled by IGOs cannot give NGOs the protection or guarantees they need in order to carry out, in complete independence, the functions which they have assumed.

NGOs and International Status

To fill the gaps arising from the juxtaposition of the various national provisions and strengthen the position of the NGOs vis-à-vis the IGOs, there is only one solution – it is to give NGOs *an international status guaranteeing them minimum rights and a degree of freedom of action vis-à-vis the various national or international authorities* with which they have relations.

This is no new idea and has already given rise to a whole series of proposals, some of which have taken the form of conventions ready to be signed by the states. Backed by the authority of these experts the NGOs have made numerous representations to IGOs, so far without success. If we consider the reasons for this failure we shall be better able to understand the remaining obstacles.

(a) *As it stands, international law allows only states to make rules of law, including those which confer legal personality and legal capacity on entities other than themselves* (cf. the opinion of the ICJ in the Bernadotte case on the legal personality of the UN). *The instinct of self-preservation ensures that states are somewhat disinclined to grant legal personality and legal capacity to private organizations when this might prejudice their own authority.*

(b) Supposing that this obstacle were removed, it would still be necessary to decide *in what framework and under whose jurisdiction this status could be prepared.* Ideally, one might think in terms of a universal conference, possibly under the patronage of an organization such as the United Nations. *In view of the varying nature of the political systems involved and the fact that each 'camp' has diametrically opposed conceptions of the role of private enterprise, the likelihood of agreement in this context is practically nil.*

In theory, the task is easier in regional organizations (such as the Council of Europe) because there is a minimum of consensus among members on the importance of private enterprise in developing international co-operation. Supposing that the undertaking did succeed it would produce a status whose scope would, necessarily, be restricted to the territories of the member states. That would in itself constitute a considerable step forward; but *it would not in any way solve the questions raised by the existence of world-wide NGOs which, beyond the frontiers of Western Europe, would come up against the same old obstacles.*

(c) As far as states are concerned, NGOs form a genuine nebula including both giants and dwarfs. But the *differences in size and power are not the only ones.* Experts well know that *the label NGO covers a wide variety of articles* – from the scientific or humanitarian association whose activities are presumed to be beneficial, to so-called 'professional associations' which frequently mask powerfully organized interests. To grant them all the same status and privileges (conferring exemptions from the ordinary law, particularly with regard to taxation, customs, labour regulations etc) would be tantamount to giving identical treatment to a learned or charitable society and to the directors of a multinational company or consortium. Experts also realize that though the activities of most NGOs benefit society as a whole *the term international association sometimes serves to cover up subversive or terrorist activities which can threaten internal security. The danger of infiltration of that sort would be increased if members of such an organization could claim privileges deriving from an international status* vis-à-vis the authorities of the host state.

(d) *In view of this instinctive mistrust on the part of governments it would be unreasonable to expect the community of states (even at regional level) to produce any other solution than the adoption of a sort of 'outline status', the application of which would necessarily be left to the judgment of the various states concerned.*

We would point out that the same applies to the recognition of states (or governments), since under the rules of international law every government can decide at its own discretion on the legitimacy of a newly created state or of a change of government as the result of a revolution. It is hardy conceivable that private organizations should be treated differently. In other words, *even if international status defining the rights and privileges of NGOs were adopted the problem of designation of organizations to benefit from that status would still remain unsolved.*

It is hard to imagine any international body making, upon its own authority, a selection from the thousands of NGOs listed by the UIA and from among the new candidates which would not fail to present themselves; it is even more difficult to imagine that a list of organizations enjoying international status could be imposed upon states. The latter would demand the right to examine and approve the credentials and good standing of the private organization in question before conferring a status which grants exemptions from the provisions of domestic law. Failure to take account of that legitimate requirement would rule out any prospect of international status for NGOs.

Conclusion

In the strict sense of the term this report can have no conclusion ... The only object to the two remarks that follow is to place the preceding observations in a wider context.

(a) *The problem raised by the legal status of NGOs must be looked at from the point of view of re-shaping the structure and organization of the international community.* The nation states have taken centuries to emerge and, for the time being, have their hands firmly on the controls in the international community. The rise of the *'transnational private sector'* constitutes a genuine challenge to this situation. Much time and patience will no doubt be needed to form a combination of *'public'* and *'private'* action so as to include transnational forces in the decision-making process.

(b) *The spontaneity and variety which are among the most positive attributes of international associations, still constitute a handicap vis-à-vis the coalition of states and will continue to do so for a long time to come.*

Appendix Two

UN CONSULTATIVE ARRANGEMENTS

2.1 ECONOMIC AND SOCIAL COUNCIL RESOLUTION 1296 (XLIV) ON ARRANGEMENTS FOR CONSULTATION WITH NON-GOVERNMENTAL ORGANIZATIONS

The Economic and Social Council,
Having regard to Article 71 of the Charter of the United Nations,
Recognizing that arrangements for consultation with non-governmental organizations provide an important means of furthering the purposes and principles of the United Nations.
Considering that consultations between the Council and its subsidiary organs and the non-governmental organizations should be developed to the fullest practicable extent,
Approves the following arrangements, which supersede those set out in its resolution 288 B (X) of 27 February 1950:

ARRANGEMENTS FOR CONSULTATION WITH NON-GOVERNMENTAL ORGANIZATIONS

Part I
PRINCIPLES TO BE APPLIED IN THE ESTABLISHMENT OF CONSULTATIVE RELATIONS
The following principles shall be applied in establishing consultative relations with non-governmental organizations

1. The organization shall be concerned with matters falling within the competence of the Economic and Social Council with respect to international economic, social, cultural, educational, health, scientific, technological and related matters and to questions of human rights.
2. The aims and purposes of the organization shall be in conformity with the spirit, purposes and principles of the Charter of the United Nations.
3. The organization shall undertake to support the work of the United Nations and to promote knowledge of its principles and activities, in accordance with its own aims and purposes and the nature and scope of its competence and activities.

4. The organization shall be of representative character and of recognized international standing; it shall represent a substantial proportion, and express the views of major sections, of the population or of the organized persons within the particular field of its competence, covering, where possible, a substantial number of countries in different regions of the world. Where there exist a number of organizations with similar objectives, interests and basic views in a given field, they shall, for the purposes of consultation with the Council, form a joint committee or other body authorized to carry on such consultation for the group as a whole. It is understood that when a minority opinion develops on a particular point within such a committee, it shall be presented along with the opinion of the majority.
5. The organization shall have an established headquarters, with an executive officer. It shall have a democratically adopted constitution, a copy of which shall be deposited with the Secretary-General of the United Nations, and which shall provide for the determination of policy by a conference, congress or other representative body, and for an executive organ responsible to the policy-making body.
6. The organization shall have authority to speak for its members through its authorized representatives. Evidence of this authority shall be presented, if requested.
7. Subject to paragraph 9 below, the organization shall be international in its structure, with members who exercise voting rights in relation to the policies or action of the international organization. Any international organization which is not established by intergovernmental agreement shall be considered as a non-governmental organization for the purpose of these arrangements, including organizations which accept members designated by governmental authorities, provided that such membership does not interfere with the free expression of views of the organization.
8. The basic resources of the international organization shall be derived in the main part from contributions of the national affiliates or other components or from individual members. Where voluntary contributions have been received, their amounts and donors shall be faithfully revealed to the Council Committee on Non-Governmental Organizations. Where, however, the above criterion is not fulfilled and an organization is financed from other sources, it must explain to the satisfaction of the Committee its reasons for not meeting the requirements laid down in this paragraph. Any financial contribution or other support, direct or indirect, from a Government to the international organization shall be openly declared to the Committee through the Secretary-General and fully recorded in the financial and other records of the organization and

shall be devoted to purposes in accordance with the aims of the United Nations.

9. *National organizations shall normally present their views through international non-governmental organizations to which they belong. It would not, save in exceptional cases, be appropriate to admit national organizations which are affiliated to an international non-governmental organization covering the same subjects on an international basis. National organizations, however, may be admitted after consultation with the Member State concerned in order to help achieve a balanced and effective representation of non-governmental organizations reflecting major interests of all regions and areas of the world or where they have special experience upon which the Council may wish to draw.*
10. Consultative arrangements shall not normally be made with an international organization which is a member of a committee or group composed of international organizations with which consultative arrangements have been made.
11. In considering the establishment of consultative relations with a non-governmental organization, the Council will take into account whether the field of activity of the organization is wholly or mainly within the field of a specialized agency, and whether or not it could be admitted when it has, or may have, a consultative arrangement with a specialized agency.

Part II

PRINCIPLES GOVERNING THE NATURE OF THE CONSULTATIVE ARRANGEMENTS

12. *A clear distinction is drawn in the Charter of the United Nations between participation without vote in the deliberations of the Council and the arrangements for consultation. Under Articles 69 and 70, participation is provided for only in the case of States not members of the Council, and of specialized agencies. Article 71, applying to non-governmental organizations, provides for suitable arrangements for consultation. This distinction, deliberately made in the Charter, is fundamental and the arrangements for consultation should not be such as to accord to non-governmental organizations the same rights of participation as are accorded to States not members of the Council and to the specialized agencies brought into relationship with the United Nations.*
13. The arrangements should not be such as to overburden the Council or transform it from a body for co-ordination of policy and action, as contemplated in the Charter, into a general forum for discussion.
14. Decisions on arrangements for consultation should be guided by *the principle that consultative arrangements are to be made, on the one hand,*

for the purpose of enabling the Council or one of its bodies to secure expert information or advice from organizations having special competence in the subjects for which consultative arrangements are made, and, on the other hand, to enable organizations which represent important elements of public opinion in a large number of countries to express their views. Therefore, the arrangements for consultation made with each organization should involve only the subjects for which that organization has a special competence or in which it has a special interest. The organizations given consultative status should be limited to those whose international activities in fields set out in paragraph 1 above qualify them to make a significant contribution to the work of the Council and should, in sum, as far as possible *reflect in a balanced way the major viewpoints or interests in these fields in all areas and regions of the world.*

Part III
ESTABLISHMENT OF CONSULTATIVE RELATIONSHIPS

15. In establishing consultative relationships with each organization, regard shall be had to the nature and scope of its activities and to the assistance it may be expected to give to the Council or its subsidiary bodies in carrying out the functions set out in Chapters IX and X of the Charter of the United Nations.
16. In establishing consultative relations with organizations, the Council will distinguish between:
    (a) Organizations which are concerned with most of the activities of the Council and can demonstrate to the satisfaction of the Council that they have marked and sustained contributions to make to the achievement of the objectives of the United Nations in the fields set out in paragraph 1 above, and are closely involved with the economic and social life of the peoples of the areas they represent and whose membership, which should be considerable, is broadly representative of major segments of population in a large number of countries (to be known as organizations in general consultative status, category I);
    (b) Organizations which have a special competence in, and are concerned specifically with, only a few the fields of activity covered by the Council, which are known internationally within the fields for which they have or seek consultative status (to be known as organizations in special consultative status, category II).
17. Organizations accorded consultative status in category II because of their interest *in the field of human rights should have a general international concern with this matter, not restricted to the interests of a*

particular group of persons, a single nationality of the situation in a single State or restricted group States. Special consideration shall be given to the applications of organizations in this field whose aims place stress on combating colonialism, apartheid, racial intolerance and other gross violations of human rights and fundamental freedoms.

18. Major organizations one of whose primary purposes is to promote the aims, objectives and purposes of the United Nations and a furtherance of the understanding of its work may be accorded consultative status in category II.
19. Other organizations which do not have general or special consultative status but which the Council, or the Secretary-General of the United Nations, in consultation with the Council or its Committee on Non-Governmental Organizations, considers can make occasional and useful contributions to the work of the Council or its subsidiary bodies or other United Nations bodies within their competence shall be included in a list (to be known as the Roster). This list may also include organizations in consultative status or similar relationship with a specialized agency or a United Nations body. These organizations shall be available for consultation at the request of the Council or its subsidiary bodies. The fact that an organization is on the Roster shall not in itself be regarded as a qualification for general or special consultative should an organization seek such status.

Part IV

CONSULTATION WITH THE COUNCIL

Provisional agenda

20. The provisional agenda of the Council shall be communicated to organizations in categories I and II and to those on the Roster.
21. Organizations in category I may propose to the Council Committee on Non-Governmental Organizations that the Committee request the Secretary-General to place items of special interest to the organizations on the provisional agenda of the Council.
22. Organizations in categories I and II may designate authorized representatives to sit as observers at public meetings of the Council and its subsidiary bodies. Those on the Roster may have representatives present at such meetings concerned with matters within their field of competence.

WRITTEN STATEMENTS

23. Written statements relevant to the work of the Council may be submitted by organizations in categories I and II on subjects in which these

organizations have special competence. Such statements shall be circulated by the Secretary-General of the United Nations to the members of the Council, except those statements which have become obsolete, for example, those dealing with matters already disposed of and those which had already been circulated in some other form.

24. The following conditions shall be observed regarding the submission and circulation of such statements:

...

Hearings

25. (a) The Council Committee on Non-Governmental Organizations shall make recommendations to the Council as to which organizations in category I should be heard by the Council or by its sessional committees and on which items they should be heard. Such organizations shall be entitled to make one statement to the Council or the appropriate sessional committee, subject to the approval of the Council or of the sessional committee concerned. In the absence of a subsidiary body, of the Council with jurisdiction in a major field of interest to the Council and to an organization in category II, the Committee may recommend that an organization in category II be heard by the Council on the subject in its field of interest.

(b) Whenever the Council discusses the substance of an item proposed by a non-governmental organization in category I and included in the agenda of the Council, such an organization shall be entitled to present orally to the Council or a sessional committee of the Council, as appropriate, an introductory statement of an expository nature. Such an organization may be invited by the President of the Council or the Chairman of the committee, with the consent of the relevant body, to make, in the course of the discussion of the item before the Council or before the committee, an additional statement for purposes of clarification.

Part V

CONSULTATION WITH COMMISSIONS AND OTHER SUBSIDIARY ORGANS OF THE COUNCIL

26. The provisional agenda of sessions of commissions and other subsidiary organs of the Council shall be communicated to organizations in categories I and II and those on the Roster.

27. Organizations in category I may propose items for the provisional agenda of commissions, subject to the following conditions:

...

Attendance at Meetings

28. Organizations in categories I and II may designate authorized representatives to sit as observers at public meetings of the commissions and other subsidiary organs of the Council. Organizations on the Roster may have representatives present at such meetings which are concerned with matters within their field of competence.

Written Statements

29. Written statements relevant to the work of the commissions or other subsidiary organs may be submitted by organizations in categories I and II on subjects for which these organizations have a special competence. Such statements shall be circulated by the Secretary-General to members of the commission or other subsidiary organs, except those statements which have become obsolete, for example those dealing with matters already disposed of and those which have already been circulated in some other form to members of the commission or other subsidiary organs.
30. The following conditions shall be observed regarding the submission and circulation of such written statements:

    ...

Hearings

31. (a) The commission or other subsidiary organs may consult with organizations in categories I and II either directly or through a committee or committees established for the purpose. In all cases, such consultations may be arranged on the request of the organization.
    (b) On the recommendation of the Secretary-General and at the request of the commission or other subsidiary organs, organizations on the Roster may also be heard by the commission or other subsidiary organs.

Special Studies

32. Subject to the relevant rules of procedure on financial implications, a commission may recommend that an organization which has special competence in a particular field should undertake specific studies or investigations or prepare specific papers for the commission. The limitations of paragraph 30 (d) and (e) above shall not apply in this case.

Part VI
CONSULTATIONS WITH AD HOC COMMITTEES OF THE COUNCIL

33. The arrangements for consultation between ad hoc committees of the Council authorized to meet between sessions of the Council and organizations in categories I and II and on the Roster shall follow those approved for commissions of the Council, unless the Council or the committee decides otherwise.

Part VII
CONSULTATION WITH INTERNATIONAL CONFERENCES CALLED BY THE COUNCIL

34. The Council may invite non-governmental organizations in categories I and II and on the Roster to take part in conferences called by the Council under Article 62, paragraph 4, of the Charter of the United Nations. The organizations shall be entitled to the same rights and privileges and shall undertake the same responsibilities as at sessions of the Council itself, unless the Council decides otherwise.

Part VIII
SUSPENSION AND WITHDRAWAL OF CONSULTATIVE STATUS

35. Organizations granted consultative status by the Council and those on the Roster shall conform at all times to the principles governing the establishment and nature of their consultative relations with the Council. In periodically reviewing the activities of the non-governmental organizations on the basis of reports submitted under paragraph 40 (b) below and other relevant information, the Council Committee on Non-Governmental Organizations shall determine the extent to which the organizations have complied with the principles governing consultative status and have contributed to the work of the Council, and may recommend to the Council suspension or exclusion from consultative status of organizations which have not met the requirements for consultative status as set forth in the present resolution.
36. The consultative status of non-governmental organizations with the Economic and Social Council and the listing of those on the Roster shall be suspended up to three years or withdrawn in the following cases:
    (a) If there exists substantiated evidence of secret governmental financial influence to induce an organization to undertake acts contrary to the purposes and principles of the Charter of the United Nations;
    (b) If the organization clearly abuses its consultative status by systematically engaging in unsubstantiated or politically motivated acts

against States Members of the United Nations contrary to and incompatible with the principles of the Charter;

(c) If, within the preceding three years, an organization had not made any positive or effective contribution to the work of the Council or its commissions or other subsidiary organs.

37. The consultative status of organizations on the categories I and II and the listing of those on the Roster will be suspended or withdrawn by the decision of the Economic and Social Council on the recommendation of its Committee on Non-Governmental Organizations.

38. An organization whose consultative status or whose listing on the Roster is withdrawn may be entitled to reapply for consultative status or for inclusion on the Roster not sooner than three years after the effective date of such withdrawal.

Part IX

COUNCIL COMMITTEE ON NON-GOVERNMENTAL ORGANIZATIONS

39. The members of the Council Committee on Non-Governmental Organizations shall be elected at the first session of the Council each year, on the basis of equitable geographic representation, in accordance with Council resolution 1099 (XL) of 4 March 1966 and rule 82 of the rules of procedure of the Council. The Committee shall elect its Chairman and other officers as necessary. A member shall serve until the next election unless it ceases to be a member of the Council.

40. The functions of the Committee shall include the following:

(a) The Committee shall hold a session before the first session of the Council each year to consider applications for consultative status in categories I and II and for listing on the Roster made by non-governmental organizations and request for changes in status, and to make recommendations thereon to the Council. Organizations shall give due consideration to any comments on technical matters which the Secretary-General of the United Nations may make in receiving such applications for the Committee. The Committee shall consider at each such session applications received by the Secretary-General not later than June 1 of the preceding year, on which sufficient data have been distributed to the members of the Committee not later than six weeks before the applications are considered by the Committee at the earliest at its first session in the second year following the session at which the substance of the previous application or request was considered, unless at the time of such consideration it was decided otherwise.

(b) Organizations in consultative status in categories I and II shall submit to the Council Committee on Non-Governmental

Organizations through the Secretary-General every fourth year a brief report of their activities, specifically as regards the support they have given to the work of the United Nations, Based on findings of the Committee's examination of the report and other relevant information, the Committee may recommend to the Council any reclassification in status of the organization concerned as it deems appropriate. However, under exceptional circumstances, the Committee may ask for such a report from an individual organization in category I or II or on the Roster, between the regular reporting dates.

(c) The Committee may consult, in connexion with sessions of the Council or at such other times as it may decide, with organizations in categories I and II on matters within their competence, other than items on the agenda of the Council or the Committee or the organization requests consultation. The Committee shall report to the Council on such consultations.

(d) The Committee may consult, in connexion with any particular session of the Council, with organizations in categories I and II on matters within the competence of the organizations concerning specific items on the provisional agenda of the Council on which the Council of the Committee or the organization requests consultation, and shall make recommendation as to which organizations, subject to the provisions of paragraph 25 (a) above, should be heard by the Council or the appropriate committee and regarding which subjects should be heard, The Committee shall report to the Council on such consultations.

(e) The Committee shall consider matters concerning non-governmental organizations which may be referred to it by the Council or by commissions.

(f) The Committee shall consult with the Secretary-General, as appropriate, on matters affecting the consultative arrangements under Article 71 of the Charter, and arising therefrom.

41. The Committee, in considering a request from a non-governmental organization in category I that an item be placed on the agenda of the Council, shall take into account, among other things:

(a) The adequacy of the documentation submitted by the organization;

(b) The extent to which it is considered that the item lends itself to early and constructive action by the Council;

(c) The possibility that the item might be more appropriately dealt with elsewhere than in the Council.

42. Any decision by the Council Committee on Non-Governmental Organizations not to grant a request submitted by a non-governmental organization in category I that an item be placed on the provisional agenda of the Council shall be considered as final unless the Council decides otherwise.

Part X

CONSULTATION WITH THE SECRETARIAT

43. The Secretariat should be so organized as to enable it to carry out the duties assigned to it concerning the consultative arrangements as set forth in the present resolution.

44. All organizations in consultative relationship shall be able to consult with officers of the appropriate sections of the Secretariat on matters in which there is a mutual interest or a mutual concern. Such consultation shall be upon the request of the non-governmental organization or upon the request of the Secretary-General of the United Nations.

45. The Secretary-General may request organizations in categories I and II and those on the Roster to carry out specific studies or prepare specific papers, subject to the relevant financial regulations.

46. The Secretary-General shall be authorized, within the means at his disposal, to offer to non-governmental organizations in consultative relationship facilities which include:

(a) Prompt and efficient distribution of such documents of the Council and its subsidiary bodies as shall in the judgement of the Secretary-General be appropriate;

(b) Access to the press documentation services provided by the United Nations;

(c) Arrangement of informal discussions on matters of special interest to groups or organizations;

(d) Use of the libraries of the United Nations;

(e) Provision of accommodation for conferences or smaller meetings of consultative organizations on the work of the Economic and Social Council;

(f) Appropriate seating arrangements and facilities for obtaining documents during public meetings of the General Assembly dealing with matters in the economic and social fields.

1520th plenary meeting, 23 May 1968

2.2 ECONOMIC AND SOCIAL COUNCIL RESOLUTION 1996/31 ON CONSULTATIVE RELATIONSHIP BETWEEN THE UNITED NATIONS AND NON-GOVERNMENTAL ORGANIZATIONS

The Economic and Social Council,
Recalling Article 71 of the Charter of the United Nations,

Recalling also its resolution 1993/80 of 30 July 1993, in which it requested a general review of arrangements for consultation with non-governmental organizations, *with a view to updating, if necessary, Council resolution 1296 (XLIV) of 23 May 1968, as well as introducing coherence in the rules governing the participation of non-governmental organizations in international conferences convened by the United Nations, and also an examination of ways and means of improving practical arrangements for the work of the Committee on Non-Governmental Organizations and the Non-Governmental Organizations Section of the Secretariat,*

Recalling further its decision 1995/304 of 26 July 1995,

Confirming the need to take into account the full diversity of the non-governmental organizations at the national, regional and international levels,

Acknowledging the breadth of non-governmental organizations' expertise and the capacity of non-governmental organizations to support the work of the United Nations,

Taking into account *the changes in the non-governmental sector, including the emergence of a large number of national and regional organizations,*

Calling upon the governing bodies of the relevant organizations, bodies and specialized agencies of the United Nations system to examine the principles and practices relating to their consultations with non-governmental organizations and to take action, as appropriate, to promote coherence in the light of the provisions of the present resolution,

Approves the following update of the arrangements set out in its resolution 1296 (XLIV) of 23 May 1968:

ARRANGEMENTS FOR CONSULTATION WITH NON-GOVERNMENTAL ORGANIZATIONS

Part I
PRINCIPLES TO BE APPLIED IN THE ESTABLISHMENT OF CONSULTATIVE RELATIONS

The following principles shall be applied in establishing consultative relations with non-governmental organizations:

1. The organization shall be *concerned with matters falling within the competence of the Economic and Social Council* and its subsidiary bodies.
2. The *aims and purposes of the organization shall be in conformity with the spirit, purposes and principles of the Charter of the United Nations.*
3. The organization shall *undertake to support the work of the United Nations and to promote knowledge of its principles and activities*, in accordance with its own aims and purposes and the nature and scope of its competence and activities.
4. Except where expressly stated otherwise, *the term 'organization' shall refer to non-governmental organizations at the national, subregional, regional or international levels.*
5. *Consultative relationships may be established with international, regional, subregional and national organizations, in conformity with the Charter of the United Nations and the principles and criteria established under the present resolution. The Committee, in considering applications for consultative status, should ensure, to the extent possible, participation of non-governmental organizations from all regions*, and particularly from developing countries, in order to help achieve a just, balanced, effective and genuine involvement of non-governmental organizations from all regions and areas of the world. The Committee shall also pay *particular attention to non-governmental organizations that have special expertise or experience upon which the Council may wish to draw.*
6. Greater participation of non-governmental organizations from developing countries in international conferences convened by the United Nations should be encouraged.
7. Greater involvement of non-governmental organizations from countries with economies in transition should be encouraged.
8. Regional, subregional and national organizations, including those affiliated to an international organization already in status, may be admitted provided that they can demonstrate that their programme of work is of direct relevance to the aims and purposes of the United Nations and, *in the case of national organizations, after consultation with the Member State concerned.* The views expressed by the Member State, if any, shall be communicated to the non-governmental organization concerned, which shall have the opportunity to respond to those views through the Committee on Non-Governmental Organizations.
9. The organization shall be of *recognized standing within the particular field of its competence or of a representative character.* Where there exist a number of organizations with similar objectives, interests and basic views in a given field, they may, for the purposes of consultation with the Council, form a joint committee or other body authorized to carry on such consultation for the group as a whole.

10. The organization shall have an *established headquarters, with an executive officer.* It shall have a *democratically adopted constitution,* a copy of which shall be deposited with the Secretary-General of the United Nations, and which shall provide for the determination of policy by a conference, congress or other representative body, and for an executive organ responsible to the policy-making body.
11. The organization shall have authority to speak for its members through its authorized representatives. Evidence of this authority shall be presented, if requested.
12. The organization shall have *a representative structure* and possess *appropriate mechanisms of accountability to its members, who shall exercise effective control over its policies and actions through the exercise of voting rights or other appropriate democratic and transparent decision-making processes. Any such organization that is not established by a governmental entity or intergovernmental agreement shall be considered a non-governmental organization for the purpose of these arrangements, including organizations that accept members designated by governmental authorities, provided that such membership does not interfere with the free expression of views of the organization.*
13. The *basic resources of the organization shall be derived in the main part from contributions of the national affiliates or other components or from individual members. Where voluntary contributions have been received, their amounts and donors shall be faithfully revealed to the Council Committee on Non-Governmental Organizations.* Where, however, the above criterion is not fulfilled and an organization is financed from other sources, it must explain to the satisfaction of the Committee its reasons for not meeting the requirements laid down in this paragraph. *Any financial contribution or other support, direct or indirect, from a Government to the organization shall be openly declared to the Committee through the Secretary-General and fully recorded in the financial and other records of the organization and shall be devoted to purposes in accordance with the aims of the United Nations.*
14. In considering the establishment of consultative relations with a non-governmental organization, the Council will take into account whether the field of activity of the organization is wholly or mainly within the field of a specialized agency, and whether or not it could be admitted when it has, or may have, a consultative arrangement with a specialized agency.
15. *The granting, suspension and withdrawal of consultative status, as well as the interpretation of norms and decisions relating to this matter, are the prerogative of Member States exercised through the Economic and Social*

Council and its Committee on Non-Governmental Organizations. A non-governmental organization applying for general or special consultative status or a listing on the Roster shall have the opportunity to respond to any objections being raised in the Committee before the Committee takes its decision.

16. The provisions of the present resolution shall apply to the United Nations regional commissions and their subsidiary bodies mutatis mutandis.
17. In recognizing the evolving relationship between the United Nations and non-governmental organizations, the Economic and Social Council, in consultation with the Committee on Non-Governmental Organizations, will consider reviewing the consultative arrangements as and when necessary to facilitate, in the most effective manner possible, the contributions of non-governmental organizations to the work of the United Nations.

Part II
PRINCIPLES GOVERNING THE NATURE OF THE CONSULTATIVE ARRANGEMENTS

18. *A clear distinction is drawn in the Charter of the United Nations between participation without vote in the deliberations of the Council and the arrangements for consultation. Under Articles 69 and 70, participation is provided for only in the case of States not members of the Council, and of specialized agencies. Article 71, applying to non-governmental organizations, provides for suitable arrangements for consultation. This distinction, deliberately made in the Charter, is fundamental and the arrangements for consultation should not be such as to accord to non-governmental organizations the same rights of participation as are accorded to States not members of the Council and to the specialized agencies brought into relationship with the United Nations.*
19. The arrangements should not be such as to overburden the Council or transform it from a body for coordination of policy and action, as contemplated in the Charter, into a general forum for discussion.
20. *Decisions on arrangements for consultation should be guided by the principle that consultative arrangements are to be made, on the one hand, for the purpose of enabling the Council or one of its bodies to secure expert information or advice from organizations* having special competence in the subjects for which consultative arrangements are made, *and, on the other hand, to enable international, regional, subregional and national organizations that represent important elements of public opinion to express their views.* Therefore, *the arrangements for consultation made*

with each organization should relate to the subjects for which that organization has a special competence or in which it has a special interest. The organizations given consultative status should be limited to those whose activities in fields set out in paragraph 1 above qualify them to make a significant contribution to the work of the Council and should, in sum, as far as possible *reflect in a balanced way the major viewpoints or interests in these fields in all areas and regions of the world.*

Part III
ESTABLISHMENT OF CONSULTATIVE RELATIONSHIPS

21. In establishing consultative relationships with each organization, regard shall be had to the nature and scope of its activities and to the assistance it may be expected to give to the Council or its subsidiary bodies in carrying out the functions set out in Chapters IX and X of the Charter of the United Nations.
22. Organizations that are *concerned with most of the activities of the Council and its subsidiary bodies* and *can demonstrate to the satisfaction of the Council that they have substantive and sustained contributions to make to the achievement of the objectives of the United Nations* in fields set out in paragraph 1 above, and *are closely involved with the economic and social life of the peoples of the areas they represent* and *whose membership, which should be considerable, is broadly representative of major segments of society in a large number of countries in different regions* of the world shall be known as *organizations in general consultative status.*
23. Organizations that have *a special competence in, and are concerned specifically with, only a few of the fields of activity covered by the Council and its subsidiary bodies,* and that are *known within the fields for which they have or seek consultative status* shall be known as *organizations in special consultative status.*
24. Other organizations that *do not have general or special consultative status* but that *the Council, or the Secretary-General of the United Nations in consultation with the Council or its Committee on Non-Governmental Organizations, considers can make occasional and useful contributions to the work of the Council or its subsidiary bodies or other United Nations bodies* within their competence shall be *included in a list* (*to be known as the Roster*). This list may also include organizations in consultative status or a similar relationship with a specialized agency or a United Nations body. These organizations *shall be available for consultation at the request of the Council or its subsidiary bodies.* The fact that an organization is on the Roster *shall not in itself be regarded as a qualification*

for general or special consultative status should an organization seek such status.

25. Organizations to be accorded special consultative status because of their interest in the field of human rights should pursue the goals of promotion and protection of human rights in accordance with the spirit of the Charter of the United Nations, the Universal Declaration of Human Rights and the Vienna Declaration and Programme of Action.
26. Major organizations one of whose primary purposes is to promote the aims, objectives and purposes of the United Nations and a furtherance of the understanding of its work may be accorded consultative status.

Part IV
CONSULTATION WITH THE COUNCIL

Provisional Agenda

27. *The provisional agenda of the Council shall be communicated to organizations* in general consultative status and special consultative status and to those on the Roster.
28. Organizations in *general consultative status may propose to the Council Committee on Non-Governmental Organizations that the Committee request the Secretary-General to place items of special interest to the organizations in the provisional agenda of the Council.*

Attendance at Meetings

29. *Organizations in general consultative status and special consultative status may designate authorized representatives to sit as observers at public meetings of the Council and its subsidiary bodies.* Those on the *Roster may have representatives present at such meetings concerned with matters within their field of competence.* These attendance arrangements may be supplemented to include other modalities of participation.

Written Statements

30. *Written statements relevant to the work of the Council may be submitted by organizations in general consultative status and special consultative status on subjects in which these organizations have a special competence.* Such statements *shall be circulated by the Secretary-General of the United Nations to the members of the Council,* except those statements that have become obsolete, for example, those dealing with matters already disposed of and those that had already been circulated in some other form.

31. The following conditions shall be observed regarding the submission and circulation of such statements:

...

Oral Presentations during Meetings

32. (a) *The Council Committee on Non-Governmental Organizations shall make recommendations to the Council as to which organizations in general consultative status should make an oral presentation to the Council* and *on which items they should be heard*. Such organizations shall be entitled to make one statement to the Council, subject to the approval of the Council. In the absence of a subsidiary body of the Council with jurisdiction in a major field of interest to the Council and to organizations in special consultative status, *the Committee may recommend that organizations in special consultative status be heard by the Council on the subject in its field of interest*;
    (b) Whenever the Council discusses the substance of an item proposed by a non-governmental *organization in general consultative status* and included in the agenda of the Council, *such an organization shall be entitled to present orally to the Council*, as appropriate, an introductory statement of an expository nature. Such an organization may be invited by the President of the Council, with the consent of the relevant body, to make, in the course of the discussion of the item before the Council, an additional statement for purposes of clarification.

Part V
CONSULTATION WITH COMMISSIONS AND OTHER SUBSIDIARY ORGANS OF THE COUNCIL

Provisional Agenda

33. *The provisional agenda of sessions of commissions and other subsidiary organs of the Council shall be communicated to organizations in general consultative status and special consultative status and those on the Roster.*
34. *Organizations in general consultative status may propose items for the provisional agenda of commissions*, subject to the following conditions:

    ...

Attendance at Meetings

35. *Organizations in general consultative status and special consultative status may designate authorized representatives to sit as observers at public meetings of the commissions and other subsidiary organs of the Council.*

Organizations *on the Roster may have representatives present at such meetings that are concerned with matters within their field of competence.* These attendance arrangements may be supplemented to include other modalities of participation.

Written Statements

36. *Written statements relevant to the work of the commissions or other subsidiary organs may be submitted by organizations in general consultative status and special consultative status on subjects for which these organizations have a special competence.* Such statements shall be circulated by the Secretary-General to members of the commission or other subsidiary organs, except those statements that have become obsolete, for example, those dealing with matters already disposed of and those that have already been circulated in some other form to members of the commission or other subsidiary organs.
37. The following conditions shall be observed regarding the submission and circulation of such written statements:

 ...

Oral Presentations during Meetings

38. (a) *The commission or other subsidiary organs may consult with organizations in general consultative status and special consultative status either directly or through a committee or committees established for the purpose.* In all cases, *such consultations may be arranged upon the request of the organization*;
 (b) *On the recommendation of the Secretary-General and at the request of the commission or other subsidiary organs, organizations on the Roster may also be heard* by the commission or other subsidiary organs.

Special Studies

39. Subject to the relevant rules of procedure on financial implications, *a commission or other subsidiary organ may recommend that an organization that has special competence in a particular field should undertake specific studies or investigations or prepare specific papers for the commission.* The limitations of paragraphs 37 (d) and (e) above shall not apply in this case.

Part VI

CONSULTATIONS WITH AD HOC COMMITTEES OF THE COUNCIL

40. The arrangements for consultation between ad hoc committees of the Council authorized to meet between sessions of the Council and organizations in general consultative status and special consultative

status and on the Roster shall follow those approved for commissions of the Council, unless the Council or the committee decides otherwise.

Part VII

PARTICIPATION OF NON-GOVERNMENTAL ORGANIZATIONS IN INTERNATIONAL CONFERENCES CONVENED BY THE UNITED NATIONS AND THEIR PREPARATORY PROCESS

41. Where non-governmental organizations have been invited to participate in an international conference convened by the United Nations, *their accreditation is the prerogative of Member States, exercised through the respective preparatory committee.* Such accreditation should be *preceded by an appropriate process to determine their eligibility.*
42. *Non-governmental organizations in general consultative status, special consultative status and on the Roster, that express their wish to attend the relevant international conferences convened by the United Nations and the meetings of the preparatory bodies* of the said conferences *shall as a rule be accredited for participation.* Other non-governmental organizations wishing to be accredited may apply to the secretariat of the conference for this purpose in accordance with the following requirements.
43. *The secretariat of the conference shall be responsible for the receipt and preliminary evaluation of requests from non-governmental organizations for accreditation to the conference and its preparatory process.* In the discharge of its functions, the secretariat of the conference shall work in close cooperation and coordination with the Non-Governmental Organizations Section of the Secretariat, and shall be guided by the relevant provisions of Council resolution 1296 (XLIV) as updated.
44. All such applications must be accompanied by information on the competence of the organization and the relevance of its activities to the work of the conference and its preparatory committee, with an indication of the particular areas of the conference agenda and preparations to which such competence and relevance pertain, and should include, inter alia, the following information:
    (a) The purpose of the organization;
    (b) Information as to the programmes and activities of the organization in areas relevant to the conference and its preparatory process and the country or countries in which they are carried out. Non-governmental organizations seeking accreditation shall be asked to confirm their interest in the goals and objectives of the conference;

(c) Confirmation of the activities of the organization at the national, regional or international level;
(d) Copies of the annual or other reports of the organization with financial statements, and a list of financial sources and contributions, including governmental contributions;
(e) A list of members of the governing body of the organization and their countries of nationality;
(f) A description of the membership of the organization, indicating the total number of members, the names of organizations that are members and their geographical distribution;
(g) A copy of the constitution and/or by-laws of the organization.

45. In the evaluation of the relevance of applications of non-governmental organizations for accreditation to the conference and its preparatory process, it is agreed that *a determination shall be made based on their background and involvement in the subject areas of the conference.*

46. The secretariat shall publish and disseminate to Member States on a periodic basis the updated list of applications received. Member States may submit comments on any of the applications on the list 14 days from receipt of the above-mentioned list by Member States. The comments of Member States shall be communicated to the non-governmental organization concerned, which shall have the opportunity to respond.

47. In cases where the secretariat believes, on the basis of the information provided in accordance with the present resolution, that the organization has established its competence and the relevance of its activities to the work of the preparatory committee, it shall recommend to the preparatory committee that the organization be accredited. In cases where the secretariat does not recommend the granting of accreditation, it shall make available to the preparatory committee its reasons for not doing so. The secretariat should ensure that its recommendations are available to members of the preparatory committee at least one week prior to the start of each session. The secretariat must notify such applicants of the reasons for non-recommendation and provide an opportunity to respond to objections and furnish additional information as may be required.

48. The preparatory committee shall decide on all recommendations for accreditation within 24 hours after the recommendations of the secretariat have been taken up by the preparatory committee in plenary meeting. In the event of a decision not being taken within this period, interim accreditation shall be accorded until such time as a decision is taken.

49. A non-governmental organization that has been granted accreditation to attend a session of the preparatory committee, including related preparatory meetings of regional commissions, may attend all its future sessions, as well as the conference itself.
50. *In recognition of the intergovernmental nature of the conference and its preparatory process, active participation of non-governmental organizations therein, while welcome, does not entail a negotiating role.*
51. *The non-governmental organizations accredited to the international conference may be given, in accordance with established United Nations practice and at the discretion of the chairperson and the consent of the body concerned, an opportunity to briefly address the preparatory committee and the conference in plenary meetings and their subsidiary bodies.*
52. *Non-governmental organizations accredited to the conference may make written presentations during the preparatory process* in the official languages of the United Nations as they deem appropriate. Those written presentations *shall not be issued as official documents* except in accordance with United Nations rules of procedure.
53. Non-governmental organizations without consultative status that participate in international conferences and wish to obtain consultative status later on should apply through the normal procedures established under Council resolution 1296 (XLIV) as updated. Recognizing the importance of the participation of non-governmental organizations that attend a conference in the follow-up process, the Committee on Non-Governmental Organizations, in considering their application, shall draw upon the documents already submitted by that organization for accreditation to the conference and any additional information submitted by the non-governmental organization supporting its interest, relevance and capacity to contribute to the implementation phase. The Committee shall review such applications as expeditiously as possible so as to allow participation of the respective organization in the implementation phase of the conference. In the interim, the Economic and Social Council shall decide on the participation of non-governmental organizations accredited to an international conference in the work of the relevant functional commission on the follow-up to and implementation of that conference.
54. The suspension and withdrawal of the accreditation of non-governmental organizations to United Nations international conferences at all stages shall be guided by the relevant provisions of the present resolution.

Part VIII

SUSPENSION AND WITHDRAWAL OF CONSULTATIVE STATUS

55. *Organizations granted consultative status by the Council and those on the Roster shall conform at all times to the principles governing the establishment and nature of their consultative relations* with the Council. In *periodically reviewing the activities of non-governmental organizations on the basis of the reports* submitted under paragraph 61 (c) below *and other relevant information, the Council Committee on Non-Governmental Organizations shall determine the extent to which the organizations have complied with the principles governing consultative status and have contributed to the work of the Council,* and *may recommend to the Council suspension of or exclusion from consultative status of organizations that have not met the requirements for consultative status* as set forth in the present resolution.

56. In cases where the Committee on Non-Governmental Organizations has decided to recommend that the general or special consultative status of a non-governmental organization or its listing on the Roster be suspended or withdrawn, *the non-governmental organization concerned shall be given written reasons for that decision and shall have an opportunity to present its response* for appropriate consideration by the Committee as expeditiously as possible.

57. *The consultative status of non-governmental organizations with the Economic and Social Council and the listing of those on the Roster shall be suspended up to three years or withdrawn in the following cases*:
   (a) If an organization, either directly or through its affiliates or representatives acting on its behalf, *clearly abuses its status by engaging in a pattern of acts contrary to the purposes and principles of the Charter of the United Nations including unsubstantiated or politically motivated acts against Member States of the United Nations incompatible with those purposes and principles*;
   (b) If there exists *substantiated evidence of influence from proceeds resulting from internationally recognized criminal activities* such as the illicit drugs trade, money-laundering or the illegal arms trade;
   (c) If, *within the preceding three years, an organization did not make any positive or effective contribution to the work of the United Nations and, in particular, of the Council or its commissions or other subsidiary organs.*

58. *The consultative status of organizations in general consultative status and special consultative status and the listing of those on the Roster shall be suspended or withdrawn by the decision of the Economic and Social*

Council on the recommendation of its Committee on Non-Governmental Organizations.

59. *An organization whose consultative status or whose listing on the Roster is withdrawn may be entitled to reapply for consultative status or for inclusion on the Roster not sooner than three years after the effective date of such withdrawal.*

Part IX

COUNCIL COMMITTEE ON NON-GOVERNMENTAL ORGANIZATIONS

60. The members of the Committee on Non-Governmental Organizations *shall be elected by the Council on the basis of equitable geographical representation,* in accordance with the relevant Council resolutions and decision[4] and rules of procedure of the Council.[5] The Committee shall elect its Chairman and other officers as necessary.

61. The *functions of the Committee shall include* the following:

    (a) The Committee shall be responsible for *regular monitoring of the evolving relationship between non-governmental organizations and the United Nations.* With a view to fulfilling this responsibility, the Committee *shall hold, before each of its sessions, and at other times as necessary, consultations with organizations in consultative status to discuss questions of interest to the Committee or to the organizations relating to the relationship between the non-governmental organizations and the United Nations.* A report on such consultations shall be transmitted to the Council for appropriate action;

    (b) The Committee shall hold its *regular session* before the substantive session of the Council each year and preferably before the sessions of functional commissions of the Council to *consider applications for general consultative status and special consultative status and for listing on the Roster* made by non-governmental organizations and *requests for changes in status,* and to *make recommendations thereon to the Council.* Upon approval by the Council, the Committee may hold *other meetings as required to fulfill its mandated responsibilities.* Organizations shall give due consideration to any comments on technical matters that the Secretary-General of the United Nations may make in receiving such applications for the Committee. The Committee shall consider at each such session applications received by the Secretary-General not later than 1 June of the preceding year, on which sufficient data have been distributed to

---

[4] Council resolutions 1099 (XL) and 1981/50 and Council decision 1995/304.

[5] Rule 80 of the rules of procedure of the Council.

the members of the Committee not later than six weeks before the applications are to be considered. Transitional arrangements, if possible, may be made during the current year only. *Reapplication by an organization for status, or a request for a change in status,* shall be considered by the Committee at the earliest at its first session in the second year following the session at which the substance of the previous application or request was considered, unless at the time of such consideration it was decided otherwise;

(c) *Organizations in general consultative status and special consultative status shall submit to the Council Committee on Non-Governmental Organizations through the Secretary-General every fourth year a brief report of their activities, specifically as regards the support they have given to the work of the United Nations. Based on findings of the Committee's examination of the report and other relevant information, the Committee may recommend to the Council any reclassification* in status of the organization concerned *as it deems appropriate.* However, *under exceptional circumstances, the Committee may ask for such a report from an individual organization in general consultative status or special consultative status or on the Roster, between the regular reporting dates*;

(d) The Committee *may consult, in connection with sessions of the Council or at such other times as it may decide, with organizations in general consultative status and special consultative status on matters within their competence, other than items in the agenda of the Council, on which the Council or the Committee or the organization requests consultation.* The Committee shall report to the Council on such consultations;

(e) The Committee may consult, in connection with any particular session of the Council, with organizations in general consultative status and special consultative status on matters within the competence of the organizations concerning specific items already in the provisional agenda of the Council on which the Council or the Committee or the organization requests consultation, and shall make recommendations as to which organizations, subject to the provisions of paragraph 32 (a) above, should be heard by the Council or the appropriate committee and regarding which subjects should be heard. The Committee shall report to the Council on such consultations;

(f) The Committee *shall consider matters concerning non-governmental organizations that may be referred to it by the Council or by commissions*;

(g) The Committee *shall consult with the Secretary-General, as appropriate, on matters affecting the consultative arrangements under Article 71 of the Charter, and arising therefrom*;

(h) An organization that applies for consultative status should attest that it has been in existence for at least two years as at the date of receipt of the application by the Secretariat. Evidence of such existence shall be furnished to the Secretariat.

62. The Committee, *in considering a request from a non-governmental organization in general consultative status that an item be placed in the agenda of the Council*, shall take into account, among other things:

(a) The adequacy of the documentation submitted by the organization;

(b) The extent to which it is considered that the item lends itself to early and constructive action by the Council;

(c) The possibility that the item might be more appropriately dealt with elsewhere than in the Council.

63. *Any decision by the Council Committee on Non-Governmental Organizations not to grant a request submitted by a non-governmental organization in general consultative status that an item be placed in the provisional agenda of the Council shall be considered final* unless the Council decides otherwise.

Part X

CONSULTATION WITH THE SECRETARIAT

64. The Secretariat should be so organized as to enable it to carry out the duties assigned to it concerning the consultative arrangements and the accreditation of non-governmental organizations to United Nations international conferences as set forth in the present resolution.

65. All organizations in consultative relationship shall be able to consult with officers of the appropriate sections of the Secretariat on matters in which there is a mutual interest or a mutual concern. Such consultation shall be upon the request of the non-governmental organization or upon the request of the Secretary-General of the United Nations.

66. The Secretary-General may request organizations in general consultative status and special consultative status and those on the Roster to carry out specific studies or prepare specific papers, subject to the relevant financial regulations.

67. The Secretary-General shall be authorized, within the means at his disposal, to offer to non-governmental organizations in consultative relationship facilities that include:

(a) Prompt and efficient distribution of such documents of the Council and its subsidiary bodies as shall in the judgement of the Secretary-General be appropriate;
(b) Access to the press documentation services provided by the United Nations;
(c) Arrangement of informal discussions on matters of special interest to groups or organizations;
(d) Use of the libraries of the United Nations;
(e) Provision of accommodation for conferences or smaller meetings of consultative organizations on the work of the Economic and Social Council;
(f) Appropriate seating arrangements and facilities for obtaining documents during public meetings of the General Assembly dealing with matters in the economic, social and related fields.

Part XI
SECRETARIAT SUPPORT

68. Adequate Secretariat support shall be required for fulfilment of the mandate defined for the Committee on Non-Governmental Organizations with respect to carrying out the wider range of activities in which the enhanced involvement of non-governmental organizations is envisaged. The Secretary-General is requested to provide the necessary resources for this purpose and to take steps for improving the coordination within the Secretariat of units dealing with non-governmental organizations.
69. The Secretary-General is requested to make every effort to enhance and streamline as appropriate Secretariat support arrangements, and to improve practical arrangements on such matters as greater use of modern information and communication technology, *establishment of an integrated database of non-governmental organizations, wide and timely dissemination of information on meetings, distribution of documentation*, provision of access and transparent, simple and streamlined procedures for the attendance of non-governmental organizations in United Nations meetings, and to facilitate their broad-based participation.
70. The Secretary-General is requested to make the present resolution widely known, through proper channels, *to facilitate the involvement of non-governmental organizations from all regions and areas of the world.*

49th plenary meeting, 25 July 1996

Appendix Three

REGIONAL ARRANGEMENTS (COUNCIL OF EUROPE)

3.1 EUROPEAN CONVENTION ON THE RECOGNITION OF THE LEGAL PERSONALITY OF INTERNATIONAL NON-GOVERNMENTAL ORGANIZATIONS

Strasbourg, 24.IV.1986

Preamble

The member States of the Council of Europe, signatories hereto,

Considering that the aim of the Council of Europe is to achieve a greater unity between its members, in particular for the purpose of safe-guarding and realizing ideals and principles which are their common heritage;

Recognizing that international non-governmental organizations carry out work of value to the international community, particularly in the scientific, cultural, charitable, philanthropic, health and education fields, and that they contribute to the achievement of the aims and principles of the United Nations Charter and the Statute of the Council of Europe;

Desiring to establish in their mutual relations rules laying down the conditions for recognition of the legal personality of these organizations in order to facilitate their activities at European level,

Have agreed as follows:

ARTICLE 1

This Convention shall apply to associations, foundations and other private institutions (hereinafter referred to as "NGOs") which satisfy the following conditions:

a. have a non-profit-making aim of international utility;
b. have been established by an instrument governed by the internal law of a Party;
c. carry on their activities with effect in at least two States; and
d. have their statutory office in the territory of a Party and the central management and control in the territory of that Party or of another Party.

Article 2

1. The legal personality and capacity, as acquired by an NGO in the Party in which it has its statutory office, shall be recognized as of right in the other Parties.
2. When they are required by essential public interest, restrictions, limitations or special procedures governing the exercise of the rights arising out of the legal capacity and provided for by the legislation of the Party where recognition takes place, shall be applicable to NGOs established in another Party.

Article 3

1. The proof of acquisition of legal personality and capacity shall be furnished by presenting the NGO's memorandum and articles of association or other basic constitutional instruments. Such instruments shall be accompanied by documents establishing administrative authorization, registration or any other form of publicity in the Party which granted the legal personality and capacity. In a Party which has no publicity procedure, the instrument establishing the NGO shall be duly certified by a competent authority. At the time of signature or of the deposit of the instrument of ratification, acceptance, approval or accession, the State concerned shall inform the Secretary General of the Council of Europe of the identity of this authority.
2. In order to facilitate the application of paragraph 1, a Party may provide an optional system of publicity which shall dispense NGOs from furnishing the proof provided for in the preceding paragraph for each transaction that they carry out.

Article 4

In each Party the application of this Convention may only be excluded if the NGO invoking this Convention, by its object, its purpose or the activity which it actually exercises:

a. contravenes national security, public safety, or is detrimental to the prevention of disorder or crime, the protection of health or morals, or the protection of the rights and freedoms of others; or
b. jeopardizes relations with another State or the maintenance of international peace and security.

Article 5

1. This Convention shall be open for signature by the member States of the Council of Europe which may express their consent to be bound ...

   ...

Article 6

...

Article 7

1. After the entry into force of this Convention, the Committee of Ministers of the Council of Europe may invite any State not a member of the Council to accede to this Convention, by a decision taken by the majority provided for in Article 20.d of the Statute of the Council of Europe and by the unanimous vote of the representatives of the Contracting States entitled to sit on the Committee.

   ...

Article 8

...

Article 9

No reservation may be made to this Convention.

Article 10

1. Any Party may at any time denounce this Convention by means of a notification addressed to the Secretary General of the Council of Europe.
2. Such denunciation shall become effective on the first day of the month following the expiration of a period of three months after the date of receipt of the notification by the Secretary General.

Article 11

The Secretary General of the Council of Europe shall notify the member States of the Council and any State which has acceded to this Convention, of:

a. any signature;
b. the deposit of any instrument of ratification, acceptance, approval or accession;
c. any date of entry into force of this Convention in accordance with Articles 6, 7 and 8;
d. any other act, notification or communication relating to this Convention.

In witness whereof the undersigned, being duly authorized thereto, have signed this Convention.

Done at Strasbourg, this 24th day of April 1986, in English and French, both texts being equally authentic ...

3.2 EUROPEAN CONVENTION ON THE RECOGNITION OF THE LEGAL PERSONALITY OF INTERNATIONAL NON-GOVERNMENTAL ORGANISATIONS

Explanatory Report

I. ...

II. The text of the explanatory report prepared by the select committee of experts and submitted to the Committee of Ministers of the Council of Europe, as amended and completed by the Euroepan Committee on Legal Co-operation (CDCJ), *does not constitute an instrument providing an authoritative interpretation of the text of the Convention, although it might be of such a nature as to facilitate the understanding of the provisions contained therein.*

I. Introduction

1. Since 1945 the number of international non-governmental organisations (NGOs) has increased considerably. The variety of their aims has also multiplied. However, NGOs, unlike associations, foundations or other private institutions having aims and activities limited to one country, pursue their activities in several countries, hold meetings in diverse places, employ personnel of various nationalities, etc., because of the international nature of their aims. All these 'transnational' activities naturally create problems, and thus the difficulties encountered by NGOs are greater and more complicated than those faced by domestic associations, foundations or other private institutions. Although several attempts have been made to alleviate their difficulties at international level, there is as yet no international instrument in force.
2. The Council of Europe recognised, as early as in 1951, the importance of the NGOs, each in its particular field, and of their contribution to the

activities of the Organisation. It therefore adopted a resolution providing for consultation of NGOs on matters within the competence of the Council of Europe. This was followed by guidelines for granting consultative status to a group of NGOs in 1954 and finally in 1972 the Committee of Ministers of the Council of Europe adopted Resolution (72) 35 containing new rules on the Council of Europe's relations with NGOs, irrespective of whether they enjoy consultative status or not.

3. The Committee of Ministers of the Council of Europe, being equally aware of the absence of any international instrument in force aimed at facilitating the activities of NGOs at international level, charged in 1981, on the proposal of the European Committee on Legal Co-operation (CDCJ), a committee of experts with an exploratory mandate to study the possibility of an *intergovernmental action in this field at European level*. Acting on a CDCJ report based on the committee's work, the Committee of Ministers charged a select Committee of experts on international non- governmental organisations (CJ-R-OR) with the task of drawing up an appropriate instrument on NGOs.
4. ...

II. Commentary on the Articles of the Convention

Article 1

5. This article sets out to define *the conditions which an international non-governmental organisation must satisfy in order to qualify for the advantages conferred by the Convention.*
   These conditions, which *have to be satisfied permanently as a fundamental requirement for continuing to benefit from the recognition provided for in the Convention* are as follows:

a. Nature of the NGO

6. The NGO must be an association, a foundation or other private institution. In the law and practice of member States, an association means a number of persons uniting together for some specific purpose and which, when it has legal personality, also has separate identity to take legal action, to acquire property, to enter into contracts, etc. A foundation is an identified property devoted to a given purpose. The term 'other private institution' is added to cover certain institutions with legal personality (for example, religious congregations, trade unions, mutual companies) which in certain States have aims and structures similar to those of associations but which are not legally considered as such.
7. The introductory sentence to Article 1 makes it a requirement that associations, foundations and other institutions should be 'private'.

It follows that the Convention covers any entity which, whatever the legal nature of the provision of domestic law whereby an NGO is created (public law or private law in States where this distinction exists), *does not exercise prerogatives of a public authority.*

b. Non-profit-making aim of international utility

8. An NGO *must not have a profit-making aim*. This condition distinguishes NGOs from commercial companies or other bodies which exist to distribute financial benefits among their members. However, an NGO may make a profit, without altering its character, in connection with a given operation (for example, by renting a property, selling a publication, etc.) if that operation is to serve its non-profit-making aim. *Furthermore, the aim of an NGO must be of international utility and not simply of national or local utility, that is, it must be of benefit to the international community. This would therefore exclude political parties and other political organisations whose aims and activities are centred on the domestic problems of a given country.*
9. *The Convention does not define the expression 'international utility'. However, the Preamble to the Convention affords a number of useful pointers to its interpretation, since it refers to 'work of value to the international community', the requirement that it should contribute to achieving the aims and principles of the United Nations Charter and the Statute of the Council of Europe, and the scientific, cultural, etc., nature of the activity.* This last-mentioned element also makes it easier to circumscribe the concept of 'non-profit-making aim'.

c. Establishment by an instrument governed by internal law

10. In order to be covered by the Convention, *the instrument whereby an NGO is established must be governed by the internal law of a State. Consequently, organisations and institutions set up by treaties or other instruments governed by public international law are excluded.* This provision is *justified by the fact that such entities are subject to public international law and not to the domestic law of a contracting State, so that the problem of recognition by other states does not arise.*

d. Activities carried on in at least two States

11. This is *the logical consequence of the international nature of the non-profit-making aim of an NGO.* The important point here is that there is no requirement for activities to be carried on in at least two Council of Europe member states, but simply *in two different states*. Therefore NGOs established in a member state and carrying out their activities in another State which is not a member of the Council of Europe (for example, to fight famine in a third world country) are not excluded.

e. Statutory office in a contracting State

12. Sub-paragraph *d* lays down two conditions for the NGO to benefit from the Convention: it *must have its statutory office in a contracting State and the central management and control in that State or another contracting State.* The first requirement is developed in Article 2, which is the fundamental article of the Convention (see paragraphs 13–15 below). The second requirement was adopted in order to protect the interests of persons concluding contracts with an NGO by ensuring that some of its assets are located in a contracting State.

Article 2

13. Paragraph 1 of the article lays down *the rule of recognition as of right in all contracting States of the legal personality and capacity acquired in one contracting State.* Consequently, *no special procedure has to be followed* to obtain recognition of legal personality.

    The principle is that *the law which governs the substance of the NGO's legal personality and capacity is the law of the State in which the statutory office of the NGO, as stated in the memorandum and articles of association, is situated.*

14. The fundamental criterion of the statutory office was adopted for two main reasons. The first of these is the fact that *in deciding on its statutory office the NGO manifested a wish to be subject to a given system of law, and that wish should be respected.* The second reason is an essentially practical one, since this principle makes it possible to avoid any break in continuity in the legal personality of an NGO when its real seat changes because the newly elected president or secretary general resides in another State.

15. The principle of the statutory office does of course entail an important change in the law of States where the rules of private international law are based on the concept of the real seat.

    Such a change is justified not only on practical grounds (to avoid situations in which the applicable law changes too often when the administrative seat changes) but also by the fact that the Council of Europe is a community where respect for human rights and democratic principles constitutes the unifying element, that is, a homogeneous legal grouping characterised by a measure of mutual recognition as between legal systems. In addition, the economic reasons underlying the principle of the real seat in the case of commercial companies are less important in the case of NGOs, which pursue non-profit-making aims.

16. *The principle of the statutory office means that the NGO will have the same legal capacity and personality in all the contracting States as are required in the State where that office is located.*
17. However, it was recognised that *such a rule could not be an absolute one.* In some States, important public interests are at the root of some restrictions or special procedures applied to, the exercise of rights which together constitute legal capacity. For example, some States require that authorisation be granted for the acquisition of real estate. These *restrictions, limitations or special procedures laid down by domestic law for national entities analogous to foreign NGOs may be applicable to the latter by virtue of paragraph 2 when they are required by essential public interest.*
    It should be noted that these must be restrictions or limitations not on the legal capacity per se but on the 'exercise' of the rights through which legal capacity manifests itself.
18. Furthermore, *if a State lays down general limits applicable to all foreigners, an NGO which has obtained legal personality in another State will be subject to those limits.*

Article 3

19. This article deals with the question of proof of the NGO's existence to be presented to the authorities of the State in which the NGO wishes to be recognised. When it seeks recognition in another State an NGO is to supply evidence that it has already been established in the State of its statutory office and enjoys legal personality and capacity.
20. ...
21. ...
22. ...

Article 4

23. This article constitutes a guarantee clause designed to *counterbalance the effects of automatic recognition of legal personality.*
    It should be noted that the application of this article is independent of the application of Article 1.
24. Article 1 (see paragraph 5 et seq. above) sets out *the conditions which have to be satisfied in order to invoke the Convention. These conditions must be met not only at the time when the NGO is seeking recognition but also throughout the period of that NGO's activity in a State. Failure to satisfy any of these conditions automatically removes the right to invoke the Convention.*

On the other hand, Article 4 can apply even if the conditions of Article 1 are met.

25. It was decided not to refer generically to the 'public policy' (*ordre public*) of the State but, following the example of Article 11, paragraph 2, of the European Convention on Human Rights, to specify the grounds on which a refusal of the recognition of legal personality in another State can be based.
26. This was done in order to avoid using the expression 'public policy' (*ordre public*) which can give rise to difficulties where NGOs are concerned. In some States the concept of public policy is twofold: the first meaning encompasses all binding national rules, while the second concept refers only to the fundamental legal principles of the legal system (this second concept being 'public policy as defined in private international law').

    The first concept would mean that an NGO which did not satisfy any binding provision of domestic law could not be recognised. If the second concept were employed, recognition could only be withheld for infringement of a fundamental principle of the legal system.
27. The concept of public policy as defined in private international law could of course have been used in Article 4, but it is not a concept known to the legal systems of all States. Consequently, the enumeration based on Article 11 of the European Convention on Human Rights has been adopted.
28. In order to complete the grounds contained in sub-paragraph *a*, which are of an internal character, sub-paragraph *b* introduces an international element.

    It would in fact be unacceptable, in view of the ideals of peace and democracy enshrined in the Council of Europe's Statute, for an NGO to be accepted in a State where its activities would be legal when it is common knowledge that the aim of that NGO is to engage, either in the State in question or in another State, in activities which would damage the latter. This would run counter to the development of peace and good relations between States.

3.3 COUNCIL OF EUROPE, COMMITTEE OF MINISTERS, RESOLUTION RES(2003)8 ON PARTICIPATORY STATUS FOR INTERNATIONAL NON-GOVERNMENTAL ORGANISATIONS WITH THE COUNCIL OF EUROPE

(Adopted by the Committee of Ministers on 19 November 2003 at the 861st meeting of the Ministers' Deputies)

The Committee of Ministers,

Recalling the Council of Europe statutory aim to achieve a closer unity between its members for the purpose of safeguarding and realising the ideals and principles which are their common heritage, and facilitating their economic and social progress;

Bearing in mind the missions entrusted to the Council of Europe by the Vienna and Strasbourg Summits and by the Budapest Declaration for a Greater Europe without Dividing Lines;

Considering that the achievement of this goal and the fulfilment of these missions cannot be realised without *constant sensitivity to public opinion and to the driving forces in European society, which are constantly evolving*;

Considering that *the existence of an active civil society and its non-governmental organisations (hereafter NGOs), which are a vital component of European society, is an important and indispensable element of democracy*;

Considering *the essential role of counterbalance played by NGOs in a pluralist democracy, to intensify the active participation of all citizens in conducting public affairs, and promoting responsible democratic citizenship* based on human rights and equality between women and men;

Convinced that *initiatives, ideas and suggestions emanating from civil society can be considered as a true expression of European citizens*;

Recalling that, in this spirit, the Council of Europe has, over the years, developed fruitful working relations with NGOs since it first created a consultative status for international non-governmental organisations in 1952;

Considering that the system of co-operation introduced by consultative status largely permitted the development and strengthening of co-operation between the Council of Europe and the voluntary sector, giving positive and particularly encouraging results for both parties;

Considering that it is indispensable that *the rules governing the relations between the Council of Europe and NGOs evolve to reflect the active participation of international non-governmental organisations (INGOs) in the Organisation's policy and work programme*, and *to facilitate INGO participation and access to such bodies as the steering committees and governmental expert committees, and other subsidiary bodies of the Committee of Ministers*. This participation will allow the INGOs to continue to draw the Council of Europe's attention to the effects of changes in European societies and the problems facing them;

Noting that the development and reinforcement of this co-operation between INGOs and the Committee of Ministers and its subsidiary bodies, as well as with the Parliamentary Assembly and the Congress of Local and

Regional Authorities of Europe has led to the "Quadrilogue" which is, within the Council of Europe, an expression of democratic pluralism and an essential element for the further development of a citizens' Europe;

Wishing, through the present rules, to reflect the active and constructive role of NGOs, and *to clarify, facilitate and intensify the co-operation between the Council of Europe and the INGOs, in particular underlining its participatory character*;

Recognising the important role to be played by the Liaison Committee as the democratically elected representative body of all of the INGOs enjoying participatory status with the Council of Europe, and by the INGO thematic groupings as their collective voice and, thus, of millions of European citizens, working in each of the fields represented by them;

Recognising the importance of the co-operation between the Council of Europe and national NGOs, provided for in Resolution Res(2003)9 on the status of partnership between the Council of Europe and national NGOs;

Hereby decides to *adopt the rules for participatory status appended to this resolution which replace the rules for consultative status* established by Resolution (93) 38.

Appendix to Resolution Res(2003)8

Rules for participatory status for INGOs at the Council of Europe

1. The Council of Europe may establish working relations with INGOs by granting them participatory status.

Conditions to be met by INGOs

2. Participatory status may be granted by the Council of Europe to INGOs:
   a. which are *particularly representative in the field(s) of their competence*, fields of action shared by the Council of Europe;
   b. which are *represented at European level*, that is to say which have *members in a significant number of countries throughout greater Europe*;
   c. which are able, through their work, to support the achievement of that closer unity mentioned in Article 1 of the Council of Europe's Statute;
   d. are capable of contributing to and participating actively in Council of Europe deliberations and activities;
   e. which are able to make known the work of the Council of Europe among European citizens.

Modalities of co-operation

3. The INGOs with participatory status *may be invited to be represented* by the Liaison Committee or the thematic groupings *at events organised by the Secretariat General.*
4. The steering committees, committees of governmental experts and other bodies of the Committee of Ministers, *may involve the INGOs enjoying participatory status in the definition of Council of Europe policies, programmes and actions in particular by granting observer status to the Liaison Committee and to the INGO thematic groupings*, in accordance with the terms of Committee of Ministers' Resolution (76) 3.
5. The committees of the Parliamentary Assembly and of the Congress of Local and Regional Authorities of Europe are invited to study ways of intensifying co-operation with and facilitating INGO participation in their work, for example *by granting observer status or by inviting the Liaison Committee or INGO thematic groupings to provide their expertise.*
6. The Commissioner for Human Rights is also encouraged to maintain close co-operation with the INGOs enjoying participatory status.
7. Additionally, considering their role as advisers in questions concerning civil society, *the Secretary General may consult the INGOs, the Liaison Committee or the INGO thematic groupings, in writing or by means of a hearing, on questions of mutual interest.*
8. The INGOs enjoying participatory status:
   a. may *address memoranda* to the Secretary General for submission to the committees mentioned above, as well as to the Commissioner for Human Rights;
   b. may be invited to provide, through their specific activity or experience, *expert advice* on Council of Europe policies, programmes and actions;
   c. shall *receive the agenda* and public documents of the Parliamentary Assembly in order to facilitate their *attendance at public sittings* of the Parliamentary Assembly;
   d. shall be *invited to public sittings* of the Congress of Local and Regional Authorities of Europe;
   e. shall be invited to activities organised for them by the Secretariat;
   f. shall be invited to attend seminars, conferences, colloquies of interest to their work according to the applicable Council of Europe rules.
9. The INGOs enjoying participatory status shall undertake to:
   a. keep themselves regularly informed of Council of Europe activities and developments in standards by means of the numerous sources of information available, including the Internet;

b. furnish, either spontaneously or at the request of the Council of Europe's different bodies, information, documents or opinions relating to their own field(s) of competence on matters which are under consideration or which could be addressed by the Council of Europe;

c. work to promote the respect of the Council of Europe's standards, conventions and legal instruments in the member states, and assist in the implementation of these standards, and this in close contact with local, regional and national NGOs;

d. give maximum publicity to the initiatives and achievements of the Council of Europe in their own field(s) of competence;

e. disseminate information on Council of Europe standards, instruments and activities, as well as information from the INGO thematic groupings, to their members, on a regular basis, and ensure that they too work actively to fulfil the requirements of the participatory status;

f. submit every four years a report to the Secretary General which should specify:

- their participation in the work of the various Council of Europe bodies (see paragraphs 4 and 6 of this appendix), the capacity in which they attended and their contribution;
- their attendance at events organised by the Secretariat General, the capacity in which they attended, the contribution they made and any follow-up action;
- their attendance at and contributions to the meetings of the INGO thematic groupings;
- any meetings which they themselves have organised, in particular those which have dealt with the promotion of the Council of Europe's aims, standards and legal instruments;
- any action they have undertaken with a view to ensuring respect of Council of Europe standards and to publicising its work.

Procedure for the granting of participatory status

10. The Secretary General shall keep the list of INGOs enjoying participatory status with the Council of Europe.

11. Any INGO wishing to be entered on this list shall submit to the Secretary General of the Council of Europe three copies of an application, in French or English, and, preferably, in both of these official languages of the Council of Europe, which must contain the following documents:

a. the INGO's statute;
b. a list of its member organisations with a French or English translation of the title of these organisations as well as an approximate number of members of each of these organisations;
c. a report on its activities covering the previous two years;
d. a declaration to the effect that it accepts the principles set out in the statute and other basic texts of the Council of Europe;
e. the official application form on which it states clearly:
  - why it is applying for participatory status with the Council of Europe;
  - how it considers it will be able to contribute to and participate in the activities of the Council of Europe (as set out in its current programme of activities);
  - in what way it feels able to make such a contribution (studies, reports, previous work in the field concerned, expertise of its members in the area concerned, etc.);
  - what practical co-operation has already been established with the Council of Europe departments concerned;
  - by what means and to which audience it would publicise the work of the Council of Europe.

12. *The decision to grant participatory status to an INGO shall be taken by the Secretary General* of the Council of Europe *based on the criteria mentioned above.* The Secretary General may also take into consideration the main priorities of the Council of Europe's programme of activities and the possible proliferation of INGOs in a given sector of activity.
13. The Secretary General will communicate the list of INGOs to which he or she intends to grant participatory status to the INGO Liaison Committee for its opinion. The INGO Liaison Committee's opinion must be expressed within two months of the Secretary General's Communication.
14. At the end of this time-limit, *the decision of the Secretary General will be submitted for tacit approval* to the Committee of Ministers, to the Parliamentary Assembly and to the Congress of Local and Regional Authorities. This decision will be accompanied by the names of the INGOs concerned, those items from the relevant files which are necessary for the assessment of each case, the Secretary General's reasons for suggesting they be added to the list, as well as any comments received from the Liaison Committee. In the absence of any objection founded on the conditions set out in paragraph 15 below, the said INGOs will be added three months later to the list of those enjoying participatory status.
15. During the three-month period, a member of the Committee of Ministers or ten members of the Parliamentary Assembly from five different

national delegations or ten members of the Congress of Local and Regional Authorities of Europe from five different national delegations may request that an examination be made of the file of any applicant INGO. In the former case, the examination shall be made and the decision to add the name to the list shall be taken by the Committee of Ministers. In the latter case, the Committee of Ministers shall defer its decision until it has received a recommendation from the Parliamentary Assembly or the Congress of Local and Regional Authorities of Europe acting on a report from their competent committees.

Withdrawal of participatory status

16. Any INGO already on the list may be removed from it by the Secretary General if, in his or her opinion:
    a. it has failed to comply with its obligations under the rules set out in paragraphs 2 and 9 above;
    b. it is represented twice as a result of affiliation to a larger organisation working in the same field of activity which is itself on the list;
    c. no longer has any activity included in the Council of Europe's work programme;
    d. it has taken any action which is not in keeping with its status as an INGO.

    To this end, the Secretary General shall review periodically the list of INGOs with participatory status. The review shall be based on the report submitted by the INGOs every four years.
    However, the Secretary General shall first inform the INGO in question of his or her intention to withdraw its participatory status in order to give it an opportunity to present its observations within two months.
17. The reasoned decision to remove an organisation from the list shall be taken by the Secretary General of the Council of Europe in accordance with the above rules.
18. The Secretary General will communicate the list of INGOs from which he or she intends to withdraw participatory status to the INGO Liaison Committee for its opinion. The Liaison Committee's opinion must be expressed within two months of the Secretary General's communication.
19. At the end of this time limit, the decision of the Secretary General will be submitted for tacit approval to the Committee of Ministers, to the Parliamentary Assembly and to the Congress of Local and Regional Authorities. This decision will be accompanied by the names of the INGOs concerned and his or her reasons for suggesting they be removed from the list of those enjoying participatory status, as well as any

comments received from the Liaison Committee. In the absence of any objection founded on the conditions described in paragraph 15 above, the names of the INGOs that have thus been communicated shall be removed from the list three months later.

20. During the three-month period, a member of the Committee of Ministers or ten members of the Parliamentary Assembly from five different national delegations or ten members of the Congress of Local and Regional Authorities of Europe from five different national delegations may request that an examination be made of the file of each INGO whose name has been communicated to them. In the former case, the examination shall be made and the decision to remove the name from the list shall be taken by the Committee of Ministers. In the latter, the Committee of Ministers shall defer its decision until it has received a recommendation from the Parliamentary Assembly or the Congress of Local and Regional Authorities of Europe acting on a report from their competent committees.

Sundry provisions

21. The procedures described above shall not restrict the right of the Council of Europe bodies to initiate any action concerning other NGOs in pursuance of their respective rules of procedure.
    It should also not prevent the Secretariat of the Council of Europe from considering practical co-operation on an ad hoc basis with other NGOs in any field of mutual interest.
22. An INGO whose application has been refused or which has been removed from the list of those enjoying participatory status may submit a fresh application only after a period of two years following the date of the decision.
23. The present rules will enter into force following their adoption by the Committee of Ministers. From that date, *the INGOs enjoying consultative status will have participatory status.*
24. The INGOs enjoying participatory status will be required to submit their first report four years after the entry into force of these rules.

3.4 COUNCIL OF EUROPE, COMMITTEE OF MINISTERS, RESOLUTION RES(2003)9 ON STATUS OF PARTNERSHIP BETWEEN THE COUNCIL OF EUROPE AND NATIONAL NON-GOVERNMENTAL ORGANISATIONS

(*Adopted by the Committee of Ministers on 19 November 2003 at the 861st meeting of the Ministers' Deputies*)

The Committee of Ministers,

Recalling the Council of Europe statutory aim to achieve closer unity between its members for the purpose of safeguarding and realising the ideals and principles which are their common heritage, and facilitating their economic and social progress;

Bearing in mind the missions entrusted to the Council of Europe by the Vienna and Strasbourg Summits and by the Budapest Declaration for a Greater Europe without Dividing Lines;

Considering that the achievement of this goal and the fulfilment of these missions cannot be realised without constant sensitivity to public opinion and to the driving forces in European society, which are constantly evolving;

Considering that the existence of an active civil society and its non-governmental organisations (hereafter NGOs), which are a vital component of European society, is an important and indispensable element of democracy;

Considering the essential role of counterbalance played by NGOs in a pluralist democracy, to intensify the active participation of all citizens in conducting public affairs, and promoting responsible democratic citizenship based on human rights and equality between women and men;

Convinced that initiatives, ideas and suggestions emanating from civil society can be considered as a true expression of European citizens;

Recalling that, in this spirit, the Council of Europe has, over the years, developed fruitful working relations with NGOs since it first created a consultative status for international non-governmental organisations in 1952;

Considering the need to support the development and consolidation of a strong civil society attached to democratic values;

Recognising that a number of activities in the Council of Europe's Programme of Activities have been carried out in partnership with national and international NGOs, reflecting not only a general effort to strengthen a democratic and open society, but also the extent to which civil society itself has developed in those countries;

Wishing, *through the present rules, to take account of the active and constructive role of national NGOs in the implementation of the Council of Europe's Programme of Activities*, and *to recognise this co-operation, in particular by underlining its partnership character*;

Wishing, therefore, *to complement Resolution Res(2003)8 on participatory status for international NGOs* at the Council of Europe;

Hereby decides to adopt the *rules for the partnership between the Council of Europe and national NGOs*, as appended to this Resolution.

Appendix to Resolution Res(2003)9

Rules for the partnership between the Council of Europe and national NGOs

1. The Council of Europe may establish *working relations with national NGOs by concluding partnership agreements.*

Conditions to be met by national NGOs

2. *Partnership agreements* may be established by the Council of Europe *with national NGOs*:
   a. which are *particularly representative in the field(s) of their competence*, fields of action shared by the Council of Europe;
   b. which are able, through their work, to support the achievement of that closer unity mentioned in Article 1 of the Statute of the Council of Europe;
   c. which are able to make known the work of the Council of Europe in their country.

Modalities of co-operation

3. Partnership agreements may be concluded by the Council of Europe with national NGOs:
   a. which are capable of contributing, *through a specific project or programme*, to the implementation of its programme of activities, in particular those aimed at the *development and consolidation of democratic stability*;
   b. which are capable of contributing, *through a specific event or manifestation* linked to a Council of Europe field of activity, to *public awareness-raising and/or strengthening of the European idea*;
   c. which are capable of providing, through their specific activity or experience, *expert advice on the definition of Council of Europe policies, programmes and actions.*
4. The national NGOs with which partnership agreements have been concluded:
   a. have the possibility to *attend the public sittings* of the Parliamentary Assembly and the Congress of Local and Regional Authorities of Europe;
   b. have the possibility to *attend seminars, conferences and hearings of interest* to their work according to the applicable Council of Europe rules;
   c. regularly *disseminate information* to their members on the standards, activities and achievements of the Council of Europe in their own field(s) of competence;

d. furnish, either spontaneously or at the request of the Council of Europe's different bodies, *information, documents or opinions* relating to their own field(s) of competence.

Procedure for partnership agreements

5. The Secretary General keeps the list of national NGOs with which partnership agreements have been concluded.
   a. He or she may enter on this list all national NGOs with which the Council of Europe has specific agreements for the implementation of programmes, projects or events falling within the Council of Europe's programme of activities, and in particular those aiming at the development and consolidation of democratic stability.
   b. The list shall be updated every two years and shall be communicated to the Committee of Ministers, the Parliamentary Assembly, the Congress of Local and Regional Authorities of Europe, the Commissioner for Human Rights and the Liaison Committee of the International NGOs enjoying participatory status with the Council of Europe.
   c. The Secretary General may remove from the list those national NGOs having ceased their partnership relations with the Council of Europe or not fulfilling their obligations under the above- mentioned agreements.

Sundry provisions

6. The present rules will enter into force following their adoption by the Committee of Ministers for an initial period of five years after which the implementation of this Resolution shall be evaluated.

Appendix Four

NEW INITIATIVES

4.1 INTERNATIONAL NON GOVERNMENTAL ORGANIZATIONS ACCOUNTABILITY CHARTER (*2006*)

International NGO Charter of Accountability Ltd.
www.ingoaccountabilitycharter.org

Who We Are

We, international non-government organizations (INGOs) signatory to this Charter, are independent non-profit organizations that work globally to advance human rights, sustainable development, environmental protection, humanitarian response and other public goods.

Our organizations are proud and privileged to work across a wide range of countries and cultures, with a diverse range of peoples and in varied eco- and social and political systems.

Our right to act is based on universally-recognized freedoms of speech, assembly and association, on our contribution to democratic processes, and on the values we seek to promote.

Our legitimacy is also derived from the quality of our work, and the recognition and support of the people with and for whom we work and our members, our donors, the wider public, and governmental and other organizations around the world.

We seek to uphold our legitimacy by responding to inter-generational considerations, public and scientific concerns, and through accountability for our work and achievements.

By signing this Charter we seek to promote further the values of transparency and accountability that we stand for, and commit our INGO to respecting its provisions.

How We Work

NGOs can complement but not replace the over-arching role and primary responsibility of governments to promote equitable human development and well- being, to uphold human rights and to protect ecosystems.

We also seek to promote the role and responsibilities of the private sector to advance human rights and sustainable development, and protect the environment.

We can often address problems and issues that governments and others are unable or unwilling to address on their own. Through constructive challenge, we seek to promote good governance and foster progress towards our goals.

We seek to advance our mission through research, advocacy and programmes. It is common for our work to be at the international, national, regional and local levels, either directly or with partners.

We work with other organizations where this is the best way to advance our individual missions.

The Charter's Purpose

This Charter outlines our common commitment to excellence, transparency and accountability. To demonstrate and build on these commitments, we seek to:

- identify and define shared principles, policies and practices;
- enhance transparency and accountability, both internally and externally;
- encourage communication with stakeholders; and
- improve our performance and effectiveness as organizations.

We recognize that transparency and accountability are essential to good governance, whether by governments, businesses or non-profit organizations.

Wherever we operate, we seek to ensure that the high standards which we demand of others are also respected in our own organizations.

The Charter complements and supplements existing laws. It is a voluntary charter, and draws on a range of existing codes, norms, standards and guidelines.

We agree to apply the Charter progressively to all our policies, activities and operations. The Charter does not replace existing codes or practices to which signatories may also be party, except as specified by them. Its adoption does not prevent signatories from supporting or using other tools to promote transparency and accountability.

We will refine the Charter through experience, taking into account future developments, particularly those that improve accountability and transparency.

Our Stakeholders

Our first responsibility is to achieve our stated mission effectively and transparently, consistent with our values. In this, we are accountable to our stakeholders.

Our stakeholders include:

- Peoples, including future generations, whose rights we seek to protect and advance;
- Ecosystems, which cannot speak for or defend themselves;
- Our members and supporters;
- Our staff and volunteers;
- Organizations and individuals that contribute finance, goods or services;
- Partner organizations, both governmental and non-governmental, with whom we work;
- Regulatory bodies whose agreement is required for our establishment and operations;
- Those whose policies, programmes or behaviour we wish to influence;
- The media; and
- The general public.
- In balancing the different views of our stakeholders, we will be guided by our mission and the principles of this Charter.

Principles

Respect for Universal Principles

INGOs are founded on the rights to freedom of speech, assembly and association in the Universal Declaration of Human Rights. We seek to advance international and national laws that promote human rights, ecosystem protection, sustainable development and other public goods.

Where such laws do not exist, are not fully implemented, or abused, we will highlight these issues for public debate and advocate appropriate remedial action.

In so doing, we will respect the equal rights and dignity of all human beings.

Independence

We aim to be both politically and financially independent. Our governance, programmes and policies will be non-partisan, independent of specific governments, political parties and the business sector.

Responsible Advocacy

We will ensure that our advocacy is consistent with our mission, grounded in our work and advances defined public interests.

We will have clear processes for adopting public policy positions, (including for partners where appropriate,) explicit ethical policies that guide our choices of advocacy strategy, and ways of identifying and managing potential conflicts of interest among various stakeholders.

Effective Programmes

We seek to work in genuine partnership with local communities, NGOs and other organizations aiming at sustainable development responding to local needs.

Non-Discrimination

We value, respect and seek to encourage diversity, and seek to be impartial and non- discriminatory in all our activities. To this end, each organization will have policies that promote diversity, gender equity and balance, impartiality and non-discrimination in all our activities, both internal and external.

Transparency

We are committed to openness, transparency and honesty about our structures, mission, policies and activities. We will communicate actively to stakeholders about ourselves, and make information publicly available.

Reporting

We seek to comply with relevant governance, financial accounting and reporting requirements in the countries where we are based and operate.

We report at least once a year on our activities and achievements. Reports will describe each organization's:

- Mission and values;
- Objectives and outcomes achieved in programme and advocacy;
- Environmental impact;
- Governance structure and processes, and main office bearers;
- Main sources of funding from corporations, foundations, governments, and individuals;
- Financial performance;
- Compliance with this Charter; and
- Contact details.

Audit

The annual financial report will conform to relevant laws and practices and be audited by a qualified independent public accountant whose statement will accompany the report.

Accuracy Information

We will adhere to generally-accepted standards of technical accuracy and honesty in presenting and interpreting data and research, using and referencing independent research.

Good Governance

We should be held responsible for our actions and achievements. We will do this by: having a clear mission, organizational structure and decision-making processes; by acting in accordance with stated values and agreed procedures; by ensuring that our programmes achieve outcomes that are consistent with our mission; and by reporting on these outcomes in an open and accurate manner.

The governance structure of each organization will conform to relevant laws and be transparent. We seek to follow principles of best practice in governance. Each organization will have at least:

- A governing body which supervises and evaluates the chief executive, and oversee programme and budgetary matters. It will define overall strategy, consistent with the organizational mission, ensure that resources are used efficiently and appropriately, that performance is measured, that financial integrity is assured and that public trust is maintained;
- Written procedures covering the appointment, responsibilities and terms of members of the governing body, and preventing and managing conflicts of interest;
- A regular general meeting with authority to appoint and replace members of the governing body.

We will listen to stakeholder's suggestions on how we can improve our work and will encourage inputs by people whose interests may be directly affected. We will also make it easy for the public to comment on our programmes and policies.

Ethical Fundraising

Donors

We respect the rights of donors: to be informed about causes for which we are fundraising; to be informed about how their donation is being used; to have their names deleted from mailing lists; to be informed of the status and authority of fundraisers; and to anonymity except in cases where the size of their donation is such that it might be relevant to our independence.

Use of Donations

In raising funds, we will accurately describe our activities and needs. Our policies and practices will ensure that donations further our organization's mission. Where donations are made for a specific purpose, the donor's request is honoured. If we invite the general public to donate to a specific cause, each organization will have a plan for handling any shortfall or excess, and will make this known as part of its appeal.

Gifts in Kind

Some donations may be given as goods or services. To retain our effectiveness and independence, we will: record and publish details of all major institutional gifts and gifts-in-kind; clearly describe the valuation and auditing methods used; and ensure that these gifts contribute towards our mission.

Agents

We seek to ensure that donations sought indirectly, such as through third parties, are solicited and received in full conformity with our own practices. This will normally be the subject of written agreement between the parties.

Professional Management

We manage our organizations in a professional and effective manner.

Our policies and procedures seek to promote excellence in all respects.

Financial Controls

Internal financial control procedures will ensure that all funds are effectively used and minimize the risk of funds being misused. We will follow principles of best practice in financial management.

Evaluation

We seek continuously to improve our effectiveness. We will have defined evaluation procedures for our boards, staff, programmes and projects on the basis of mutual accountability.

Public Criticism

We will be responsible in our public criticisms of individuals and organizations, ensuring such criticism amounts to fair public comment.

Partners

We recognize our that organizational integrity extends to ensuring that our partners also meet the highest standards of probity and accountability, and will take all possible steps to ensure that there are no links with organizations, or persons involved in illegal or unethical practices.

Human Resources

We recognize that our performance and success reflect the quality of our staff and volunteers and management practices, and are committed to investing in human resource development.

Remuneration and benefits should strike a balance between public expectations of voluntary-based, not-for-profit organizations and the need to attract and retain the staff we need to fulfill our mission. Our human resources policies seek to conform fully with relevant international and national labour regulations and apply the best voluntary sector practices in terms of employee and volunteer rights and health and safety at work. Human resources policies will include procedures for evaluating the performance of all staff on a regular basis.

Bribery and Corruption

Human resources policies will specifically prohibit acts of bribery or corruption by staff or other persons working for, or on behalf of, the organization.

Whistle-Blowers

Staff will be enabled and encouraged to draw management's attention to activities that may not comply with the law or our mission and commitments, including the provisions in this Code.

4.2 GUIDELINES ON INTERNATIONAL HUMAN RIGHTS FACT-FINDING VISITS AND REPORTS (THE LUND-LONDON GUIDELINES) (2009)

Raoul Wallenberg Institute of Human Rights and Humanitarian Law, Lund University & International Bar Association

Preamble

Human rights are the concern of all members of the international community. We all hold a right and an obligation to promote and encourage respect for human rights, as pronounced in the 1998 United Nations Declaration on the Right and Responsibility of Individuals, Groups and Organs of Society to Promote and Protect Universally Recognised Human Rights and Fundamental Freedoms.

These guidelines have been developed by the International Bar Association and the Raoul Wallenberg Institute following wide consultation and extensive analysis of human rights fact-finding reports in order to contribute to good practice in the conduct of fact-finding visits and in the compilation of reports.

Fact finding and report writing are essential to human rights monitoring. Although primarily intended for the use of non-governmental organisations (NGOs), the present guidelines can provide direction to all those engaged in this exercise with a view to improving accuracy, objectivity, transparency and credibility in human rights fact finding.

The independence and integrity of NGOs must be respected, but fact-finding missions must nevertheless be, and be seen to be, conducted in a bona fide manner. Reports must be clearly objective and properly sourced, and the conclusions in them reached in a transparent manner.

If a report has been compiled in accordance with these guidelines it indicates that the allegations, observations and conclusions in it can be reasonably relied upon, thus enhancing the efficacy and credibility of the report. This will enhance fact finding as a step in a constructive process to improve the general climate of human rights compliance and to protect the victims of human rights violations.

Definition of Fact Finding

1. For the purpose of these guidelines, fact finding means a mission or visit mandated by an NGO to ascertain the relevant facts relating to and elucidating a situation of human rights concern, whether allegedly committed by state or non-state actors. In many instances this activity will result in a report. These guidelines do not prejudice the use of other methods of collecting information, other ventures or the use of fact finding in other contexts.

Instigation of a Fact-Finding Mission

2. Where a situation of concern is identified, a fact-finding mission should be considered in the light of the mandate, priorities, resources and procedures of the NGO. The NGO should consider the possible negative consequences of undertaking a mission.
3. The NGO should take into account the work that other relevant organisations have done or are doing on the same situation and of the effect

any previous missions or public statements relating to the situation have had. In order to strengthen efforts and maximise the effective use of resources, cooperation with those other organisations should be considered.

Terms of Reference for the Mission

4. The terms of reference must be determined prior to the mission. These should relate to the specific situations under investigation bearing in mind the NGO's mandate.
5. The terms of reference must not reflect any predetermined conclusions about the situation under investigation.
6. The terms of reference should be clear, concise and relevant. However, they should be sufficiently flexible to permit the investigation of and reporting on any other related relevant circumstances.
7. If unforeseen situations arise which are outside of the mission's terms of reference the delegation should report those to the relevant NGO contact person as soon as possible. If the new situation falls within the mandate and expertise of the NGO, it may decide to extend the terms of reference or create a second mission. If the former, the NGO should be confident that the delegation has the competence and expertise to deal with the new situation. If the new situation falls outside the mandate and expertise of the NGO, it should refer the matter to another organisation which can take action.

Composition of the Delegation

8. The mission's delegation should comprise individuals who are and are seen to be unbiased. The NGO should be confident that the delegation members have the competence, experience and expertise relevant to the matters pertaining to the terms of reference.
9. The NGO should ensure that delegation members have sufficient time for pre-mission briefings and/or training for implementation of the mission and any proposed follow-up work, including contributing to the report.
10. The NGO should ensure that all members of the delegation are aware that they must, at all times, act in an independent, unbiased, objective, lawful and ethical manner.
11. The NGO should ensure appropriate gender balance in the composition of the delegation. Where relevant, the NGO may wish to consider such issues as geographic, racial, ethnic or other types of balance and diversity when selecting the delegation members. The NGO may also

vwish to consider the importance of linguistic expertise and/or in-country knowledge.

12. The NGO should identify a leader of the delegation and/or a rapporteur.
13. As and where appropriate, delegations should be comprised of people with relevant expertise and skills in interviewing members of specific victim groups, especially when these are children, women, victims of torture or other vulnerable groups and internally displaced persons. See also paragraph 45.
14. When appointing a member of a delegation, the NGO should take into account any potential risk in appointing people of specific nationalities or members of particular religious groups, and any other reasons which might make it too dangerous for an individual to participate in the mission, or create danger for that person's family or others. This possibility should always be kept under review by the delegation and the NGO both before and during the visit.

Interpreters and Other Persons Associated with the Mission and/or Report

15. The NGO should ensure that all persons associated with a mission and/or a report are aware that they must, at all times, act in an independent, unbiased, objective, lawful and ethical manner.
16. The NGO should ensure that the delegation and other persons associated with the mission in the field develop inclusive operational methods that encourage the development of a participatory and unified team spirit.
17. The delegation should maintain as a principal consideration the safety of all persons associated with a mission and/or report, keeping personal details confidential. If there is a risk to any such person during the mission or afterwards, the NGO should seek assurances from the government that they will not be persecuted, victimised or otherwise put in a worse position for having worked with the delegation.
18. Where necessary, interpreters should be used during the course of the mission. Every care must be taken in selection to ensure that interpreters are expert in the required languages and relevant technical concepts, as well as independent and professional.
19. If the interpretation is not satisfactory, if the interpreters are not independent, or if they pose a risk to the safety of the delegation or those being interviewed, the delegation must desist from using the interpreters and where possible make alternative arrangements.

Pre-Visit

20. The NGO should provide a pre-visit briefing for members of the delegation, which includes balanced material relating to the reason for the visit and any relevant cultural, economic, political, historical and legal information. Where necessary, any relevant material should be translated.
21. The NGO should also provide a briefing on local logistical issues, operating procedures, medical issues (including preparation for travel), appropriate conduct in-country and other relevant matters. All members of the delegation should be provided with a copy of these guidelines.
22. The NGO should ensure that the members of the delegation are confident that they have been adequately briefed and understand the terms of reference, the initial reason for the visit and the mandate of the NGO. If any member of the delegation is not sufficiently confident that their briefing has been adequate, the NGO should be informed and it should then provide additional briefing.
23. The NGO should ensure that the members of the delegation understand the need to be unbiased and not pre-judge any issues during the mission. The NGO must also ensure that the delegation understands the need to act in an ethical manner and in accordance with the laws of the country and internationally accepted human rights standards. Awareness training, including gender sensitivity, should be provided where necessary.
24. The NGO should ensure that members of the delegation and persons associated with the mission receive clear and consistent messages about the mission, specifically its objectives and limitations, to ensure that the mission can be clearly explained to the people with whom they meet, so as to manage expectations and avoid miscommunication.
25. Where necessary, the NGO should ensure that all members of the delegation are fully briefed on recognising and managing stress and psychosocial trauma to prepare them properly for the realities of the situation and to promote the well-being of persons they interview, persons otherwise associated with the mission, and themselves.
26. The NGO is responsible for organising the visit, including the security, health and safety of the delegation. The NGO should ensure that appropriate emergency procedures are in place and that the delegation is fully briefed. It is the responsibility of the members of the delegation to act in accordance with any risk assessment made by the NGO and any formal requirements such as visa conditions as required by the laws of the country.

27. The NGO should as appropriate inform the government of the state in which the mission is to take place or any other relevant authorities that the mission will take place.
28. The NGO should consider what, if any, media strategy is appropriate for the delegation and for the mission overall. The NGO should ensure that all members of the mission are familiar with any strategy adopted.

Working Methods

General

29. The NGO has overall responsibility for the delegation and the mission.
30. The members of the delegation must conduct themselves with integrity, professionalism and in accordance with international human rights law standards at all times during the mission.
31. If a member of the delegation, or any other person associated with the mission, conducts him- or herself in a way which jeopardises the mission, the safety of others or the confidentiality of sources, or in any other way acts without sufficient professionalism or integrity, that person should be required to leave the mission. In such situations it will be for the NGO, in consultation with the leader of the delegation, to determine whether to abandon the mission or replace that person. If the team leader is implicated, or is otherwise unavailable, any other member of the delegation may draw the matter to the attention of the NGO.
32. If it transpires during the course of the mission that there is a conflict of interest or other circumstances involving any member of the delegation which might jeopardise their independence and impartiality, or which might give the appearance that their independence and integrity is compromised, the leader of the delegation should inform the NGO and that member should desist from participating in a particular meeting, or where necessary from the remainder of the mission. If the team leader is implicated, or is otherwise unavailable, any other members of the delegation may draw the matter to the attention of the NGO.
33. Any threats to, or intimidation of, the delegation must be reported immediately to the NGO. Where appropriate, the NGO will need to seek assurances from the government as to the safety of the delegation and should initiate emergency procedures should they be required.

Agenda

34. The NGO, in collaboration with the delegation, should determine criteria for selecting the people and locations it wishes to visit, make the necessary arrangements and draw up a schedule for the visit, as far as

possible. In so doing, the NGO should take into account the safety and security of potential interviewees and persons associated with them. It may be necessary to amend the schedule as the mission progresses.

35. Wherever possible the delegation should interview all parties relevant to the situation under consideration in order to achieve a balanced, comprehensive picture. This might include members of the government, judiciary, parliamentarians, opposition party members, journalists, NGO personnel, academics, staff of intergovernmental organisations, or any other person who could reliably shed light on the situation under review.
36. The delegation is under no obligation to advise the government of the people it intends to meet. If the government or any other party finds out this information and there are concerns as to the safety of an interviewee, then the NGO may wish to cancel the interview or to abandon the mission and should seek a guarantee from the government that the interviewee or prospective interviewee will not be persecuted, victimised or otherwise put in a worse position for having been willing to cooperate with the delegation. The same principle applies if the interviewee is threatened as a result of identification by other people.
37. The delegation may wish to operate as a whole group, or may wish to separate into smaller groups for specific assignments.

Interviews

38. The delegation must take into account the safety and security of the interviewees.
39. The delegation should be mindful that the venues for interviews will ensure the protection and confidentiality of all involved and are culturally appropriate.
40. Interviews should be scheduled with sufficient time for the ascertainment of all the relevant facts and to give the interviewee an opportunity to express their opinion.
41. The delegation should inform interviewees of the terms of reference, as well as giving reasons for the visit, prior to or at the meeting, in a language they understand.
42. The delegation should take a careful note of whether an interviewee provides informed consent to be interviewed and identified or quoted and of future possible uses of their statements. If they do not consent, their wishes must be respected.
43. Where appropriate, interviews should be conducted by at least two members of the delegation. It should be clarified in all cases whether

interviewees wish to have a supporting person present, or wish for some person to absent themselves during the interview.

44. Interviews should be consistent and thorough and be conducted in a professional manner.
45. Members of the mission should be especially aware of the vulnerabilities of particular categories of potential interviewees and such interviewees should be approached with the utmost care. Interviews of vulnerable groups must only be undertaken by those with the relevant expertise and skill (see paragraph 13). Particular methodological techniques should be considered in certain cases: for example, female victims of sexual abuse should be offered the choice of being interviewed by a female member of the delegation and a clear explanation given of the possible future need for testimony in criminal or other proceedings.
46. Members of the delegation should be alert to the possibility of stress or trauma experienced by interviewees and be ready to terminate the interview if necessary. Wherever possible, the delegation members should ensure that interviewees are referred to appropriate victim support services.
47. Members of the delegation should be alert to the humanitarian needs of interviewees and, wherever possible, should ensure that interviewees are referred to appropriate humanitarian or other organisations which might be able to meet those needs.

Information Gathering

48. It is essential that the delegation make use of all data collection techniques available. In addition to interviews, these may include site visits, collation of documents, or assessment of local laws and practices. Where the delegation relies upon information gathered by a third party, the delegation should take all reasonable measures to verify the objectivity of that information gathering process in order to rely on the evidence collected. See also paragraph 60 (ix).
49. The delegation should take full and fair notes or, where necessary, ensure that these are being taken on the delegation's behalf.
50. The delegation should endeavour to obtain and review all relevant written materials and documents.
51. The delegation must ensure that all materials and information are collated for the drafter of the report.
52. All notes, transcripts and documents, including electronic date, together with other materials from the visit, should be kept secure at all times. If confidentiality cannot be secured, the interviewee should be informed in accordance with paragraph 42.

53. The delegation should document any relevant obstacles it has met during its visit and in relation to the collection of information.
54. In making their findings the delegation should try to verify alleged facts with an independent third party or otherwise. Where this is not possible, it should be noted.
55. In making their findings the delegation should work independently having regard to the terms of reference, the situation giving rise to the visit, and the mandate of any reasonable directions from the NGO.
56. The delegation should assess all the information gathered and reach conclusions to its reasonable satisfaction based on this assessment.

Fact-Finding Report

57. If not already decided, the delegation and the NGO should identify the person or persons with responsibility for drafting the report. Unless there are exceptional circumstances, this should be a person or persons who was a delegate or who participated in the mission.
58. The delegation as a whole should reach its conclusions and make recommendations where required by the terms of reference. Where possible, recommendations should attempt to outline possible practical solutions. Every effort should be made to reach a consensus on conclusions and recommendations. If there is a dissenting viewpoint, the NGO should consider publishing it.
59. In order to enhance the overall quality and credibility of the report, it must be accurate, clear and drafted objectively so that the processes of the mission are transparent. It should fairly reflect all the information gathered and must refrain from bias. It is good practice to identify the standards against which the delegation members weigh the information obtained.
60. As good practice, reports should include:
    i) an executive summary;
    ii) the mandate of the sending NGO;
    iii) the reason for the visit and terms of reference of the mission;
    iv) the names of the delegation members, including brief particulars as to their relevant expertise and experience, to assure transparency;
    v) the dates of the visit;
    vi) sufficient background information to enable readers to contextualize the evidence;
    vii) the methodology used during the visit, especially regarding interviews;

viii) as appropriate and where safety and confidentiality would not be compromised, a list of the sites visited and organisations and categories of people interviewed;
ix) identification of any other sources of information relied upon, including disclosure of unverified third party evidence (see paragraph 48);
x) disclosure of the source of funding for the mission;
xi) the applicable law;
xii) where applicable, complementary secondary sources should be identified as such;
xiii) identification of any circumstances relevant to the mission, including anything that impeded it;
xiv) the findings of the report;
xv) an acknowledgment of any contributions by people or organisations who rendered assistance to the delegation or NGO, where it would not compromise their safety;
xvi) conclusions and recommendations, indicating to whom the latter are addressed;
xvii) details of any significant developments occurring after the conclusion of the mission.

61. Where it is the practice for the NGO to submit the report to the government for its response in advance of publication, any comments received should be included if the government consents. Any failure of the government to respond should be noted in the report.
62. The report should be written and published within a reasonable time following the conclusion of the mission.

Translation

63. The report should be made available in the languages of the NGO and of the country being investigated, or in a language of common use in that country.
64. Every effort should be made to ensure the translation is of the highest quality.

Publication

65. The NGO has overall responsibility for decisions about the publication and dissemination of the report.
66. The NGO should, wherever possible, widely publicise and disseminate the report, particularly in the locality of the visit, including to relevant governments, individuals or organisations.

67. The NGO should consider what, if any, media strategy is appropriate for disseminating the report.

Follow-up

68. The safety of those interviewed or engaged by a fact-finding delegation should continue to be monitored by the NGO, particularly where safety concerns were already present. Any post-mission threats or hostile acts should be acted upon immediately by the NGO including, where necessary, notifying the government, assisting with protective measures and alerting the wider international community.
69. The NGO should offer post-mission debriefing to members of the delegation and persons associated with the mission where necessary to deal with stress and psychosocial trauma that may be experienced after a mission.
70. The NGO should consider any opportunities to cooperate with other NGOs, international organisations and relevant governments working on the same situation, subject area or country so as to maximise the effectiveness of the report.
71. The NGO should consider the best means by which to encourage governments and other relevant entities to be receptive of its report and to act upon its recommendations.
72. The NGO may wish to monitor any relevant developments in the country which is the subject of the report, occurring after the report has been published. In such a case a follow-up mission and/or report may be considered.
73. The NGO should review all aspects of the mission, including the delegation's performance and the adequacy of the NGO's procedures. The NGO should endeavour to disseminate the lessons learned within the NGO and to others, in order to promote the development of good practice and the implementation of these guidelines.

NGOs working in the field of human rights recognise that fact finding is not an end in itself. It is a crucial vehicle for the implementation of human rights in all countries or situations under examination.

INDEX

Accountability 48 (see also: INGOs Accountability Charter)
Accountability holders fn. 16(50)
Accountability mechanisms 76
vs. 'Better performance' fn. 16(50)
Debate about fn. 16(50)
Demands for 47, 88
vs. Democratic representation fn. 16(50), fn. 24(76)
Fashionable topic fn. 16(49)
of INGOs fn. 13(71), 72, 77, 88
of International actors fn. 1(47)
Literature on fn. 16(49)
Mutual accountability model fn. 1(47), fn. 16(50)
by National authorities 73
of NSAs 60, 72
Relational concept fn. 16(49)
Advocacy (see also: International Non-Governmental Organizations)
Responsible advocacy fn. 16(50)
American Society of International Law fn. 20(9)
Amnesty International fn. 2(47) (see also: INGOs Accountability Charter)
Article 71 UN Charter (see also: Consultative status arrangements; Charter of the UN; ECOSOC) 13, 21, 22, 23, 61, 66, 70
Controversial operation of 15
Interpretations of 14
NGOs' drafting of fn. 44(14)
Rules of Procedure of 14
Scope of application of 14
the Term 'INGO' 13
Western-biased 15

von Bar, C. L. 5, 8, 10, 12, 18
Bastid, S. 27
Beckett, Sir E. 29, 30
British Institute of International and Comparative Law fn. 28(52)

'Cardoso report' – see Report of the Panel of Eminent Persons on United Nations-Civil Society Relations
Charnovitz, S. fn. 6(2), fn. 32(12), 87
Charter of the UN 13, 24 (see also: Article 71 UN Charter; ECOSOC; Drafting conference of fn. 44(14) Consultative status arrangements)
CIVICUS fn. 2(47) (see also: INGOs Accountability Charter)
Clemens Nathan Research Center fn. 28(52)
Code of Conduct for Special Procedures Mandate-Holders of the Human Rights Council fn. 37(54), 73
Cold War 13
Committee on NGOs – see ECOSOC
Conference of Consultative Status Non-Governmental Organizations (CCNGOs) 17, 22, 28, 83
1948 Proposal 18
1949 Proposal 21 (see also: Preliminary Draft Agreement Designed to Facilitate the Work of NGOs having Consultative Status)
Study Committee 18, 19, 23
UN General Assembly Resolution on the Granting of International Juridical Personality to Certain Consultative NGOs, draft proposal of 18
Conflicts-of-Laws problem – see International Non-Governmental Organizations, legal status of
Constitution – see International Non-Governmental Organizations, legal status of
Consultative Council of Jewish Organizations (CCJO) fn. 28(52)
Consultative status arrangements (see also: Article 71 UN Charter; ECOSOC) 13, 33, 36, 63, 66, 78, 83
Accreditation/verification process 16
Consultative INGOs – see International Non-Governmental Organizations
Critical approach towards fn. 124(36)
De-facto legal status 17

ECOSOC Res. 1296 (XLIV), Arrangements for Consultation with NGOs (May 23, 1968) 14, Appendices 2.1
ECOSOC Res. 1996/31, Consultative Relationship between the United Nations and Non-Governmental Organizations (July 25, 1996) 15, Appendices 2.2
as Functionalist appeal 70
vs. ILP 17
Instrumental approach towards INGOs 39
& National NGOs 15
& NSAs' legal 'status' 61
& Participatory rights fn. 86(62)
Political considerations 16
Purposes of 14
State-centric approach 15
Western-biased 15
Control, problem of 18
Control system, universal 8
Convention Concerning Recognition of the Legal Personality of Foreign Companies, Associations, and Institutions (HCPIL, 1956) 31
Council of Europe (see also: European Convention on the Recognition of the Legal Personality of International NGOs (CoE, 1986)) 35
Conference of INGOs of the Council of Europe – see Participatory status arrangements (CoE)
Consultative status arrangements 39
& INGOs accountability fn. 17(72)
INGOs' offices in 37
& INGOs' participatory rights 63
& national NGOs fn. 139(39)
Participatory status arrangements fn. 139(39), fn. 87(62), 63 (see also: Participatory status arrangements (CoE))

Democratic pluralism – see Pluralism, democratic
Democratic representation fn. 16(50) (see also: Accountability)
Draft Convention on Facilitating Activity of International NGOs (UIA, 1959) 32
Draft Convention on the Legal Status of International Associations (Institute, 1912) 5, 6, 65
Draft Convention Relating to the Position of International Associations (Institute, 1923) 7, fn. 81(22), 65

ECOSOC 13, 14, 21 (see also: Consultative status arrangements; Article 71 UN Charter)
Committee on NGOs 16
Diplomats of fn. 69(19)
as International registration bureau 18
NGOs in consultative status with fn. 39(13)
Political organ 19
Res. 1296(XLIV) 1968 – see Consultative status arrangements
Res. 1996/31 – see Consultative status arrangements
Europe
'European Law on Associations' 44
Intellectual/political environment 35, 45, 84, 85
European Community (EC) 41
'Association movement' in 43, 45
EC Associations statute 43
EC Commission 42, 44
European Parliament 42
European Parliament Resolution on Non-Profit Making Associations in the European Communities 1986 43
Freedom of association & membership 43
INGOs & regional integration 42, 43, 44
Integrative momentum 42, 43
1992 Internal Market 43
Limited Community action 45
Mutual recognition system 43
& National associations 45
Report on Non-Profit-Making Associations in the EC (1986) 44
Resolution on the Role and Administration of Associations and the Law Governing Them in the EC (1984) 42

Supranational arrangements/ institutions 41, 42
European Convention on the Recognition of the Legal Personality of International NGOs (Council of Europe, 1986) 37, 38, 44
Application requirements fn. 137(38)
vs. EC action 45
French Declaration to fn. 138(39)
as Functionalist appeal 70
vs. International legal status 40
National legal personality 41
& NSAs' legal 'status' 61
Objective of 40
& Participatory rights 63
'Real administrative seat' fn. 134(38)
Reciprocity and mutuality 41
'Statutory office' rule 38, 40
Travaux préparatoirs 40
vs. UN consultative arrangements 38, fn. 138(39)

Fact-Finding (see also: Guidelines on International Human Rights Fact-Finding Visits and Reports (The 'Lund-London Guidelines', 2009); International Non-Governmental Organizations)
Discipline of fn. 34(53)
Procedural standards for 53
Importance of fn. 35(54)
Fairness, notion of 70, 89
Functionalism 70
vs. Democratic pluralism 71
Funding, ethical – see International Non-Governmental Organizations

Global Conscience – see International Non-Governmental Organizations
Global Civil Society (GCS) 78
Forum of 48 (see also: INGOs Accountability Charter)
& INGOs' legal status 91
Notion of 67, 75, fn. 7(89), 90
Global elections fn. 24(76)
Globalization, processes of 46, fn. 4(67), 89
Global interdependence 89
Notion of 90
Governance, global/international 58, 67, 88, 90
Definition of fn. 60(58)
INGOs involvement in 73, 84, 88, 93
Notion of 75
NSAs participation in 59, 60, 67
Greenpeace International fn. 2(47) (see also: INGOs Accountability Charter)
Guidelines on International Human Rights Fact-Finding Visits and Reports (The 'Lund-London Guidelines', 2009) 52, 65, 71, 73, 81, 82, 84, 85, 92, 93,
Appendices 4.2
Bias elimination 54, fn. 40(55)
Drafting process of fn. 29(52), 82
Function-based approach 81
& INGOs' legal status 53, 84
& INGOs' legitimacy 77, 78
International standard of good practice 53
Mandate of 52
Objectivity enforcement 54, fn. 40(55)
Self-regulating sector-based code-of-conduct model 73
'Soft-law' code-of-conduct 84

Hague Conference on Private International Law (HCPIL) 31
Hague Peace Conferences fn. 21(10)
Human interest 75, 76
Human rights (see also International Non-Governmental Organizations)
'Human rights situation' fn. 40(55)
Human Rights Council 73
Human Rights Watch (HRW) fn. 12(49), fn. 35(54), 81

Immunities (from enforcement/ jurisdiction) 60 (see also: International Non-Governmental Organizations, legal status of; Non State Actors)
Functional considerations 60
Institute of International Law (Institute) 5, 9, 28, 35
1912 Proposal – see Draft Convention on the Legal

Status of International Associations
1923 Proposal – see Draft Convention Relating to the Position of International Associations
1950 Proposal – see Resolution on Granting of International Status to Associations Established by Private Initiative
Intergovernmental/international conferences 10
INGOs' involvement in 10
Intergovernmental organizations (IGOs) 1, 24, 30
Accreditation procedures 73
Disenchantment with INGOs 12
Distinct from INGOs 10
ILP of 74, 75
& INGOs' accountability 72
INGOs' Participatory roles in 63
INGOs' resemblance to 23, 66, 74
Normative legitimacy of 74
Regulatory legitimacy of 74
Supervision of INGOs 23, 73
International Associations – see International Non-Governmental Organizations
International Bar Association 52 (see also: Guidelines on International Human Rights Fact-Finding Visits and Reports (The 'Lund-London Guidelines', 2009))
'International Bureau' 6 (see also: Registration, international) 23, 28, 32, 73
Composition of fn. 6(6), 7, 8, 77, 87
Diplomatic supervision of 8
ECOSOC – see ECOSOC
Legal status of fn. 6(6)
International community
Interest(s) of 7, 11, 66
Invention of fn. 39(82)
INGOs position in 65, 69, 74
Nation-based 37
Re-organization of 36
Structure/composition of fn. 8(6), 8, 23, 88
International control/supervision fn. 69(19) (see also: Political control; Registration; International Bureau)
vs. Domestic legislation 20
International Court of Justice (ICJ) 22, 24
International Criminal Court (ICC) 73
Rules of Procedure and Evidence of fn. 40(55)
International Labor Organization (ILO) fn. 21(10)
International law
Becoming transnational law 57, fn. 71(59), 94
'Customary transnational law' fn. 49(57)
Fundamental concepts of 68
Human-based fields of 63
'Inclusive process' of norm creation 57, 71
& INGOs advocacy 10
International institutional law 74
International security law 56
'Process-based' conception of 62
Rethinking of 57, 61, 71
Strengthening of 9
Traditional 'static' conception of 62
International Law Association (ILA) 5, 9, 65, 83, 84
Committee on Non-State Actors 55, 82, 85
'Non-State Actors in International Law: Aims, Approach and Scope of Project and Legal Issues', First Report of the Committee on NSAs (The Hague Conference, 2010) 55, 65, 70, 71, 75, 77, 79
'Non-State Actors in International Law: Lawmaking and Participation Rights', Second Report of the Committee on NSAs (Sofia Conference, 2012) 62
Report on Preliminary Issues for the International Law Association Conference in Rio de Janeiro (2008), Committee on NSAs 56, 65, 70
International Legal Personality (ILP) 58, 60, 61, 65, 75, 83 (see also: International Non-Governmental Organizations, legal status of)
vs. Consultative status 17
as Customary rule 69
of IGOs 24, 75
Implied/functional/limited 26, 35, 45, 74, 93

of INGOs 6, 28, 35, 36, 40, 69, 70, 73, 91, 92, 93
of NSAs 56, 60, 83
Re-conceptualization of 61, 71
Recognition of 6, 23
Renouncement of 19, 27, 36
Quest for 5, 11, 66
International legal status 7, 22, 28, 35, 36, 40, 45, 57, 60, 65, 69, 91, 93, 94 (see also: International Non-Governmental Organizations, legal status of)
vs. (UN) Consultative status 16, 23
Disapproval of 26
vs. ILP fn. 12(7), 68, 71
& National NGOs 34
vs. Observer status fn. 61(16)
International Non-Governmental Organizations (INGOs)
Activity/function of fn 4(1), 3
Advocacy & campaigning fn. 1(47), 92
'Age of INGOs' 89
Association with IGOs 24, 25, 26, 29
Benefiting IGOs 32, 63
Coalitions of 1
Collective 'INGO identity' fn. 31(78)
Competition/tensions between fn. 84(22), 34, 78, 79, 80, 81, 93
Consultative status INGOs 18, 27, 83
Credibility of 12
Definition of fn. 13(7), 22, 27, 33, 34, 35, fn. 155(43), 54, 66, fn. 10(70), 77, 88, 93
'Democratic deficit' of fn. 24(76)
& Democratic process 50
Expanding functions of 69
Expertise provision 11, 12, 54, 63, 77, 92
Fact-finding missions of 53, 54
Funding of 12, 51, 79, 94
as 'Global Conscience' 1
Good governance of 73
Governance/self-government of 32, 72, 73
Governance structures of 51
vs. Governments/states 8, fn. 19(9), fn. 20(10), 10, fn. 26(11), 12, 13, 15, 17, 23, 69, 73
Grouping/ranking of 18
& Human-rights monitoring 54
Human rights reports of fn. 30(53)
Independence of 51, 54
& Intergovernmental policymaking 10, 63
Law-related INGOs fn. 20(10)
Leadership of 12, 13
Legality of 2
Legitimacy of 2, 48, 50, fn. 20(51), 54, 72, 74, 75, 76, 84, 90 (see also: Legitimacy)
Lobbying by 1, 13
Memberships of 12, 13
Monitoring international instruments 63
as National NGOs 26, 28, 29, 46, 67
vs. National NGOs 34, 79
as NSAs 56, 60
Number of 1, 12, 29, 35, fn. 10(70), 80, 88, 93
as Political actors 91
as Political allies 92
Political reliability of 12, 29, 83
& Power politics 13
Reputation of 84
Responsible advocacy of 88
Right to act 50
Selection of 73, 74
Self-awareness of fn. 20(10), fn. 1(66)
as Socio-political phenomenon 29
Stakeholders of 50
& States lawmaking 63
as Subjects of international law fn. 17(9), 16, 45
Supranational entities 42
Third-world INGOs fn. 56(16)
Transparency of 73 (see also: Transparency)
Unaccountable 2, 54
Unelected 1
Unrepresentative 2
& Violence 92
Western INGOs fn. 56(15)
International Non-Governmental Organizations (INGOs)
Accountability Charter (2006) 47, 65, 71, 80, 82, 84, 92, 93
Annual reports 52
Complaints mechanism 52
Donors rights 51
Funds & donations 51
Financial controls 51

'Five Years Strategy' 49, 80
Founding signatories fn. 2(47), 85
'Global Civil Society Forum' 48
'Global cross-sectoral accountability framework' fn. 7(48)
Global Reporting Initiative's (GRI) NGO Sector Supplement fn. 24(51)
'Global self-regulation system' 48
& Ideological diversity fn. 17(50)
Independent Review Panel (IRP) 52
INGOs Charter of Accountability Ltd Company (UK) fn. 3(48)
& INGOs' formal status 84
& INGOs' legitimacy 48, fn. 20(51), 77
& INGOs' self-governance 73
Reporting mechanism/ requirement 51, 73, 77
Responsible advocacy fn. 16(50)
Secretariat of 81
Selective-membership framework 80, 81

International Non-Governmental Organizations (INGOs), legal status of
Activities supervision 20
Administrative/fiscal difficulties 27, 33, 67
Article 71 – see Article 71 UN Charter
Consultative status – see Consultative status arrangements
Conflicts-of-Laws (problem) 19, 23, 31, 35, 44, 46, 66, 84
Customary law rule 9
De-facto status 22
Diplomatic/international convention 2, 5, 18, 21, 29, 36, 45
Extra/super-national status/ statute 5, fn. 8(6)
Freedom of assembly 50, 77
Freedom of association 29, 50, 77
Freedom to move funds 29
Freedom of speech 50, 77
Freedom of traveling 29
Functional (sectoral) approach 69, 93
Funds & property holding 29
& 'Global public good' 60
Host state 7, 27, 29
Immunity 60, fn. 13(71), 75, fn. 30(77)
Implied legal personality 26, 45
INGOs' Constitution 6
INGOs' disinterest in 82, 83
INGOs' interests 20
INGOs' Registration – see Registration, international; International Bureau
International activity/aim 33, fn. 122(34), 79
International character/'Internationality' requirement 34, 80, 93
International composition/staff 79
International law control 20
International legal liability of 60, 75, 77, 88
International/universal (legal) status 9, 11, 20, 22, 23, 31, 35, 36, 45, 57, 66, 68, 71, 91, 93, 94
Internationally secured rights/ benefits 8, 33, 36, 45, 89
Legal requirements of INGOs 23, 66, 93
Legitimate purpose principle 20
Liability for libel fn. 32(53)
'Most-favored organization' clause 28, 33, 67
Mutual state recognition fn. 19(9), 43, 45, 66
National NGO status 27
Observer status fn. 45(14), 56
Privileges and immunities 23, fn. 88(24), 25, 45, 89
Problem of legal personality 6, 66 (see also: International Legal Personality (ILP))
Recognition of 6, 19, 21, 30, 82
Refusal of recognition 6, fn. 14(8), fn. 18(9)
Regional status 44, 84
Revocation of recognition fn. 7(6)
Scholarly debate about 87
State of constitution/incorporation/ origin/registration 21, 22, 33, 45, 66
World Court appeal right 8, 22

International organizations – see Intergovernmental organizations (IGOs)

International registration – see Registration (procedure/machinery/bureau), international
International Relations 2, 9, 67, 79
Neo-liberal perceptions 46, fn. 4(67), 75
Neofunctionalism fn. 150(42)
New models/notions 46, 90
'International society movement' 36
International tribunals 53, 73
Internet 1

Kopelmanas, L. 19, 24, 27, 30, fn. 19(74)

Lador-Lederer, J. J. 24, fn. 19(74)
Langrod, A. 30
League of Nations 10
Consultative relationships with 14
Legitimacy (see also: International Non-Governmental Organizations)
Cognitive legitimacy 76, 78
Functional legitimacy 71
Normative legitimacy 74, 75, 76, 77, 78
Output legitimacy 76
Regulatory legitimacy 76
Lund-London Guidelines – see Guidelines on International Human Rights Fact-Finding Visits and Reports (The 'Lund-London Guidelines', 2009)

Mass-Media 1, fn. 7(48), 53
Mattli W. 42
Médecins Sans Frontières (MSF) fn. 12(49)
Merle, M. 35
Mutual accountability – see Accountability
Mutual recognition – see International Non-Governmental Organizations, legal status of

National/domestic non-governmental organizations (NGOs) fn. 9(6), 21
& Consultative status 15, 34
Committee of Ministers Resolution Res(2003)9, Status of Partnership between the Council of Europe and National NGOs, (Nov. 2003) fn. 139(39), Appendices 3.4
vs. INGOs 124, fn.9(6), 34, 79
International activity/aim 34, 79
International goal(s) of fn. 9(6)
& International status 34
Network model(s) 78
Non-State Actors (NSAs) 2 (see also: International Law Association (ILA))
Accreditation frameworks of 59
Challenging international law 56
& Customary international law 57
Definition of 57
Governance roles of 58, 59
in International forums 56
Immunities of 60
& Lawmaking 62, 63,
Legal personality of 56, 58, 59, 83
Legal 'status' of 57, 58, 60, 61
NGOs as prototypical NSAs 56
as Normative group 56, 57, 79
Normative position of 56
Participation/participatory right(s) of fn. 61(58), 62, 63, 64
Proliferation of 56
Rights and obligations of 58
as Subjects of international law 57, 61, 71
& Treaty adoption 57

Observer status – see International Non-Governmental Organizations, legal status of

Participation (see also: Participatory status arrangements)
Notion of 14, fn. 87(62), 63
of INGOs fn. 7(69), 89
Participatory rights – see Participatory status arrangements (CoE)
Participatory status arrangements (Council of Europe) fn. 139 (39), fn. 87(62), 63 (see also: Participation)
Participatory rights fn. 139(39), fn. 87(62)
Committee of Ministers Resolution Res(2003)8, Participatory Status for INGOs with the Council of Europe, (Nov. 2003) fn. 139(39), Appendices 3.3
Conference of INGOs of the Council of Europe fn. 139(39)

'Peoples Assembly' – see United Nations system
Permanent Court of International Justice (PCIJ) 8 (see also: International Non-Governmental Organizations, legal status of)
Pickard, B. 25, fn. 19(74)
Pluralism, democratic 70, 71
  vs. Functionalism 71
Political control (see also: Control, problem of)
  by States/IGOs 19, 23, 35
Political reliability – see International Non-Governmental Organizations
Political theory 90
Politics, international fn. 69(19)
Politis, N. S. 7, 8, 10, 12, 18, 28
Power politics 13
Preliminary Draft Agreement Designed to Facilitate the Work of NGOs having Consultative Status, Conference of Consultative Non-Governmental Organizations (1949) 21
Public opinion 1, 44
Public order/policy 7, 8, fn. 18(9), 28, 32

Raul Wallenberg Institute of Human Rights and Humanitarian Law (Lund University, Sweden) 52 (see also: Guidelines on International Human Rights Fact-Finding Visits and Reports (The 'Lund-London Guidelines', 2009))
Rechenberg, H.H.-K. 16
Recognition, system of
  & domestic jurisdiction 21
Registration (procedure/machinery/bureau), international 6, 8, 11, 20, 21, 66
  ECOSOC – see ECOSOC
  Problem of 18, 35, 70, 72, 74, 77, 79, 87, 93
  Refusal of 8
Reliability, political – see International Non-Governmental Organizations
Reparation for Injuries Suffered in the Service of the United Nations, Advisory Opinion (ICJ, 1949) 24, 58, 60, 61, 66, 70
Report of the Panel of Eminent Persons on United Nations-Civil Society Relations (*'Cardoso report'*) fn. 39(13)
Report of the Secretary General in Response to the Report of the Panel of Eminent Persons on United Nations-Civil Society Relations fn. 39(13)
Report on 'International Non-Governmental Organizations and their Legal Status', (M. Merle, Strasburg 1983) 35, 41, Appendices 1.2
  Current relevancy 35
Report on 'The Legal Status of International Non-Governmental Organizations', Conference of Non-Governmental Consultative Organizations (L. Kopelmanas, Geneva 1949) 19, Appendices 1.1
  Current relevancy 19
Reporting – see Guidelines on International Human Rights Fact-Finding Visits and Reports (The 'Lund-London Guidelines', 2009)
Representation – see Democratic representation
Resolution on Granting of International Status to Associations Established by Private Initiative (Institute, 1950) 27
Res. 1296 (XLIV), Arrangements for Consultation with NGOs (May 23, 1968) (ECOSOC) – see Consultative status arrangements
Res. 1996/31, Consultative Relationship between the United Nations and Non-Governmental Organizations (July 25, 1996) – see Consultative status arrangements
Rodgers, R.S. fn. 7(2), 24, 29, 37, fn. 19(74)

'Sans Frontiérisme', phenomenon of 80
Selection, problem of 11, 72, 74, 77, 79, 87, 93
Sovereignty, principle of 75
Soviet Union 12
State-system 2

Subjects of international law fn. 17(9), 46 (see also: International Non-Governmental Organizations)
& NSAs 57, 71
Status of 16

Terrorism/Terrorist activities
& INGOs 36, 83, 92
& NSAs fn. 46(56)
Transnational corporations 1
'Transnational private sector' 36, 88
Transparency 48, 53, 73, 77 (see also: Accountability)

UNESCO 32, 33
Union of International Associations (UIA) 5, 9, 32, 33
Foundation of fn. 1(66), 83
& INGOs' self-awareness fn. 1(66)
UIA Commission 33
United Nations (UN) system 24 (see also: ECOSOC; Article 71 UN Charter)
Functionalist INGOs institutional arrangements 70
& INGOs accountability fn. 17(72)
General Assembly fn. 39(13)
'Peoples Assembly' fn. 24(73)
Specialized agencies 14, 21
Universalist vision 62

Voluntary NGO mechanisms fn. 1(47)

Wiederkehr, M.-O. 40
Willetts, P. 70
World Congress of International Associations 5
World Wars 11, 12

www.ingramcontent.com/pod-product-compliance
Lightning Source LLC
LaVergne TN
LVHW102227300926
849160LV00005B/56